Garfield
LISTENS TO HIS GUT

BY JIM DAVIS

FEEED MEEE

Ballantine Books ● New York

A Ballantine Books Trade Paperback Original

Published in the United States by Ballantine Books, an imprint of Random House,
a division of Penguin Random House LLC, New York.

BALLANTINE and the HOUSE colophon are registered trademarks of Penguin Random House LLC.

ISBN 978-0-425-28557-2
Ebook ISBN 978-0-425-28556-5

Printed in China on acid-free paper

randomhousebooks.com

9 8 7 6 5 4 3 2 1

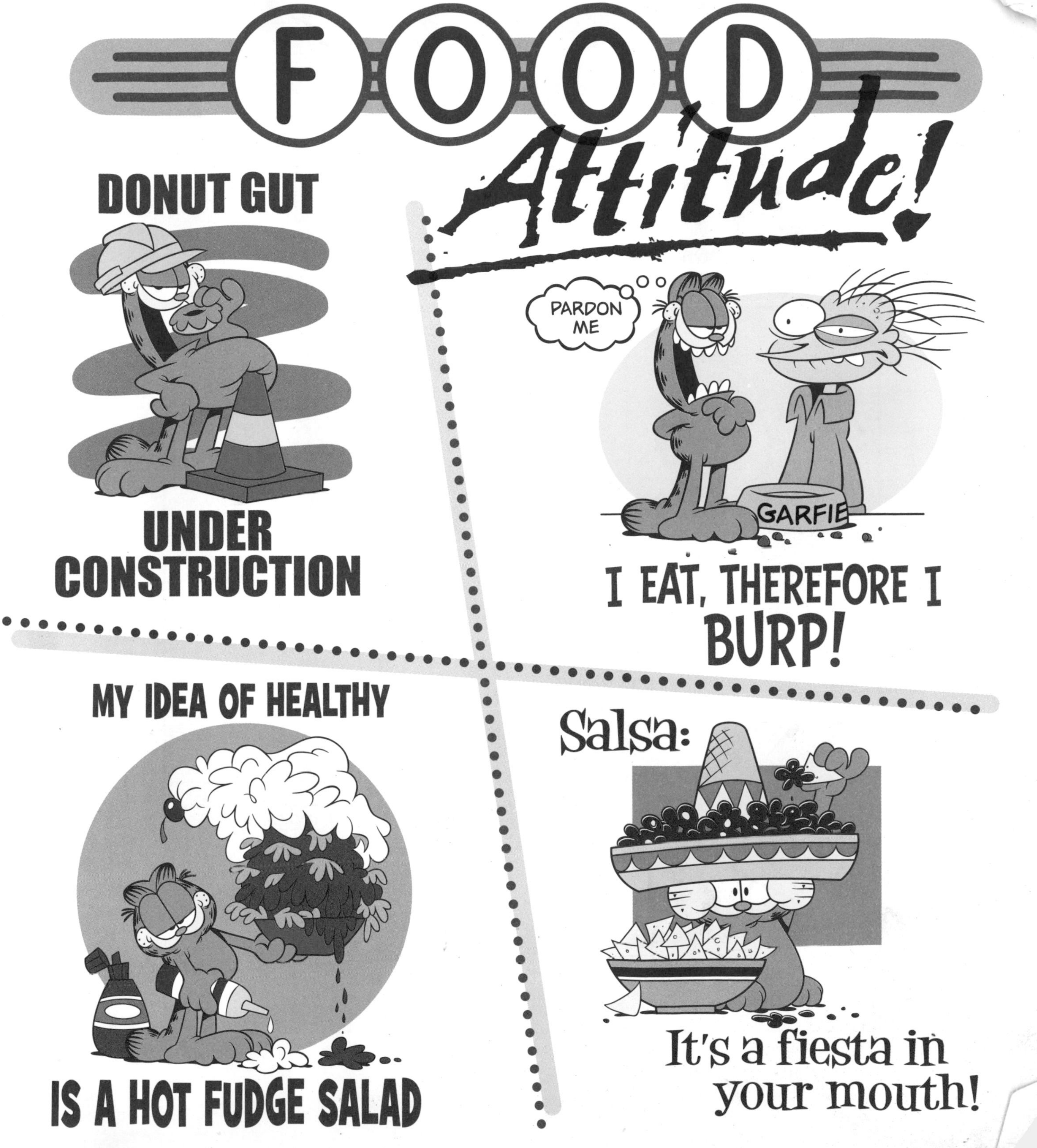
FOOD
Attitude!
DONUT GUT
UNDER CONSTRUCTION
PARDON ME
GARFIE
I EAT, THEREFORE I BURP!
MY IDEA OF HEALTHY
IS A HOT FUDGE SALAD
Salsa:
It's a fiesta in your mouth!

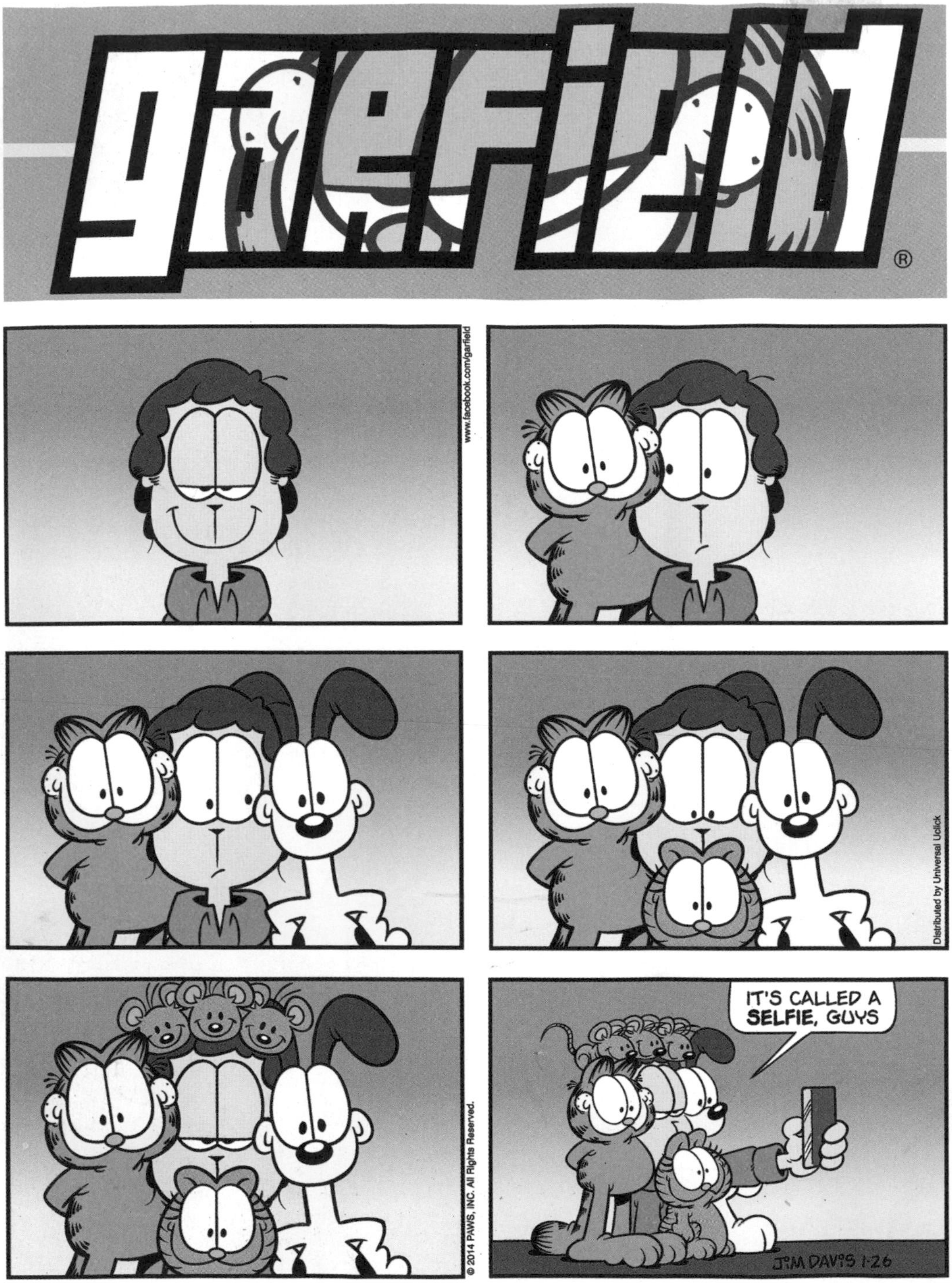
garfield®
www.facebook.com/garfield
Distributed by Universal Uclick
© 2014 PAWS, INC. All Rights Reserved.
IT'S CALLED A **SELFIE**, GUYS
JIM DAVIS 1-26

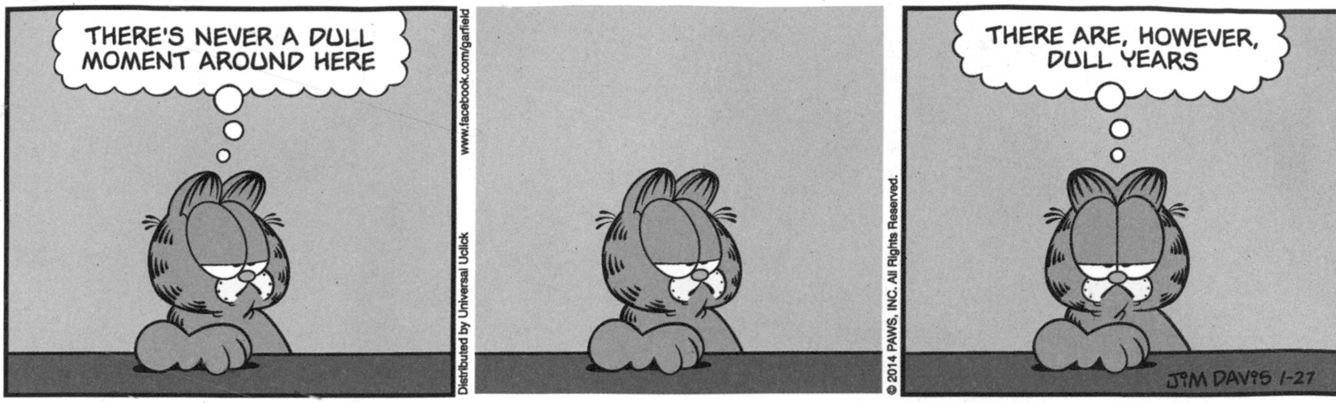
THERE'S NEVER A DULL MOMENT AROUND HERE
THERE ARE, HOWEVER, DULL YEARS
JIM DAVIS 1-27
Distributed by Universal Uclick
www.facebook.com/garfield
© 2014 PAWS, INC. All Rights Reserved.

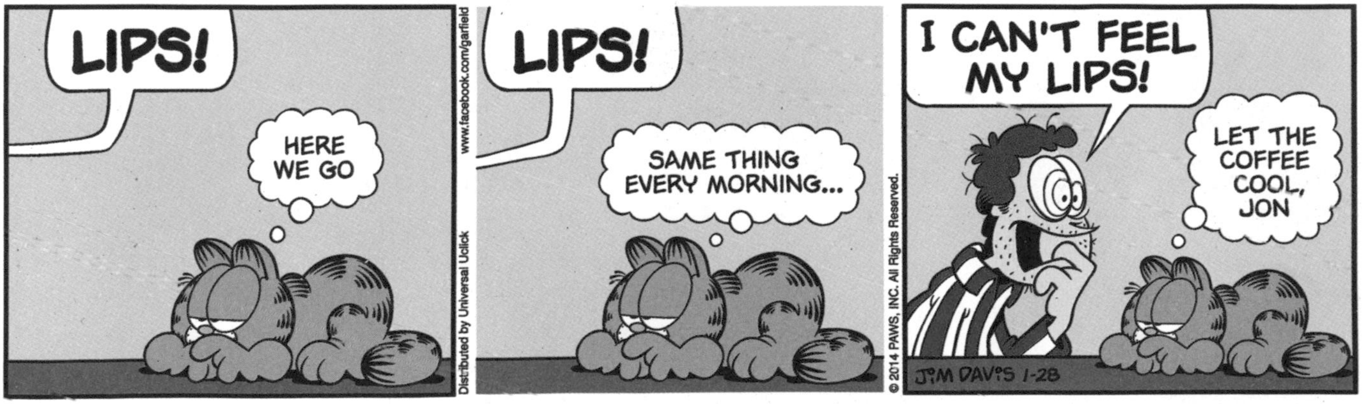
LIPS!
HERE WE GO
LIPS!
SAME THING EVERY MORNING...
I CAN'T FEEL MY LIPS!
LET THE COFFEE COOL, JON
JIM DAVIS 1-28
Distributed by Universal Uclick
www.facebook.com/garfield
© 2014 PAWS, INC. All Rights Reserved.

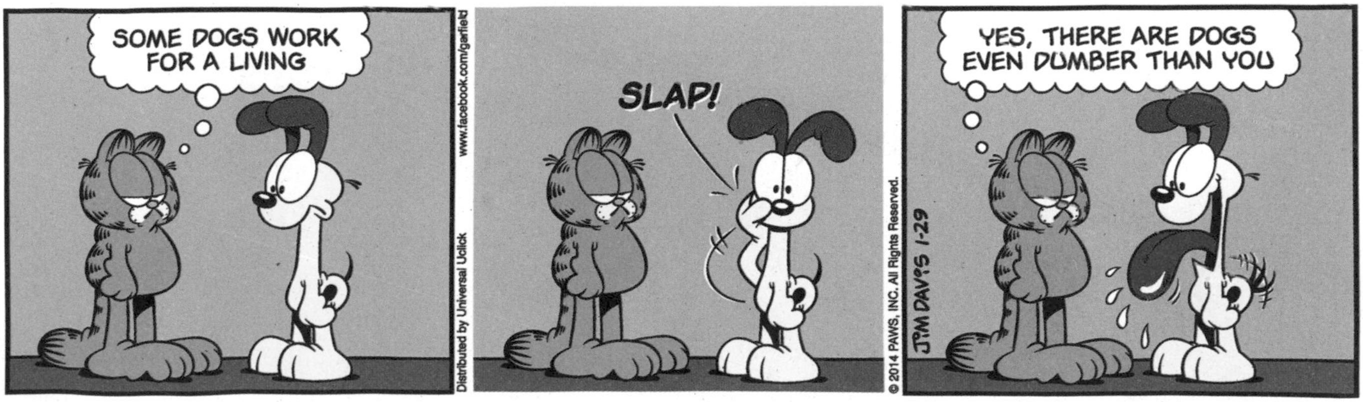
SOME DOGS WORK FOR A LIVING
SLAP!
YES, THERE ARE DOGS EVEN DUMBER THAN YOU
JIM DAVIS 1-29
Distributed by Universal Uclick
www.facebook.com/garfield
© 2014 PAWS, INC. All Rights Reserved.

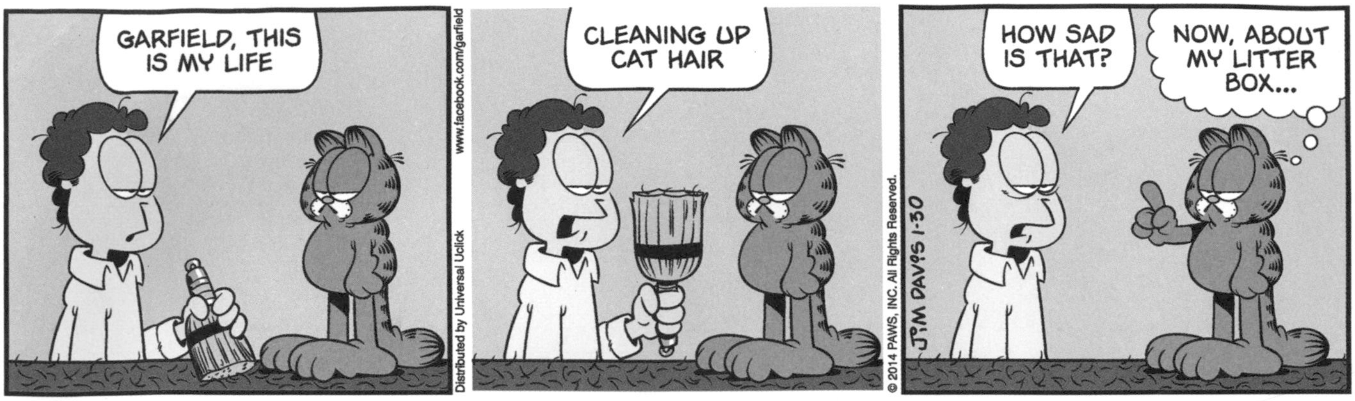
GARFIELD, THIS IS MY LIFE
CLEANING UP CAT HAIR
HOW SAD IS THAT?
NOW, ABOUT MY LITTER BOX...
Distributed by Universal Uclick www.facebook.com/garfield
© 2014 PAWS, INC. All Rights Reserved.
JIM DAVIS 1-30

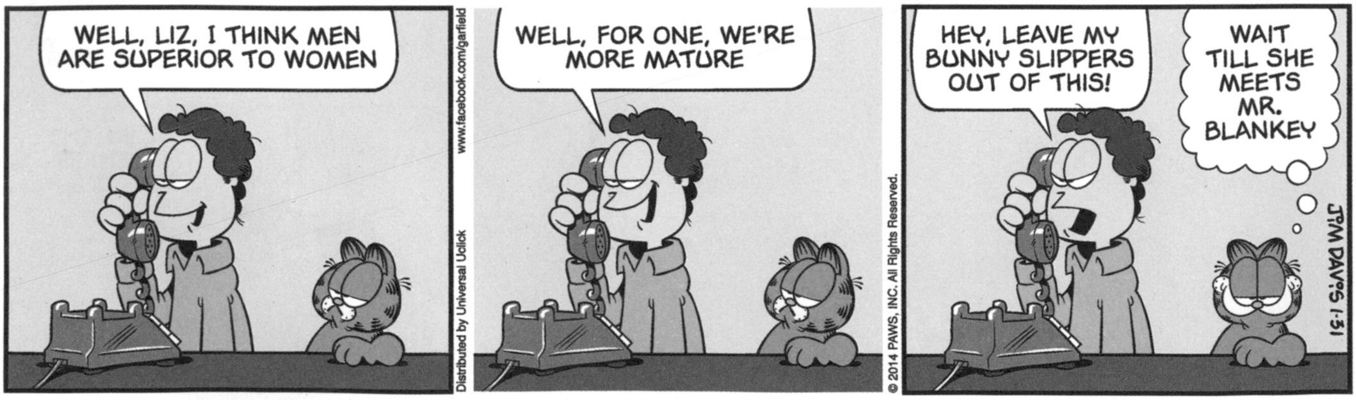
WELL, LIZ, I THINK MEN ARE SUPERIOR TO WOMEN
WELL, FOR ONE, WE'RE MORE MATURE
HEY, LEAVE MY BUNNY SLIPPERS OUT OF THIS!
WAIT TILL SHE MEETS MR. BLANKEY
Distributed by Universal Uclick www.facebook.com/garfield
© 2014 PAWS, INC. All Rights Reserved.
JIM DAVIS 1-31

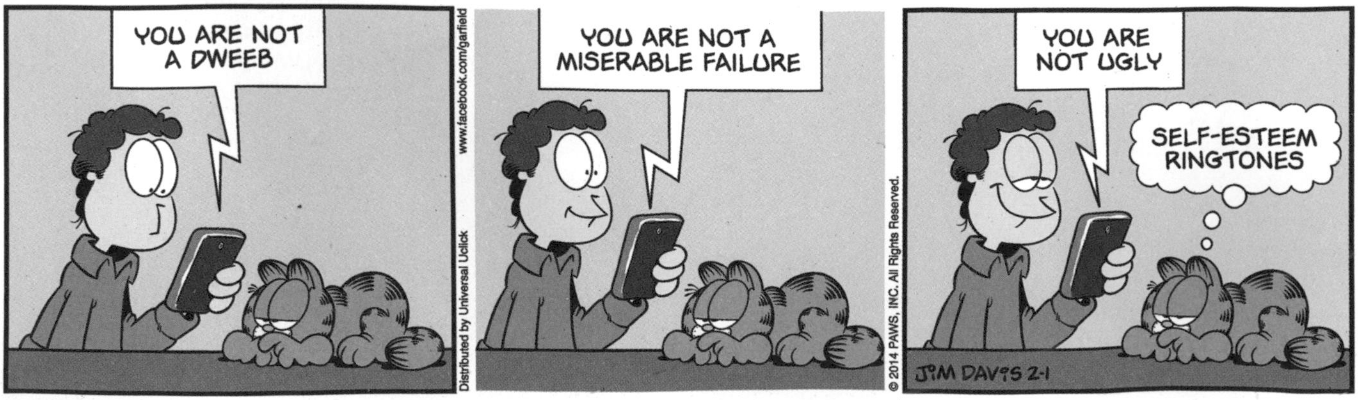
YOU ARE NOT A DWEEB
YOU ARE NOT A MISERABLE FAILURE
YOU ARE NOT UGLY
SELF-ESTEEM RINGTONES
Distributed by Universal Uclick www.facebook.com/garfield
© 2014 PAWS, INC. All Rights Reserved.
JIM DAVIS 2-1

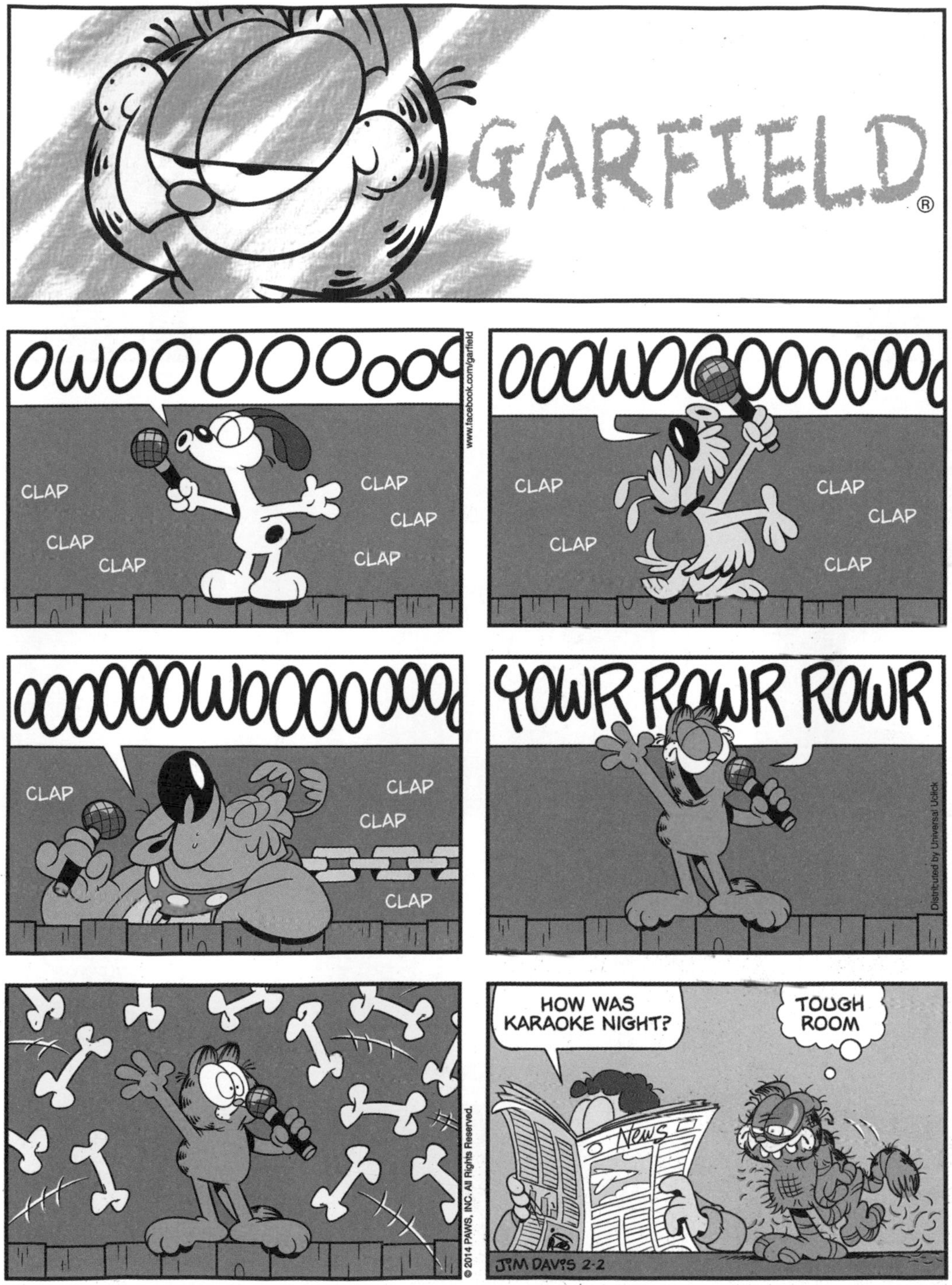
GARFIELD®
OWOOOOOOOOO
www.facebook.com/garfield
CLAP CLAP CLAP CLAP CLAP CLAP
OOOWOOOOOOOOO
CLAP CLAP CLAP CLAP CLAP
OOOOOOWOOOOOOOO
CLAP CLAP CLAP CLAP
YOWR ROWR ROWR
Distributed by Universal Uclick
© 2014 PAWS, INC. All Rights Reserved.
HOW WAS KARAOKE NIGHT?
TOUGH ROOM
NEWS
JIM DAVIS 2-2

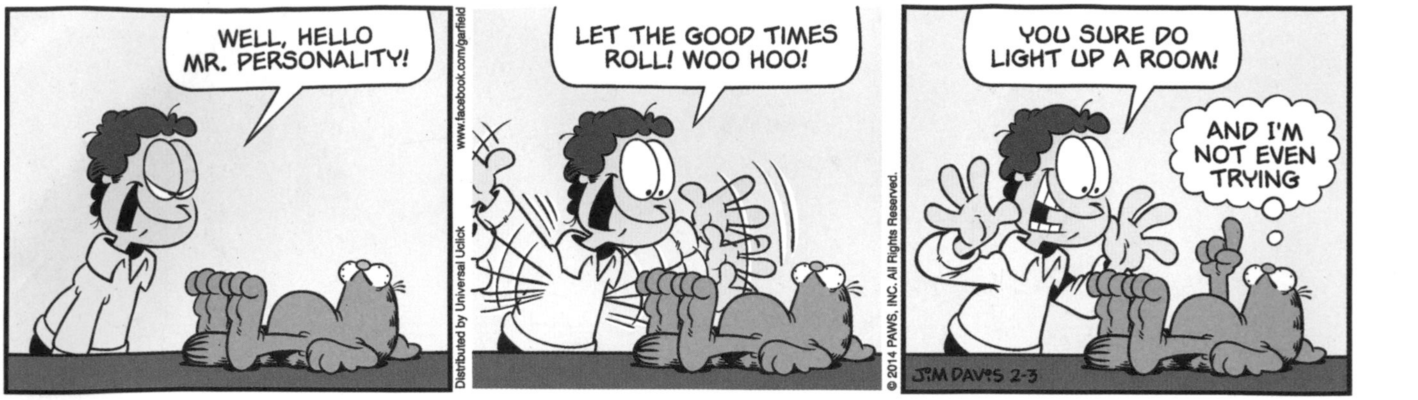
WELL, HELLO MR. PERSONALITY!
www.facebook.com/garfield
Distributed by Universal Uclick
LET THE GOOD TIMES ROLL! WOO HOO!
© 2014 PAWS, INC. All Rights Reserved.
YOU SURE DO LIGHT UP A ROOM!
AND I'M NOT EVEN TRYING
JIM DAVIS 2-3

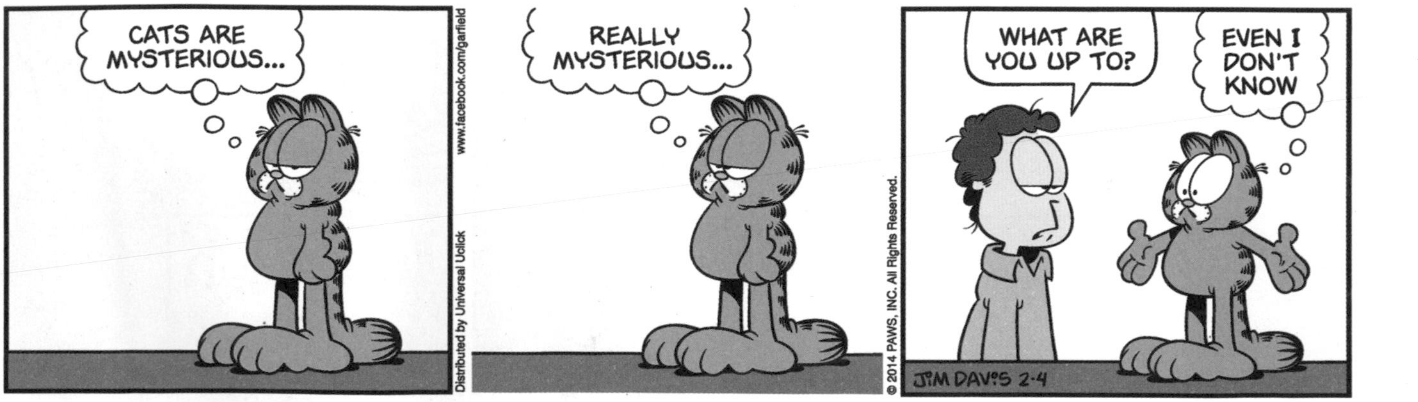
CATS ARE MYSTERIOUS...
www.facebook.com/garfield
Distributed by Universal Uclick
REALLY MYSTERIOUS...
© 2014 PAWS, INC. All Rights Reserved.
WHAT ARE YOU UP TO?
EVEN I DON'T KNOW
JIM DAVIS 2-4

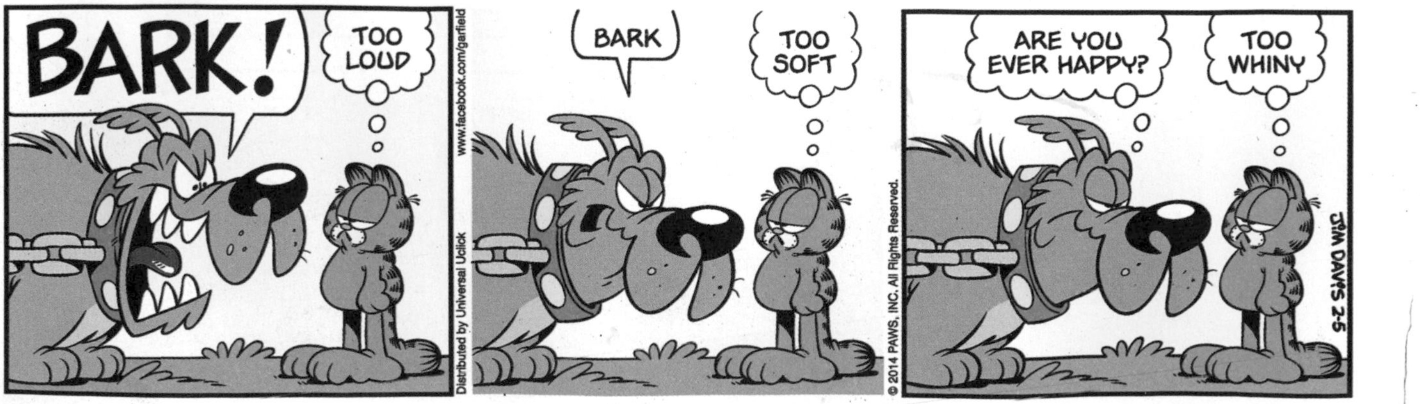
BARK!
TOO LOUD
www.facebook.com/garfield
Distributed by Universal Uclick
BARK
TOO SOFT
© 2014 PAWS, INC. All Rights Reserved.
ARE YOU EVER HAPPY?
TOO WHINY
JIM DAVIS 2-5

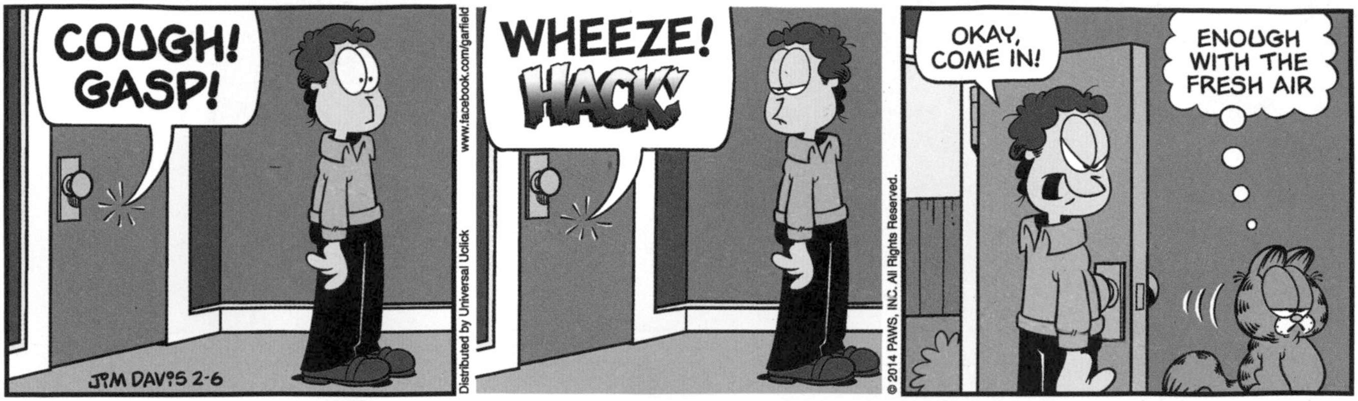
COUGH! GASP!
JIM DAVIS 2-6
Distributed by Universal Uclick www.facebook.com/garfield
WHEEZE! HACK!
© 2014 PAWS, INC. All Rights Reserved.
OKAY, COME IN!
ENOUGH WITH THE FRESH AIR

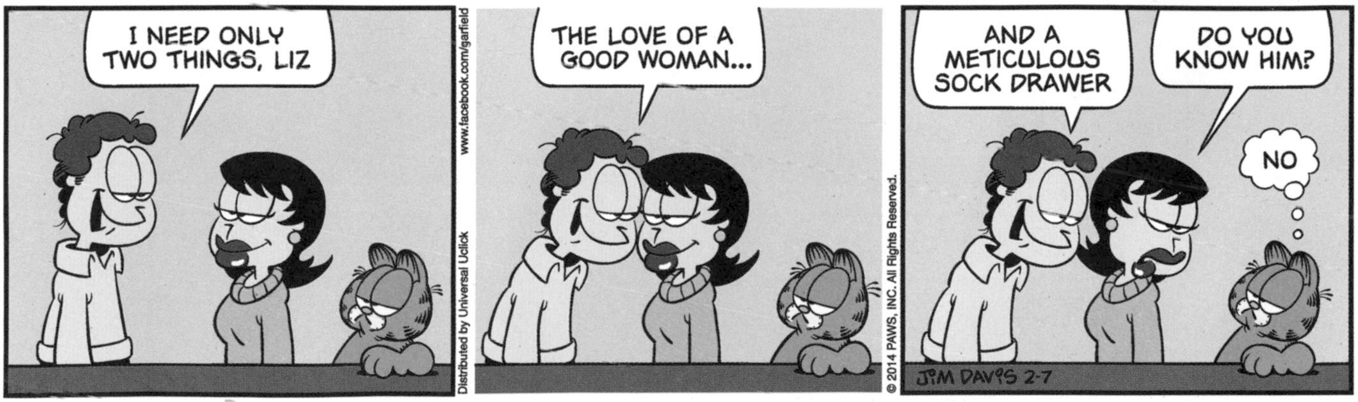
I NEED ONLY TWO THINGS, LIZ
Distributed by Universal Uclick www.facebook.com/garfield
THE LOVE OF A GOOD WOMAN...
© 2014 PAWS, INC. All Rights Reserved.
AND A METICULOUS SOCK DRAWER
DO YOU KNOW HIM?
NO
JIM DAVIS 2-7

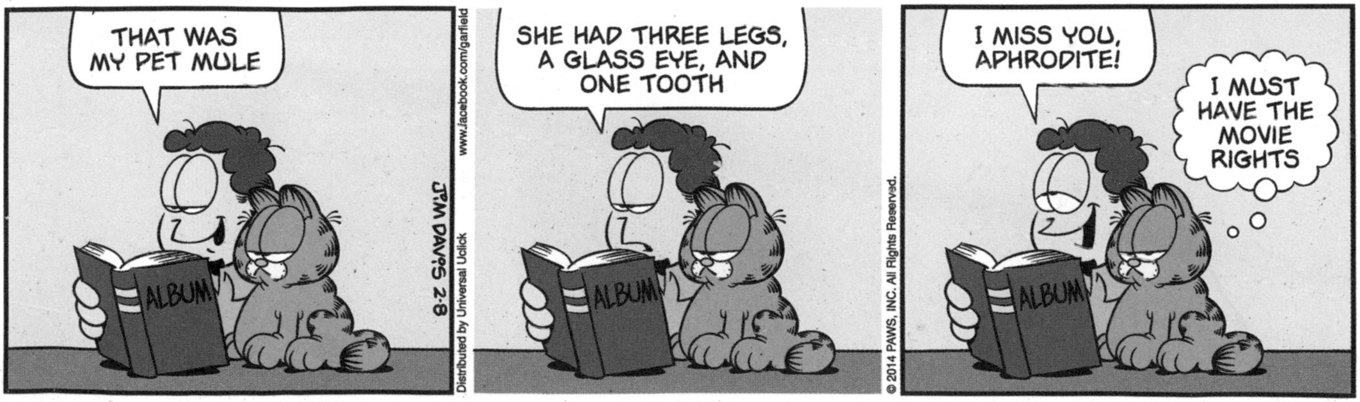
THAT WAS MY PET MULE
ALBUM
JIM DAVIS 2-8
Distributed by Universal Uclick www.facebook.com/garfield
SHE HAD THREE LEGS, A GLASS EYE, AND ONE TOOTH
ALBUM
© 2014 PAWS, INC. All Rights Reserved.
I MISS YOU, APHRODITE!
I MUST HAVE THE MOVIE RIGHTS
ALBUM

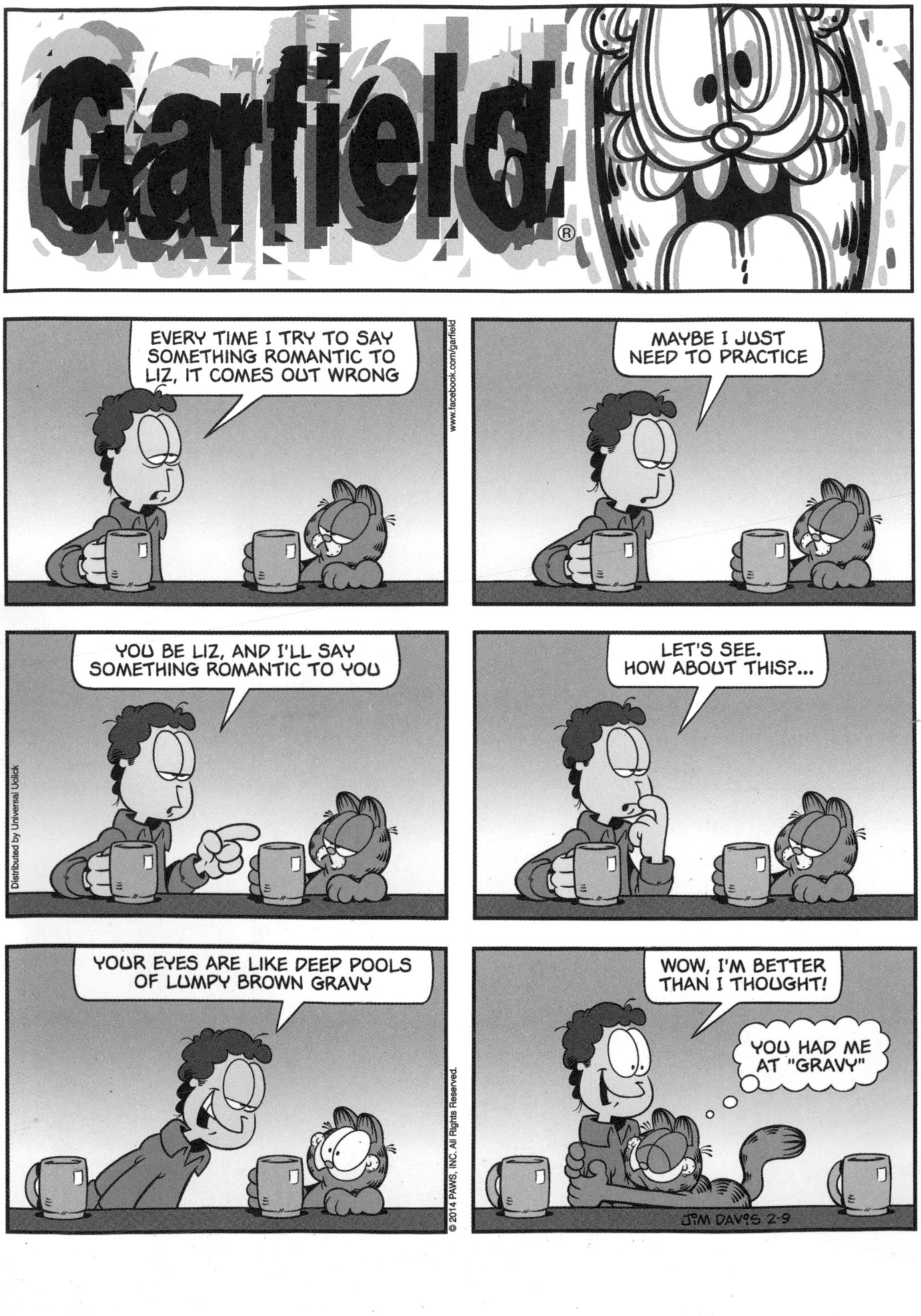
Garfield®
EVERY TIME I TRY TO SAY SOMETHING ROMANTIC TO LIZ, IT COMES OUT WRONG
www.facebook.com/garfield
MAYBE I JUST NEED TO PRACTICE
YOU BE LIZ, AND I'LL SAY SOMETHING ROMANTIC TO YOU
Distributed by Universal Uclick
LET'S SEE. HOW ABOUT THIS?...
YOUR EYES ARE LIKE DEEP POOLS OF LUMPY BROWN GRAVY
© 2014 PAWS, INC. All Rights Reserved.
WOW, I'M BETTER THAN I THOUGHT!
YOU HAD ME AT "GRAVY"
JIM DAVIS 2-9

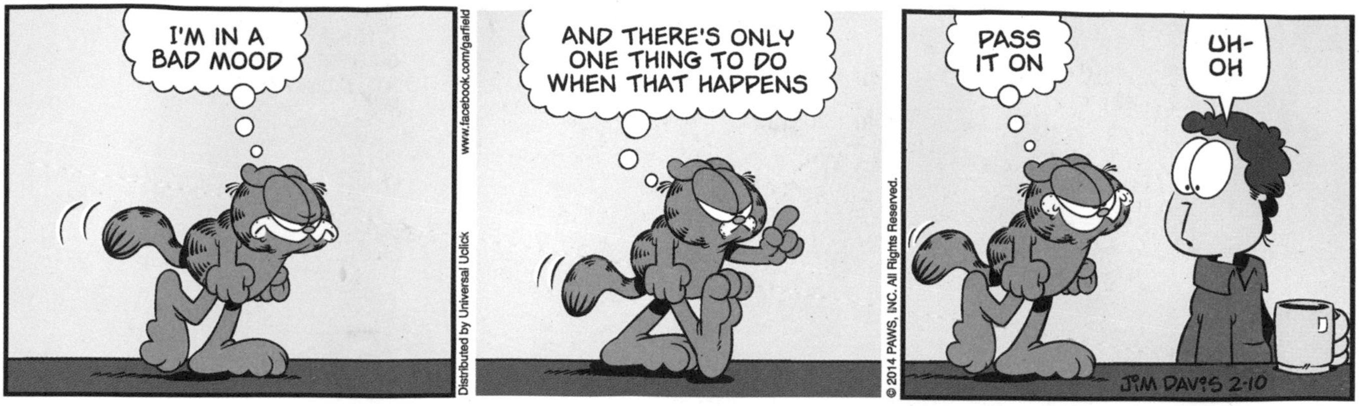
I'M IN A BAD MOOD
AND THERE'S ONLY ONE THING TO DO WHEN THAT HAPPENS
PASS IT ON
UH-OH
Distributed by Universal Uclick www.facebook.com/garfield
© 2014 PAWS, INC. All Rights Reserved.
JIM DAVIS 2-10

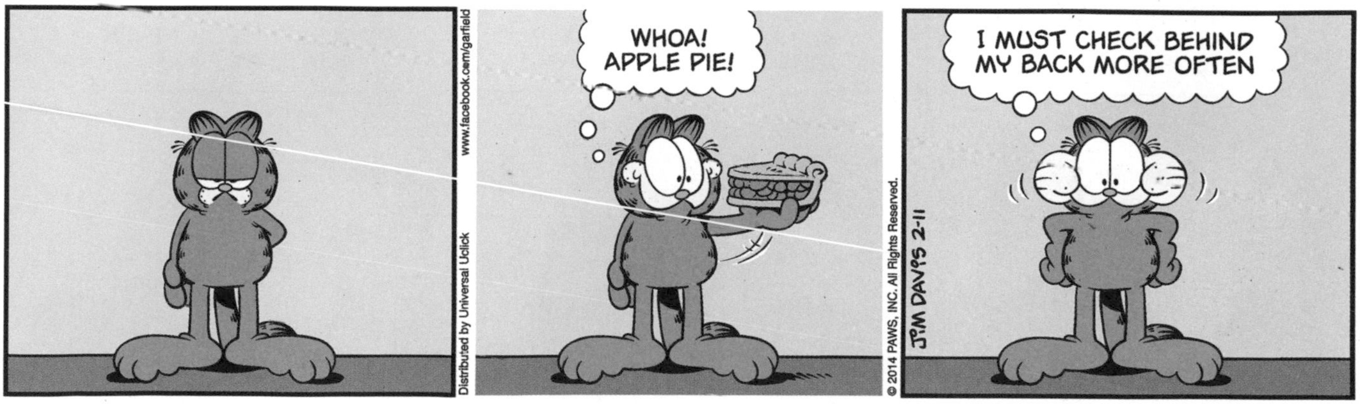
WHOA! APPLE PIE!
I MUST CHECK BEHIND MY BACK MORE OFTEN
Distributed by Universal Uclick www.facebook.com/garfield
© 2014 PAWS, INC. All Rights Reserved.
JIM DAVIS 2-11

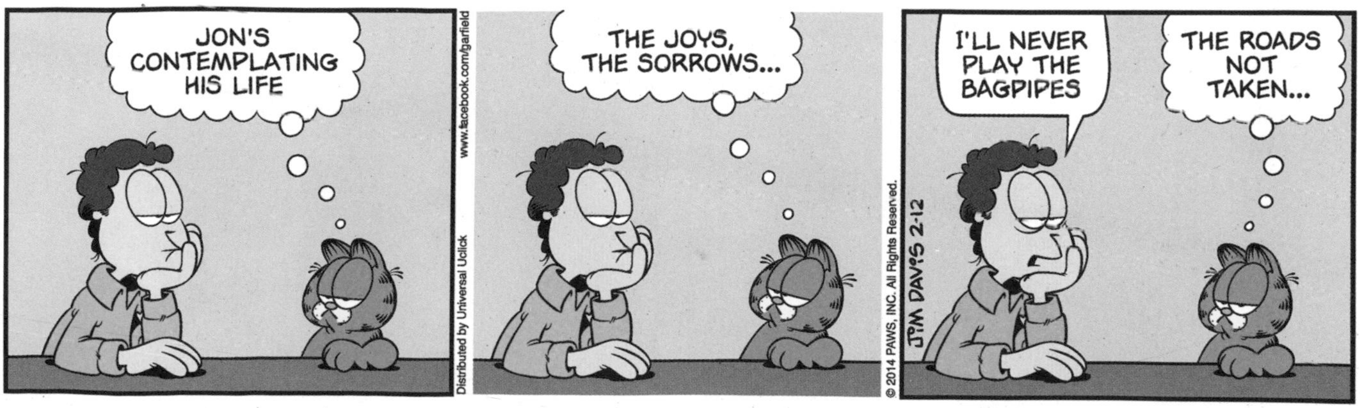
JON'S CONTEMPLATING HIS LIFE
THE JOYS, THE SORROWS...
I'LL NEVER PLAY THE BAGPIPES
THE ROADS NOT TAKEN...
Distributed by Universal Uclick www.facebook.com/garfield
© 2014 PAWS, INC. All Rights Reserved.
JIM DAVIS 2-12

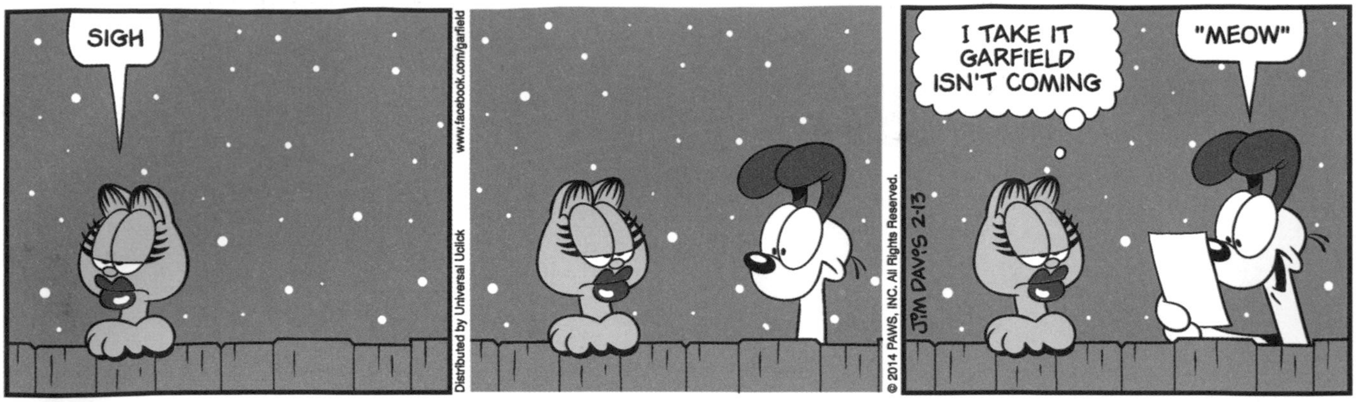
SIGH
Distributed by Universal Uclick www.facebook.com/garfield
I TAKE IT GARFIELD ISN'T COMING
"MEOW"
© 2014 PAWS, INC. All Rights Reserved.
JIM DAVIS 2-13

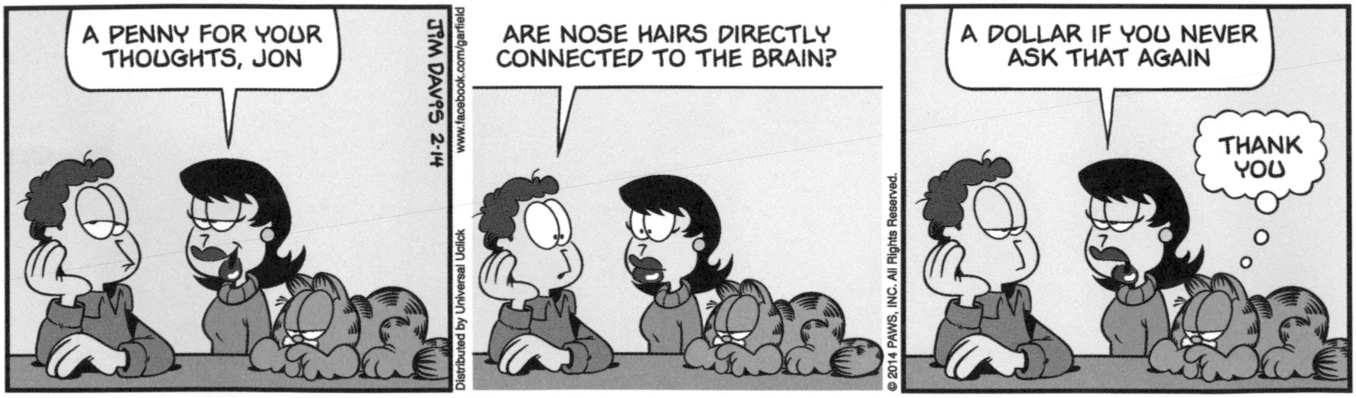
A PENNY FOR YOUR THOUGHTS, JON
JIM DAVIS 2-14
Distributed by Universal Uclick www.facebook.com/garfield
ARE NOSE HAIRS DIRECTLY CONNECTED TO THE BRAIN?
A DOLLAR IF YOU NEVER ASK THAT AGAIN
THANK YOU
© 2014 PAWS, INC. All Rights Reserved.

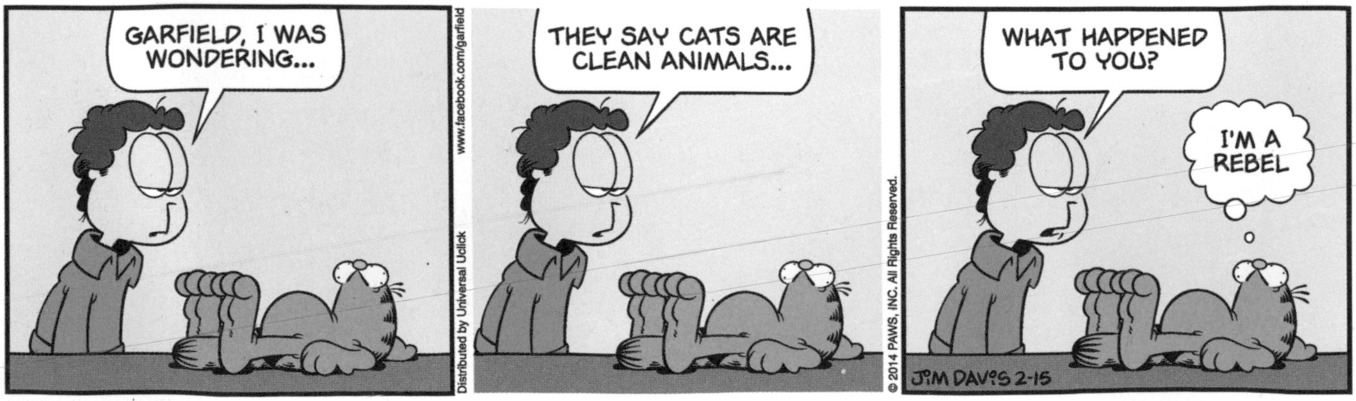
GARFIELD, I WAS WONDERING...
Distributed by Universal Uclick www.facebook.com/garfield
THEY SAY CATS ARE CLEAN ANIMALS...
WHAT HAPPENED TO YOU?
I'M A REBEL
© 2014 PAWS, INC. All Rights Reserved.
JIM DAVIS 2-15

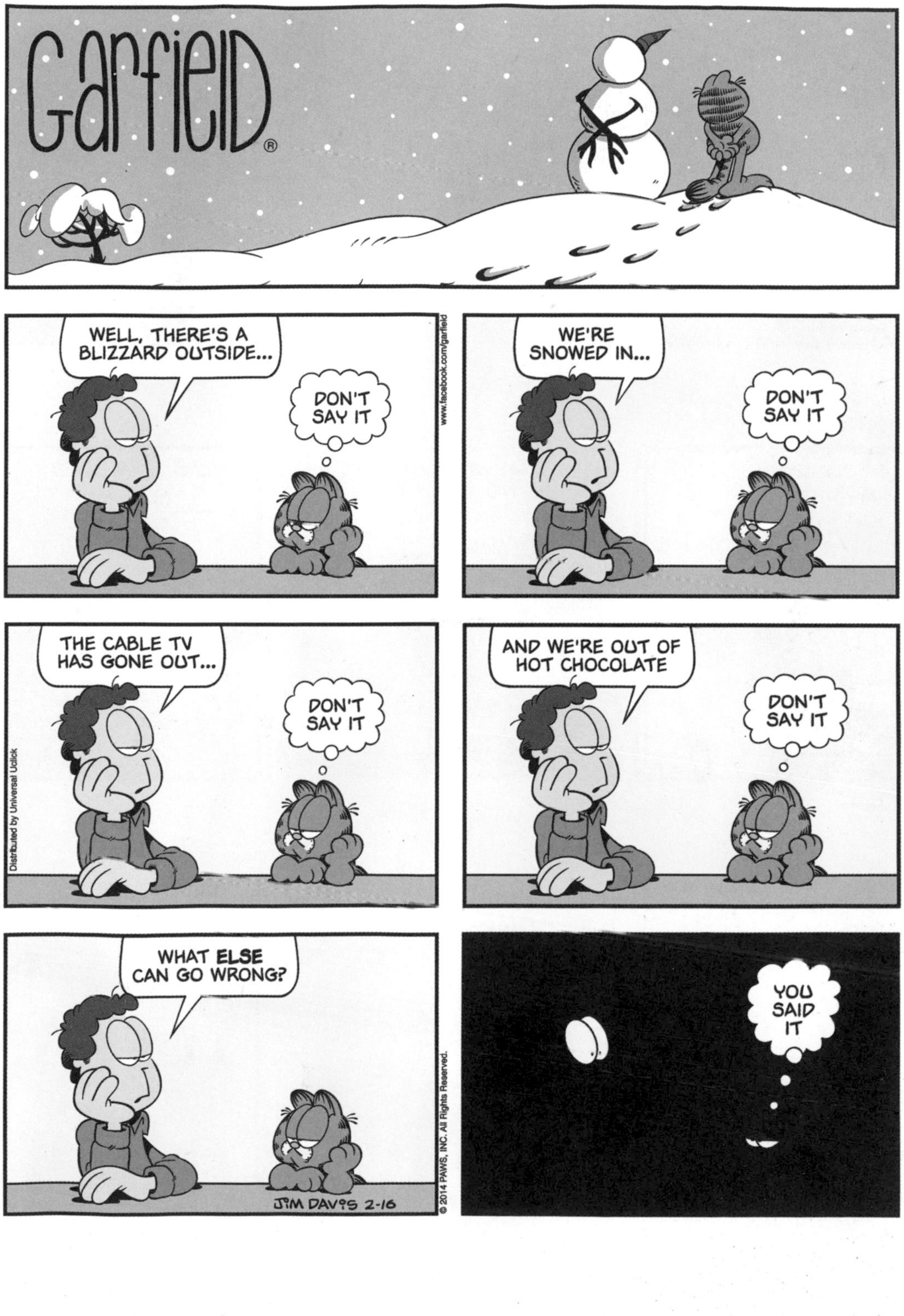
GARFIELD®
WELL, THERE'S A BLIZZARD OUTSIDE...
DON'T SAY IT
WE'RE SNOWED IN...
DON'T SAY IT
THE CABLE TV HAS GONE OUT...
DON'T SAY IT
AND WE'RE OUT OF HOT CHOCOLATE
DON'T SAY IT
WHAT ELSE CAN GO WRONG?
JIM DAVIS 2-16
YOU SAID IT
www.facebook.com/garfield
Distributed by Universal Uclick
© 2014 PAWS, INC. All Rights Reserved.

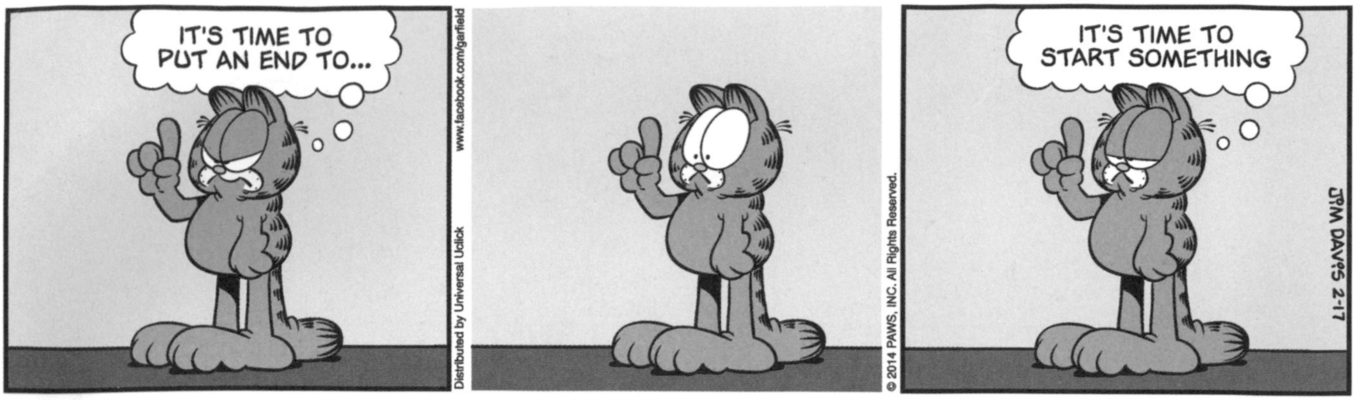
IT'S TIME TO PUT AN END TO...
IT'S TIME TO START SOMETHING
JIM DAVIS 2-17
www.facebook.com/garfield
Distributed by Universal Uclick
© 2014 PAWS, INC. All Rights Reserved.

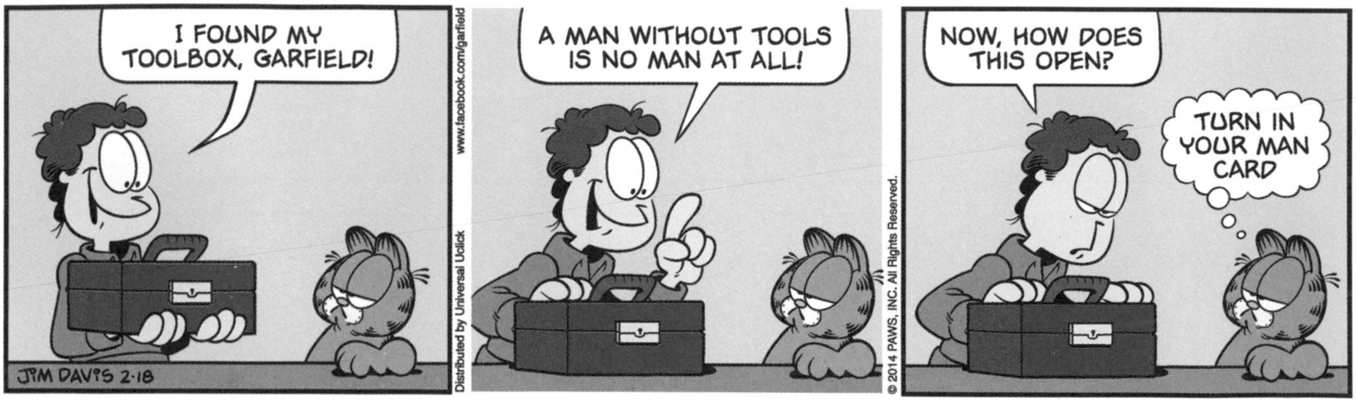
I FOUND MY TOOLBOX, GARFIELD!
JIM DAVIS 2-18
A MAN WITHOUT TOOLS IS NO MAN AT ALL!
NOW, HOW DOES THIS OPEN?
TURN IN YOUR MAN CARD
www.facebook.com/garfield
Distributed by Universal Uclick
© 2014 PAWS, INC. All Rights Reserved.

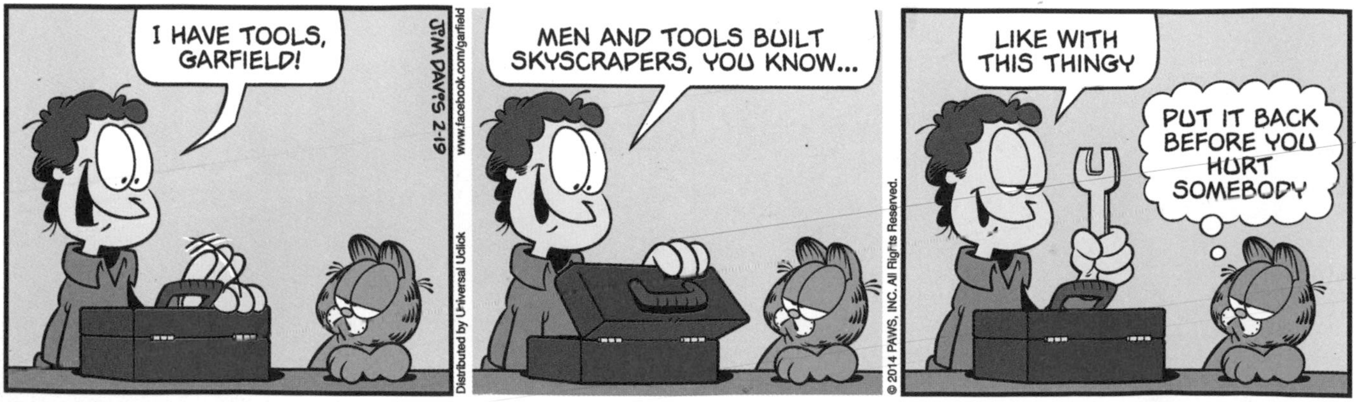
I HAVE TOOLS, GARFIELD!
JIM DAVIS 2-19
MEN AND TOOLS BUILT SKYSCRAPERS, YOU KNOW...
LIKE WITH THIS THINGY
PUT IT BACK BEFORE YOU HURT SOMEBODY
www.facebook.com/garfield
Distributed by Universal Uclick
© 2014 PAWS, INC. All Rights Reserved.

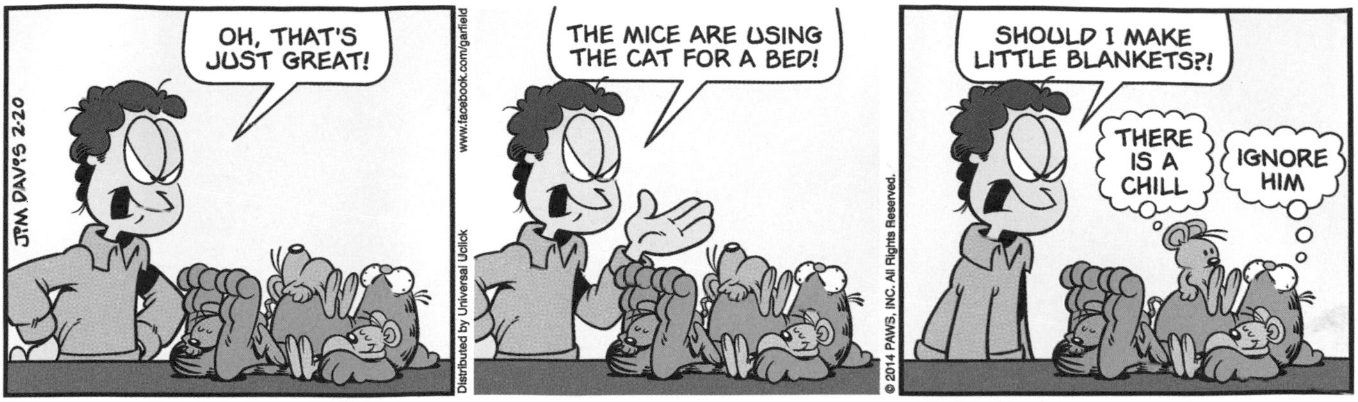
JIM DAVIS 2-20
OH, THAT'S JUST GREAT!
Distributed by Universal Uclick www.facebook.com/garfield
THE MICE ARE USING THE CAT FOR A BED!
© 2014 PAWS, INC. All Rights Reserved.
SHOULD I MAKE LITTLE BLANKETS?!
THERE IS A CHILL
IGNORE HIM

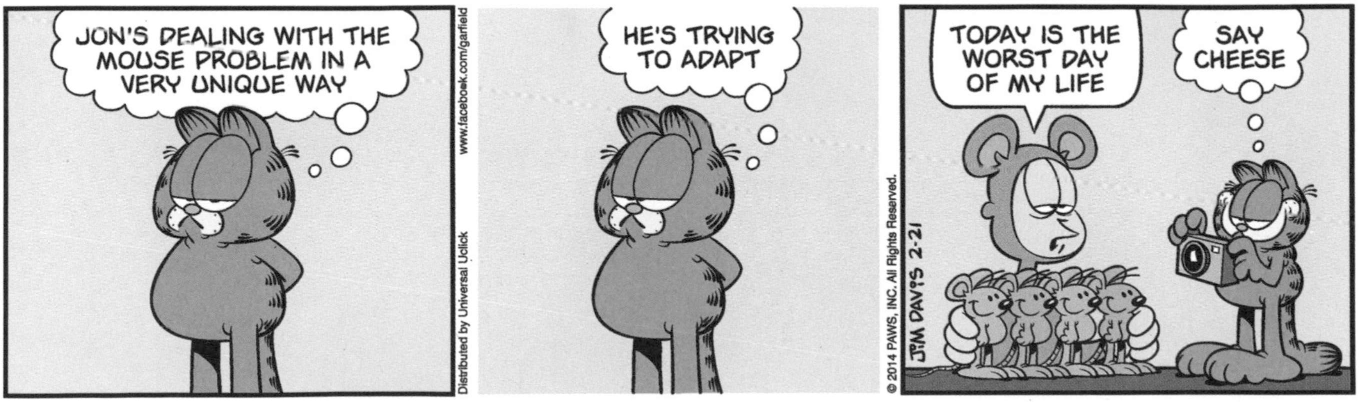
JON'S DEALING WITH THE MOUSE PROBLEM IN A VERY UNIQUE WAY
Distributed by Universal Uclick www.facebook.com/garfield
HE'S TRYING TO ADAPT
© 2014 PAWS, INC. All Rights Reserved.
TODAY IS THE WORST DAY OF MY LIFE
SAY CHEESE
JIM DAVIS 2-21

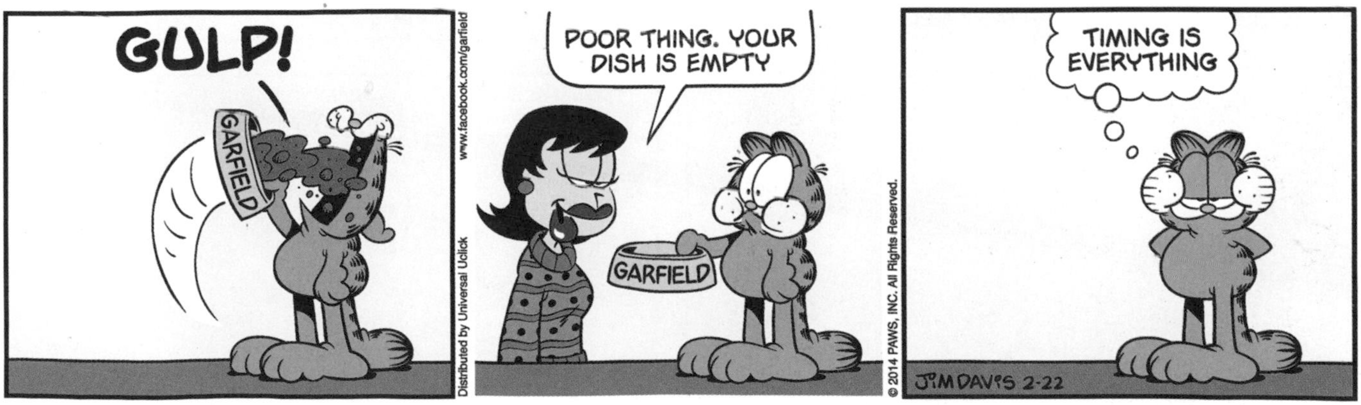
GULP!
GARFIELD
Distributed by Universal Uclick www.facebook.com/garfield
POOR THING. YOUR DISH IS EMPTY
GARFIELD
© 2014 PAWS, INC. All Rights Reserved.
TIMING IS EVERYTHING
JIM DAVIS 2-22

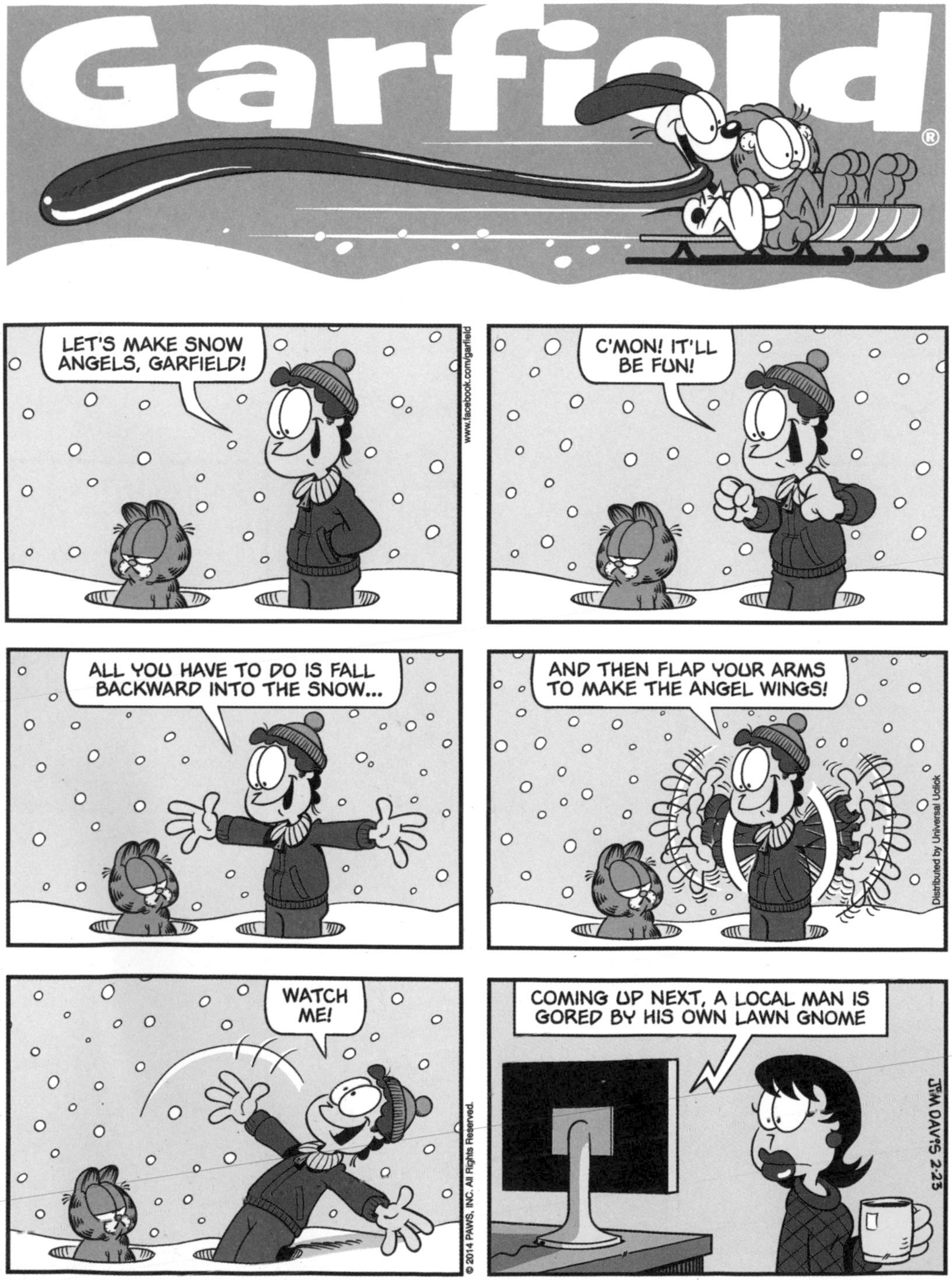
Garfield®
LET'S MAKE SNOW ANGELS, GARFIELD!
www.facebook.com/garfield
C'MON! IT'LL BE FUN!
ALL YOU HAVE TO DO IS FALL BACKWARD INTO THE SNOW...
AND THEN FLAP YOUR ARMS TO MAKE THE ANGEL WINGS!
Distributed by Universal Uclick
WATCH ME!
© 2014 PAWS, INC. All Rights Reserved.
COMING UP NEXT, A LOCAL MAN IS GORED BY HIS OWN LAWN GNOME
JIM DAVIS 2-23

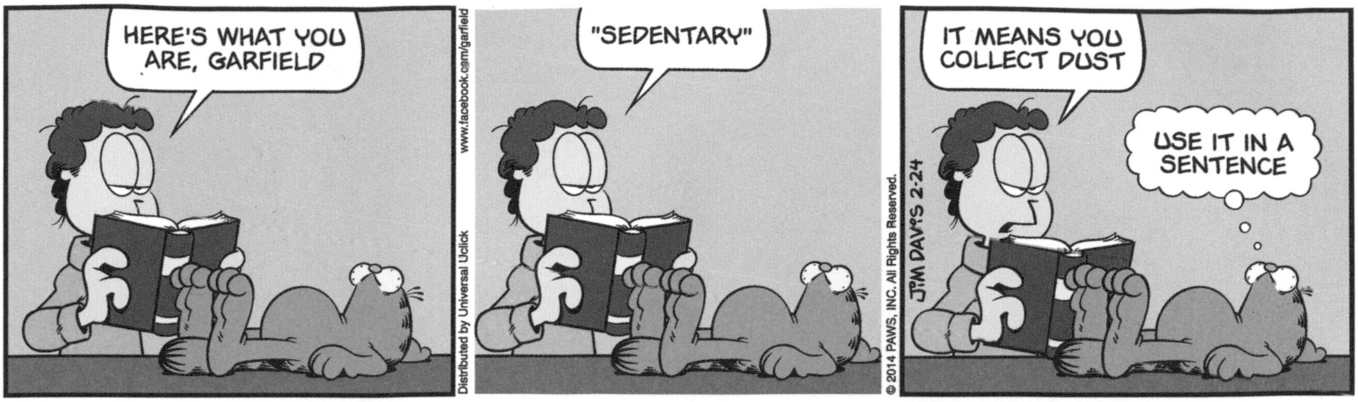
HERE'S WHAT YOU ARE, GARFIELD
"SEDENTARY"
IT MEANS YOU COLLECT DUST
USE IT IN A SENTENCE
JIM DAVIS 2-24
Distributed by Universal Uclick www.facebook.com/garfield
© 2014 PAWS, INC. All Rights Reserved.

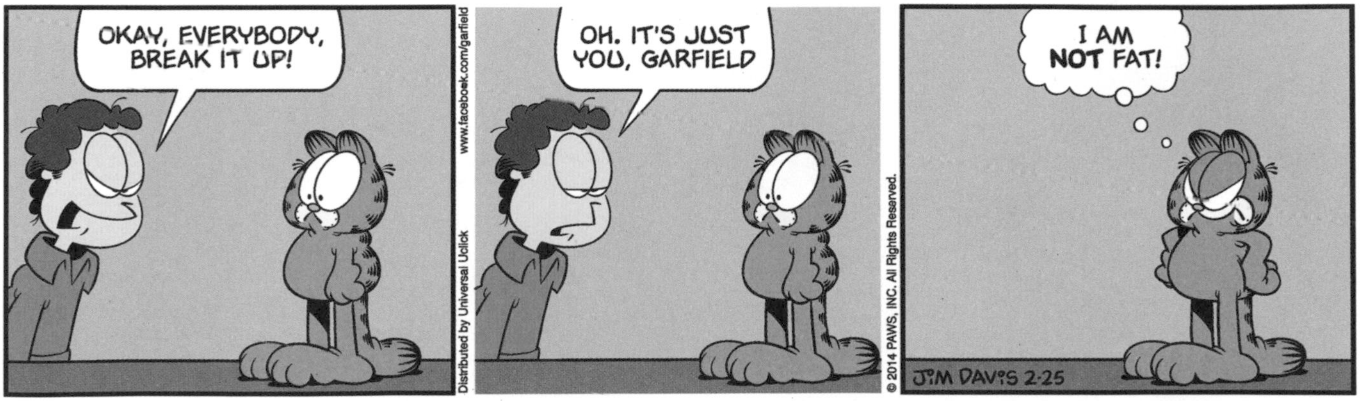
OKAY, EVERYBODY, BREAK IT UP!
OH. IT'S JUST YOU, GARFIELD
I AM **NOT** FAT!
JIM DAVIS 2-25
Distributed by Universal Uclick www.facebook.com/garfield
© 2014 PAWS, INC. All Rights Reserved.

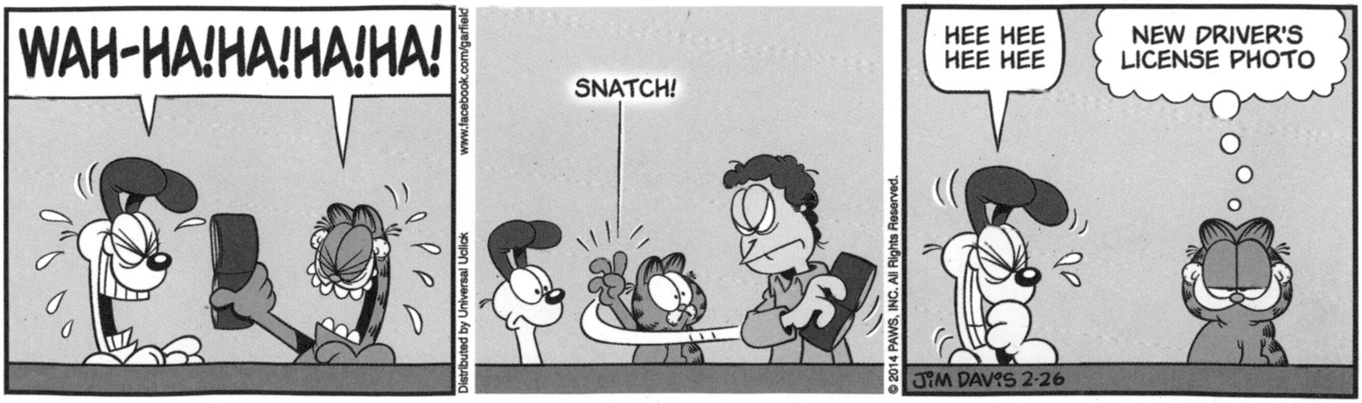
WAH-HA!HA!HA!HA!
SNATCH!
HEE HEE HEE HEE
NEW DRIVER'S LICENSE PHOTO
JIM DAVIS 2-26
Distributed by Universal Uclick www.facebook.com/garfield
© 2014 PAWS, INC. All Rights Reserved.

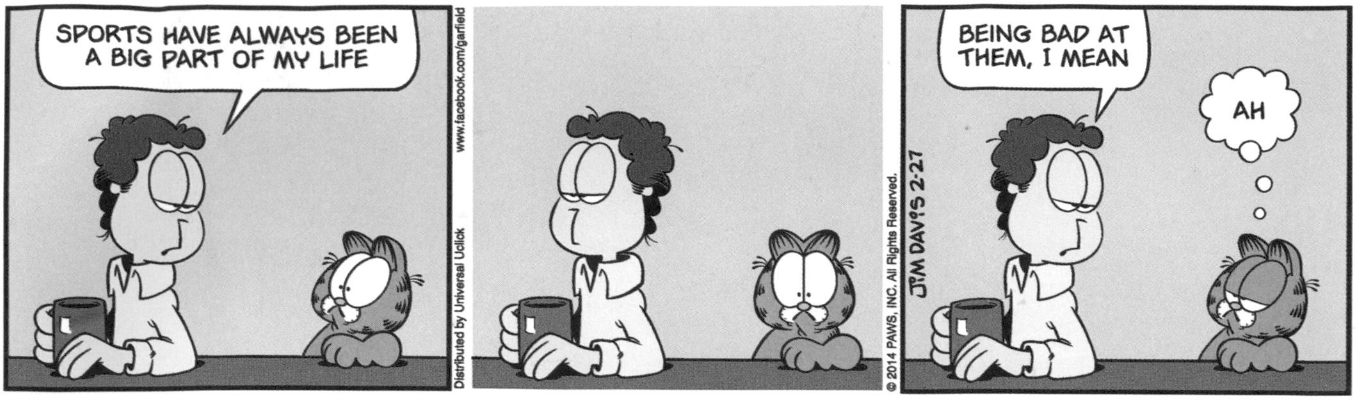
SPORTS HAVE ALWAYS BEEN A BIG PART OF MY LIFE
Distributed by Universal Uclick www.facebook.com/garfield
BEING BAD AT THEM, I MEAN
AH
© 2014 PAWS, INC. All Rights Reserved.
JIM DAVIS 2-27

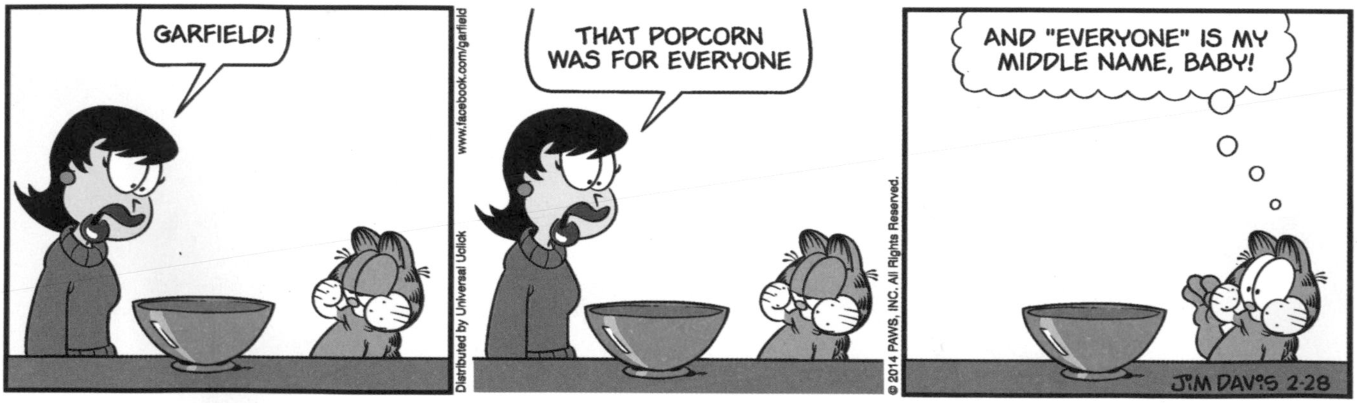
GARFIELD!
Distributed by Universal Uclick www.facebook.com/garfield
THAT POPCORN WAS FOR EVERYONE
© 2014 PAWS, INC. All Rights Reserved.
AND "EVERYONE" IS MY MIDDLE NAME, BABY!
JIM DAVIS 2-28

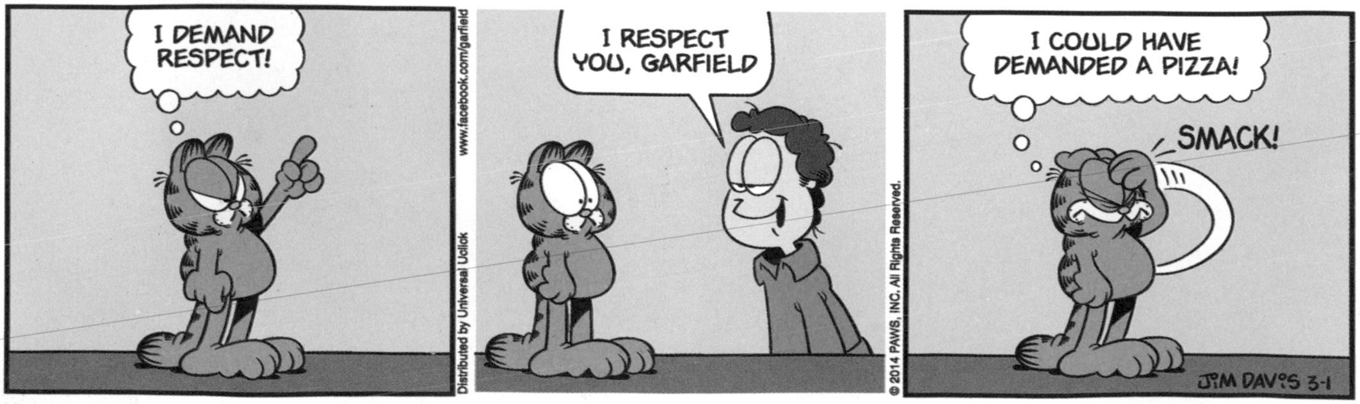
I DEMAND RESPECT!
Distributed by Universal Uclick www.facebook.com/garfield
I RESPECT YOU, GARFIELD
© 2014 PAWS, INC. All Rights Reserved.
I COULD HAVE DEMANDED A PIZZA!
SMACK!
JIM DAVIS 3-1

GARFIELD®

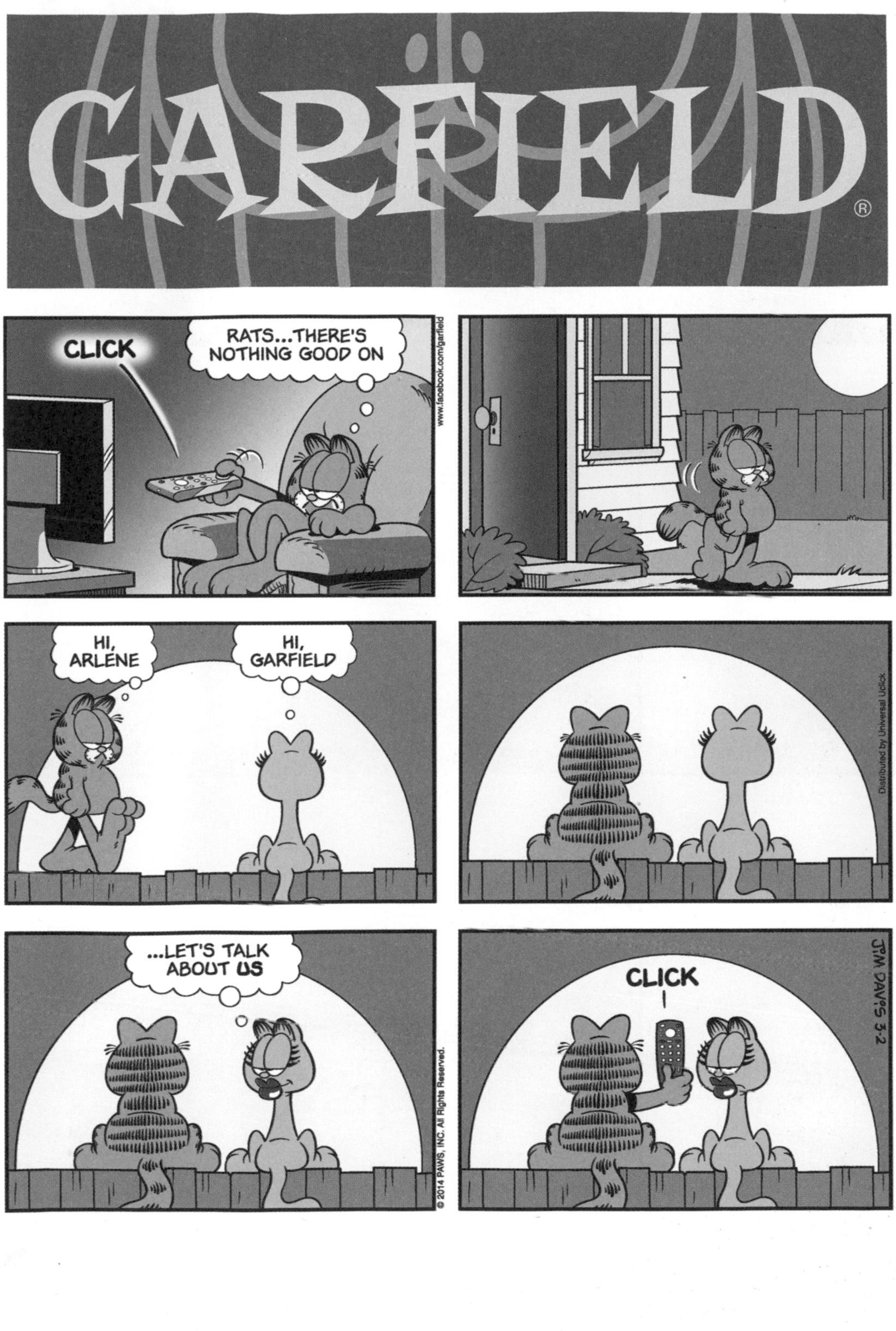
CLICK
RATS...THERE'S NOTHING GOOD ON
www.facebook.com/garfield
HI, ARLENE
HI, GARFIELD
Distributed by Universal Uclick
...LET'S TALK ABOUT US
© 2014 PAWS, INC. All Rights Reserved.
CLICK
JIM DAVIS 3-2

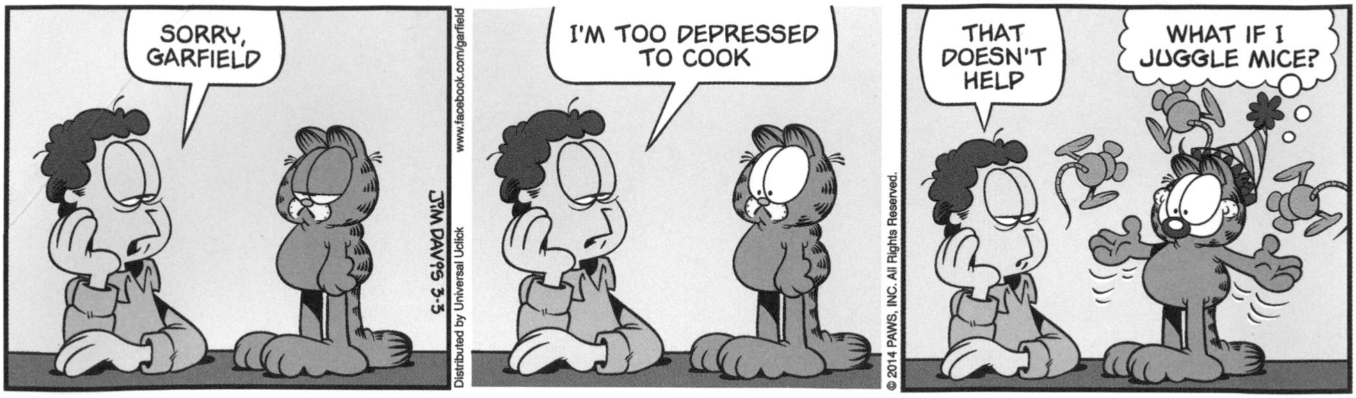
SORRY, GARFIELD
JIM DAVIS 3-3
www.facebook.com/garfield
Distributed by Universal Uclick
I'M TOO DEPRESSED TO COOK
© 2014 PAWS, INC. All Rights Reserved.
THAT DOESN'T HELP
WHAT IF I JUGGLE MICE?

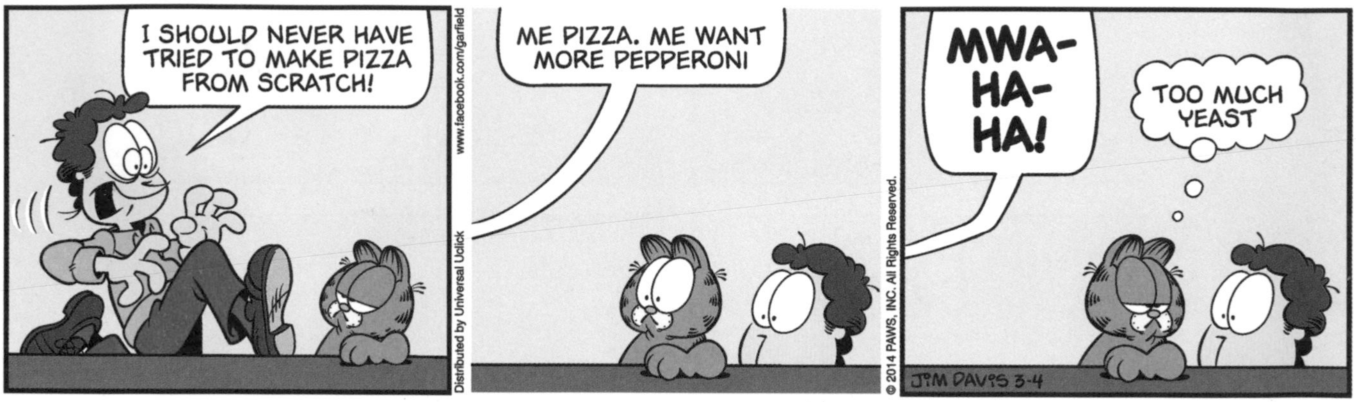
I SHOULD NEVER HAVE TRIED TO MAKE PIZZA FROM SCRATCH!
www.facebook.com/garfield
Distributed by Universal Uclick
ME PIZZA. ME WANT MORE PEPPERONI
© 2014 PAWS, INC. All Rights Reserved.
MWA-HA-HA!
TOO MUCH YEAST
JIM DAVIS 3-4

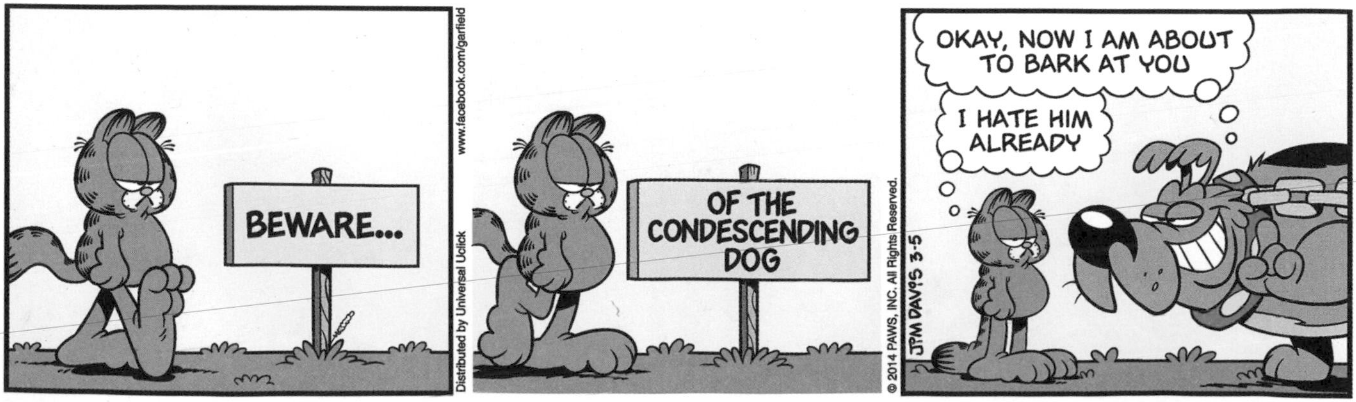
BEWARE...
www.facebook.com/garfield
Distributed by Universal Uclick
OF THE CONDESCENDING DOG
© 2014 PAWS, INC. All Rights Reserved.
JIM DAVIS 3-5
OKAY, NOW I AM ABOUT TO BARK AT YOU
I HATE HIM ALREADY

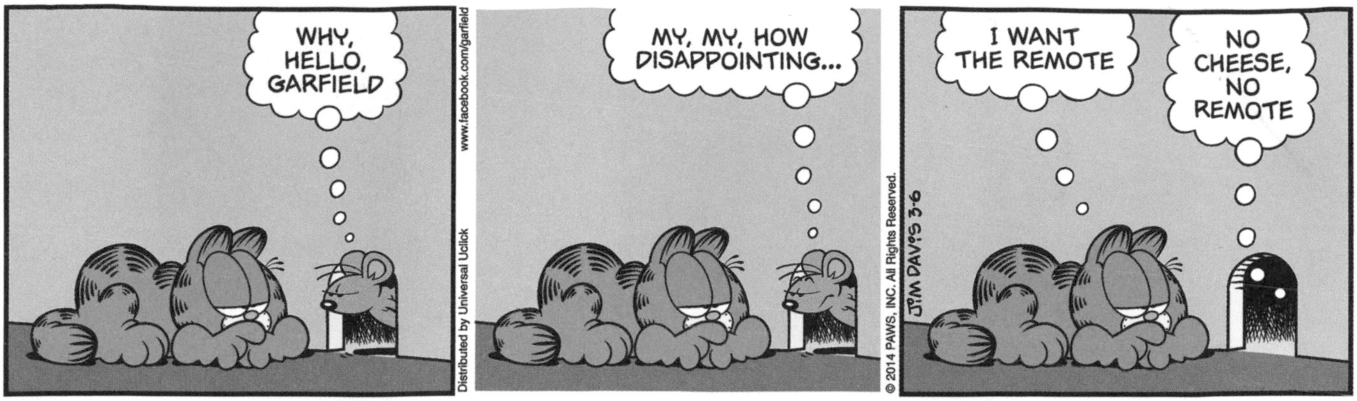
WHY, HELLO, GARFIELD
MY, MY, HOW DISAPPOINTING...
I WANT THE REMOTE
NO CHEESE, NO REMOTE
Distributed by Universal Uclick www.facebook.com/garfield
© 2014 PAWS, INC. All Rights Reserved.
JIM DAVIS 3-6

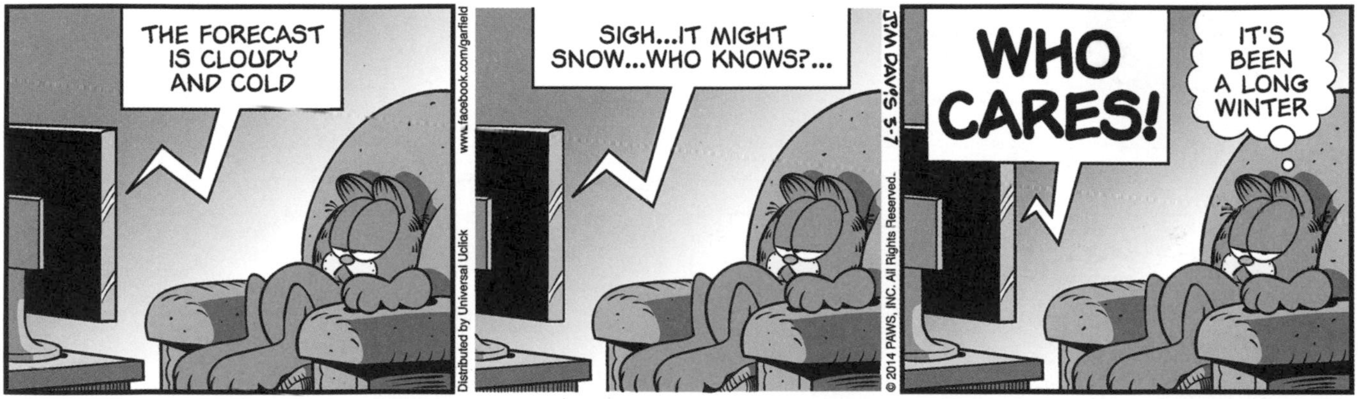
THE FORECAST IS CLOUDY AND COLD
SIGH...IT MIGHT SNOW...WHO KNOWS?...
WHO CARES!
IT'S BEEN A LONG WINTER
Distributed by Universal Uclick www.facebook.com/garfield
© 2014 PAWS, INC. All Rights Reserved.
JIM DAVIS 3-7

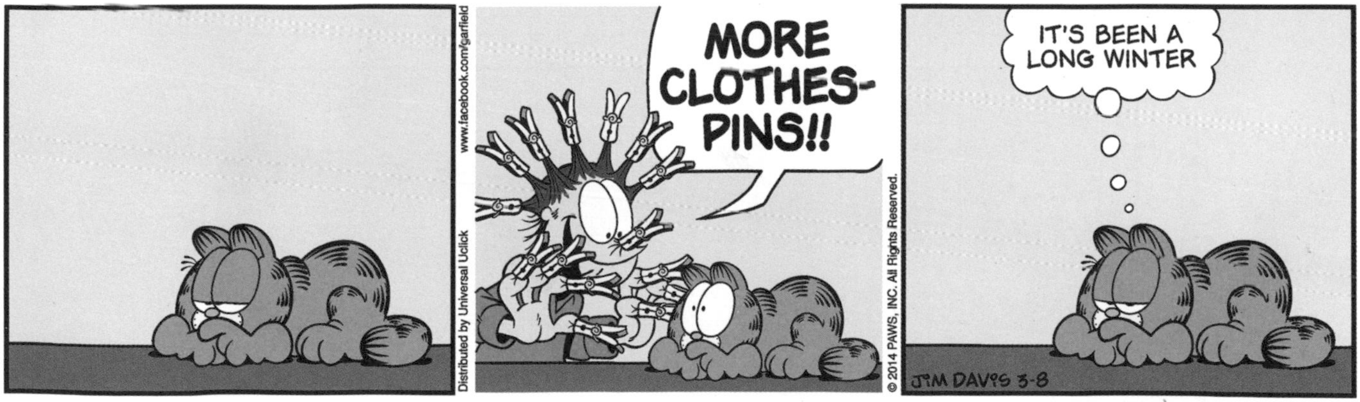
MORE CLOTHES-PINS!!
IT'S BEEN A LONG WINTER
Distributed by Universal Uclick www.facebook.com/garfield
© 2014 PAWS, INC. All Rights Reserved.
JIM DAVIS 3-8

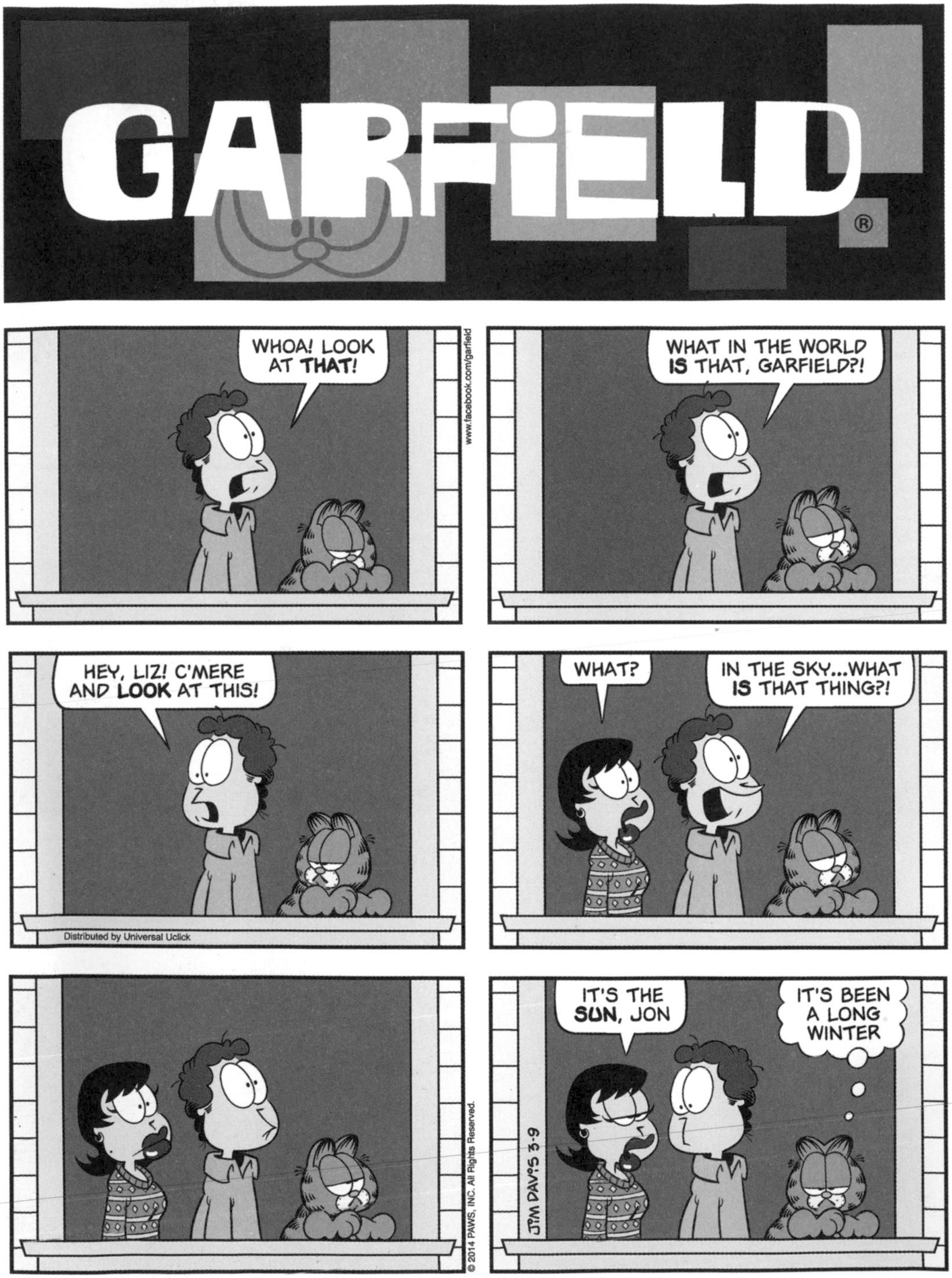
GARFIELD®
WHOA! LOOK AT THAT!
www.facebook.com/garfield
WHAT IN THE WORLD IS THAT, GARFIELD?!
HEY, LIZ! C'MERE AND LOOK AT THIS!
Distributed by Universal Uclick
WHAT?
IN THE SKY...WHAT IS THAT THING?!
© 2014 PAWS, INC. All Rights Reserved.
JIM DAVIS 3-9
IT'S THE SUN, JON
IT'S BEEN A LONG WINTER

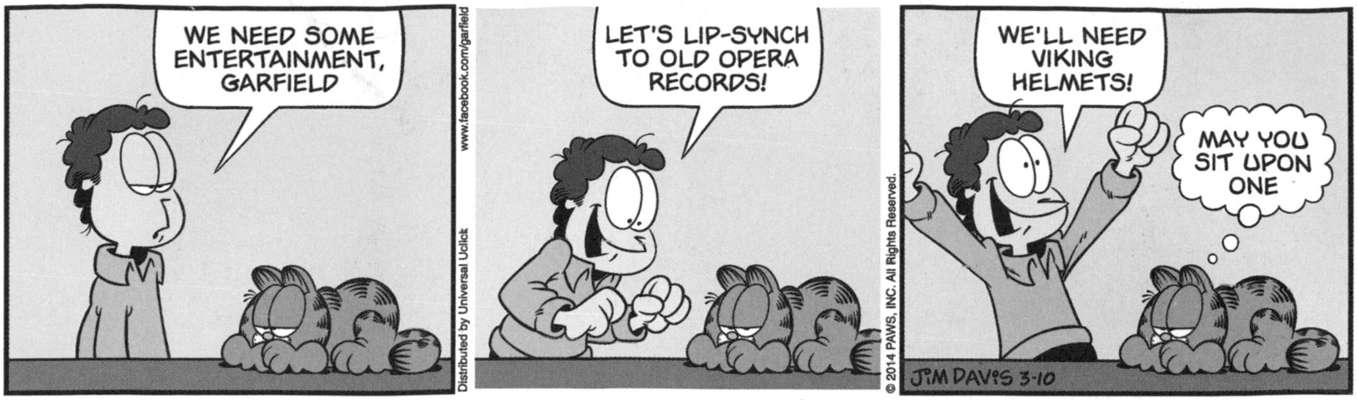
WE NEED SOME ENTERTAINMENT, GARFIELD
LET'S LIP-SYNCH TO OLD OPERA RECORDS!
WE'LL NEED VIKING HELMETS!
MAY YOU SIT UPON ONE
JIM DAVIS 3-10
Distributed by Universal Uclick www.facebook.com/garfield
© 2014 PAWS, INC. All Rights Reserved.

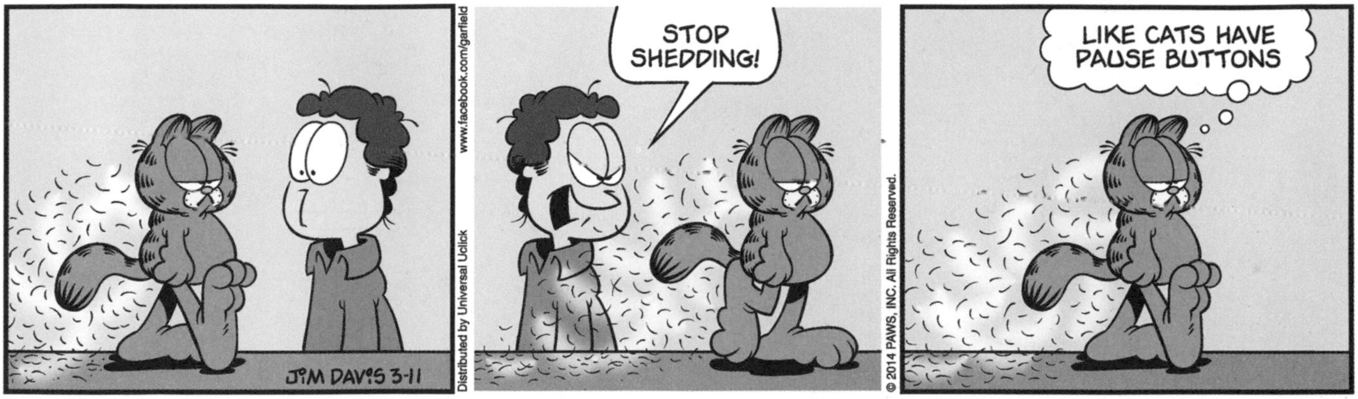
JIM DAVIS 3-11
STOP SHEDDING!
LIKE CATS HAVE PAUSE BUTTONS
Distributed by Universal Uclick www.facebook.com/garfield
© 2014 PAWS, INC. All Rights Reserved.

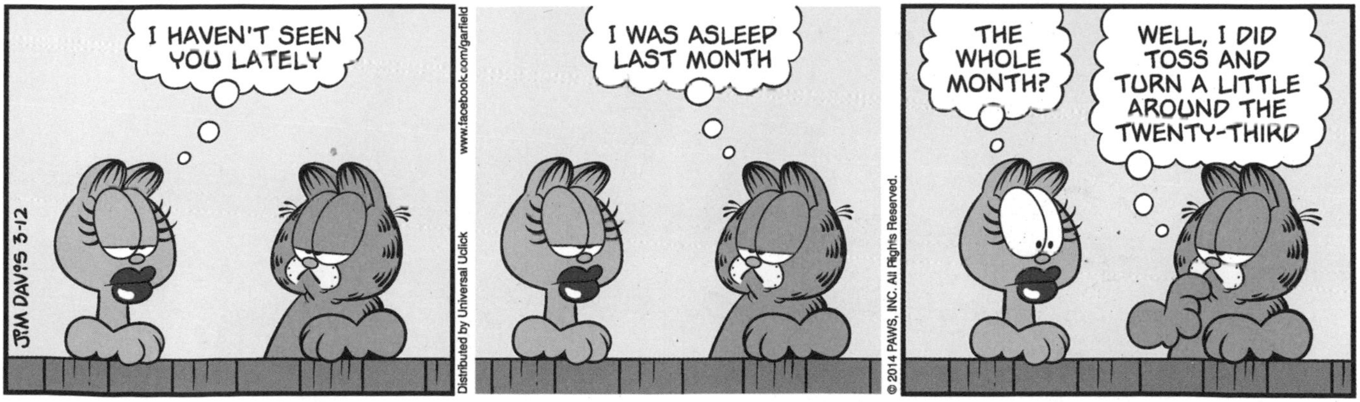
JIM DAVIS 3-12
I HAVEN'T SEEN YOU LATELY
I WAS ASLEEP LAST MONTH
THE WHOLE MONTH?
WELL, I DID TOSS AND TURN A LITTLE AROUND THE TWENTY-THIRD
Distributed by Universal Uclick www.facebook.com/garfield
© 2014 PAWS, INC. All Rights Reserved.

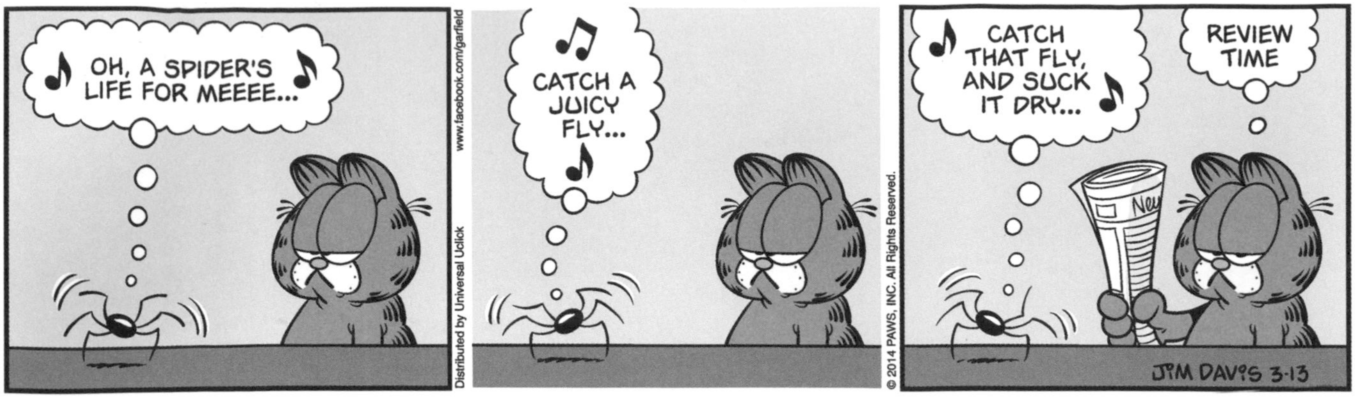
OH, A SPIDER'S LIFE FOR MEEEE...
Distributed by Universal Uclick www.facebook.com/garfield
CATCH A JUICY FLY...
© 2014 PAWS, INC. All Rights Reserved.
CATCH THAT FLY, AND SUCK IT DRY...
REVIEW TIME
JPM DAVPS 3-13

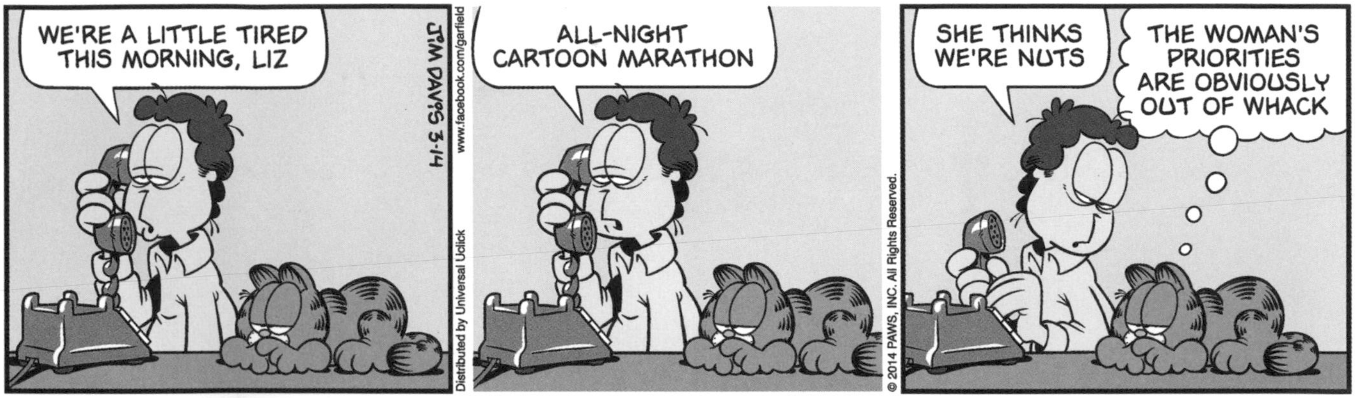
WE'RE A LITTLE TIRED THIS MORNING, LIZ
JPM DAVPS 3-14
Distributed by Universal Uclick www.facebook.com/garfield
ALL-NIGHT CARTOON MARATHON
© 2014 PAWS, INC. All Rights Reserved.
SHE THINKS WE'RE NUTS
THE WOMAN'S PRIORITIES ARE OBVIOUSLY OUT OF WHACK

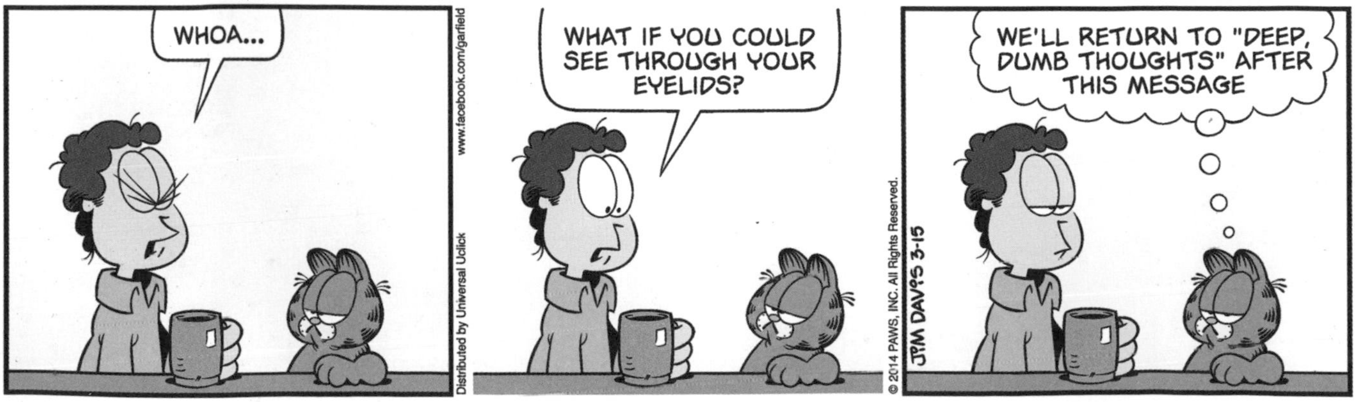
WHOA...
Distributed by Universal Uclick www.facebook.com/garfield
WHAT IF YOU COULD SEE THROUGH YOUR EYELIDS?
© 2014 PAWS, INC. All Rights Reserved.
JPM DAVPS 3-15
WE'LL RETURN TO "DEEP, DUMB THOUGHTS" AFTER THIS MESSAGE

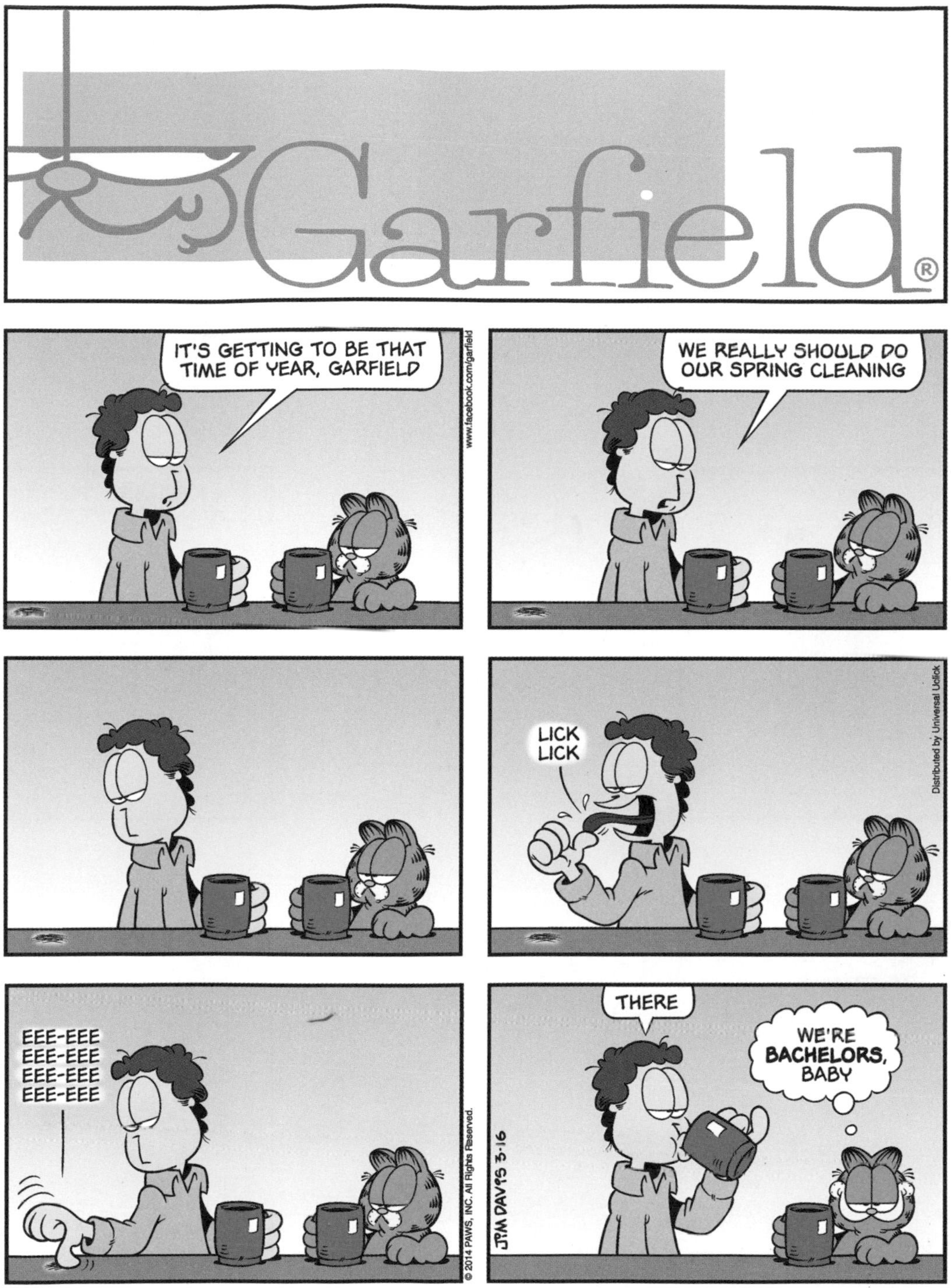
Garfield®
IT'S GETTING TO BE THAT TIME OF YEAR, GARFIELD
www.facebook.com/garfield
WE REALLY SHOULD DO OUR SPRING CLEANING
LICK LICK
Distributed by Universal Uclick
EEE-EEE EEE-EEE EEE-EEE EEE-EEE
© 2014 PAWS, INC. All Rights Reserved.
JIM DAVIS 3-16
THERE
WE'RE BACHELORS, BABY

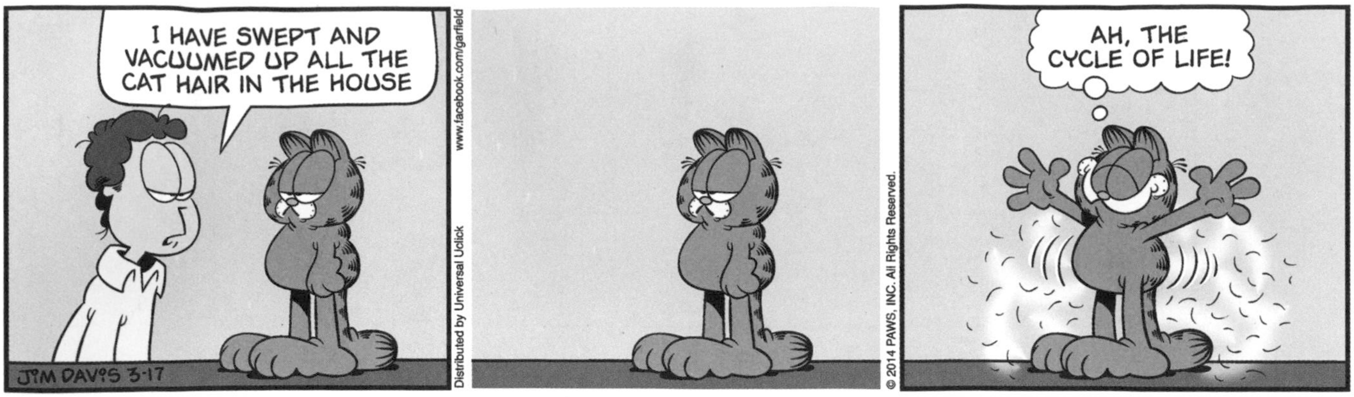
I HAVE SWEPT AND VACUUMED UP ALL THE CAT HAIR IN THE HOUSE
JIM DAVIS 3-17
Distributed by Universal Uclick www.facebook.com/garfield
© 2014 PAWS, INC. All Rights Reserved.
AH, THE CYCLE OF LIFE!

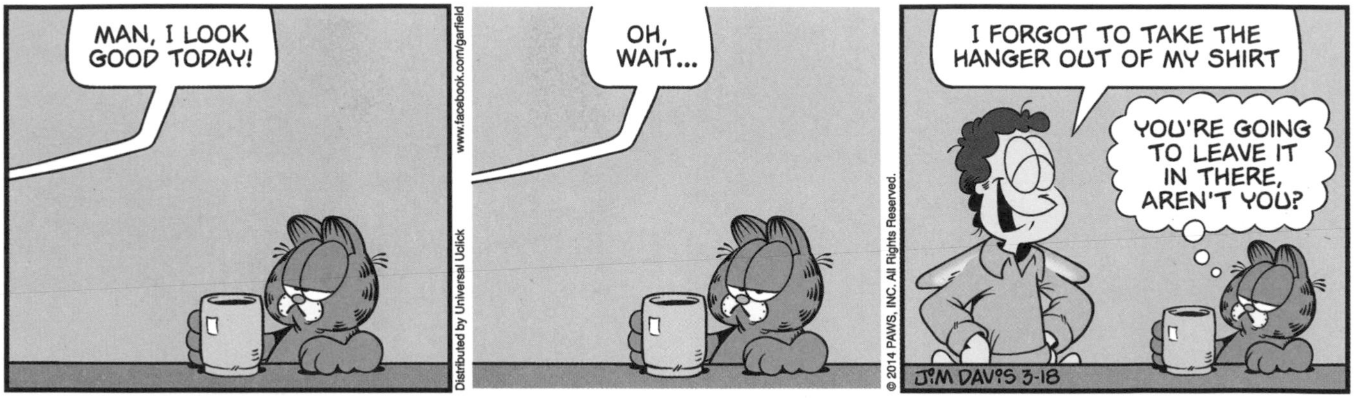
MAN, I LOOK GOOD TODAY!
Distributed by Universal Uclick www.facebook.com/garfield
OH, WAIT...
© 2014 PAWS, INC. All Rights Reserved.
I FORGOT TO TAKE THE HANGER OUT OF MY SHIRT
YOU'RE GOING TO LEAVE IT IN THERE, AREN'T YOU?
JIM DAVIS 3-18

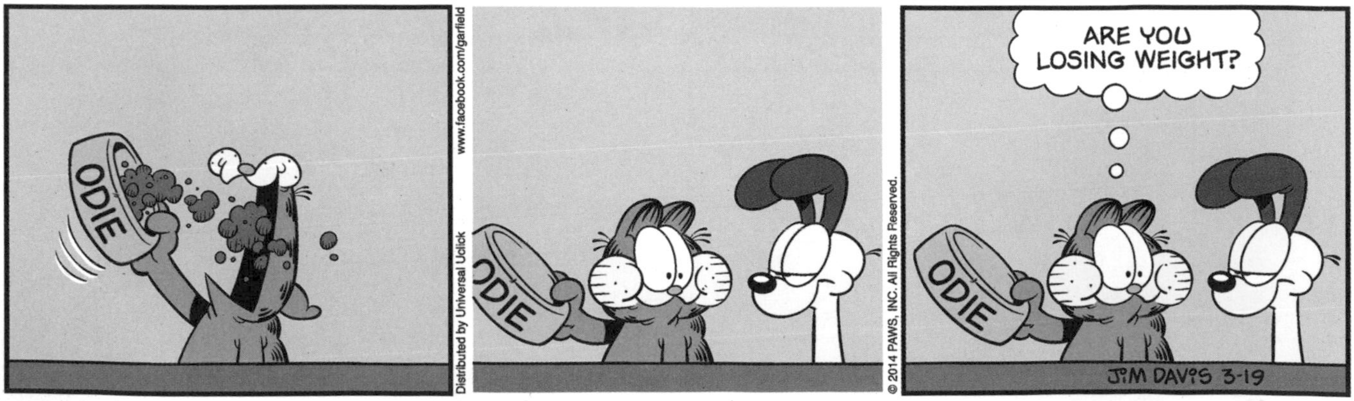
ODIE
Distributed by Universal Uclick www.facebook.com/garfield
ODIE
© 2014 PAWS, INC. All Rights Reserved.
ARE YOU LOSING WEIGHT?
ODIE
JIM DAVIS 3-19

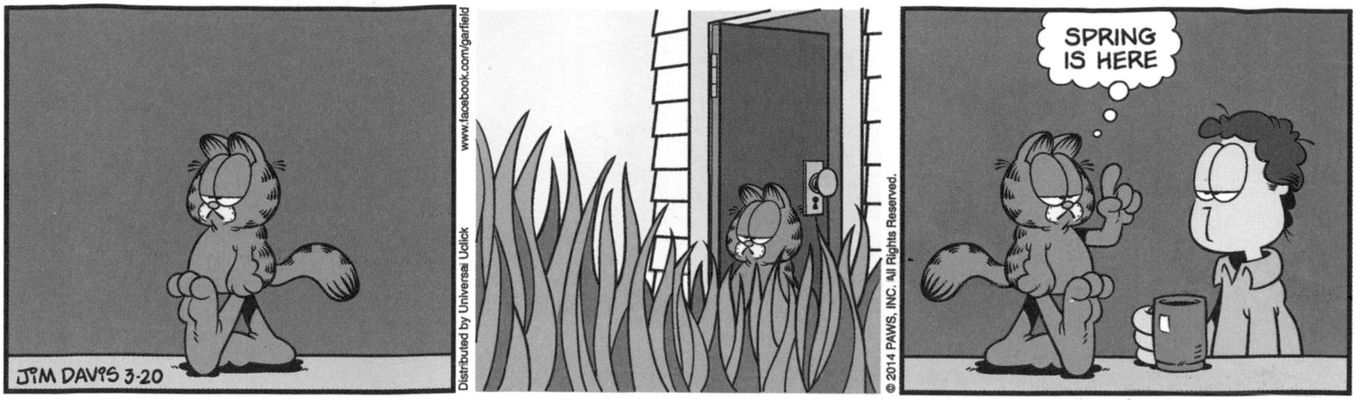
JIM DAVIS 3-20
Distributed by Universal Uclick www.facebook.com/garfield
SPRING IS HERE
© 2014 PAWS, INC. All Rights Reserved.

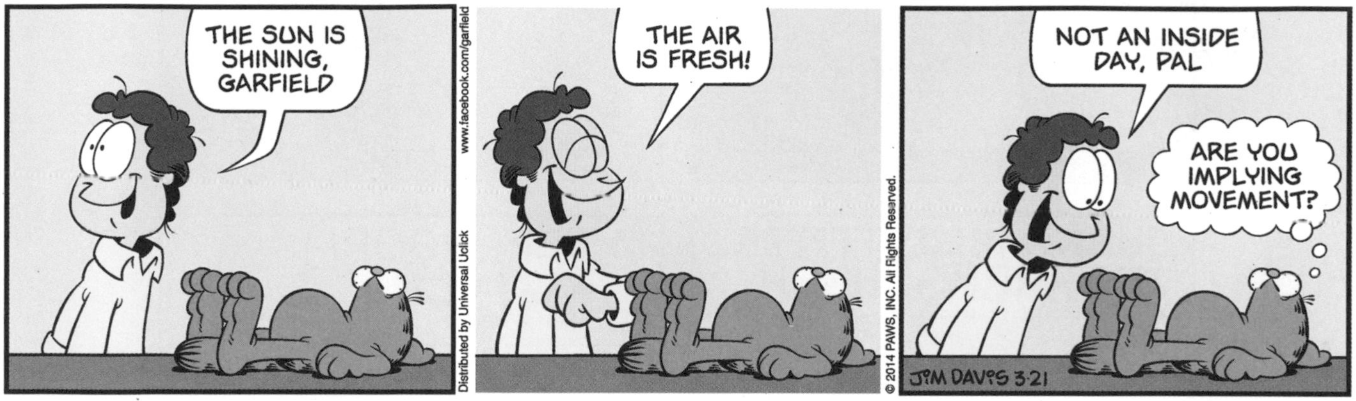
THE SUN IS SHINING, GARFIELD
Distributed by Universal Uclick www.facebook.com/garfield
THE AIR IS FRESH!
© 2014 PAWS, INC. All Rights Reserved.
NOT AN INSIDE DAY, PAL
ARE YOU IMPLYING MOVEMENT?
JIM DAVIS 3-21

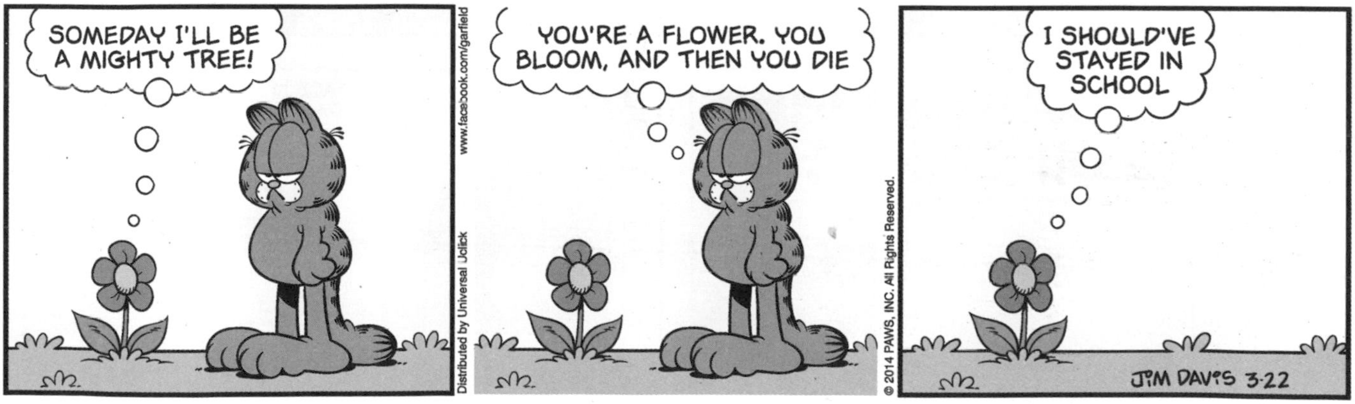
SOMEDAY I'LL BE A MIGHTY TREE!
Distributed by Universal Uclick www.facebook.com/garfield
YOU'RE A FLOWER. YOU BLOOM, AND THEN YOU DIE
© 2014 PAWS, INC. All Rights Reserved.
I SHOULD'VE STAYED IN SCHOOL
JIM DAVIS 3-22

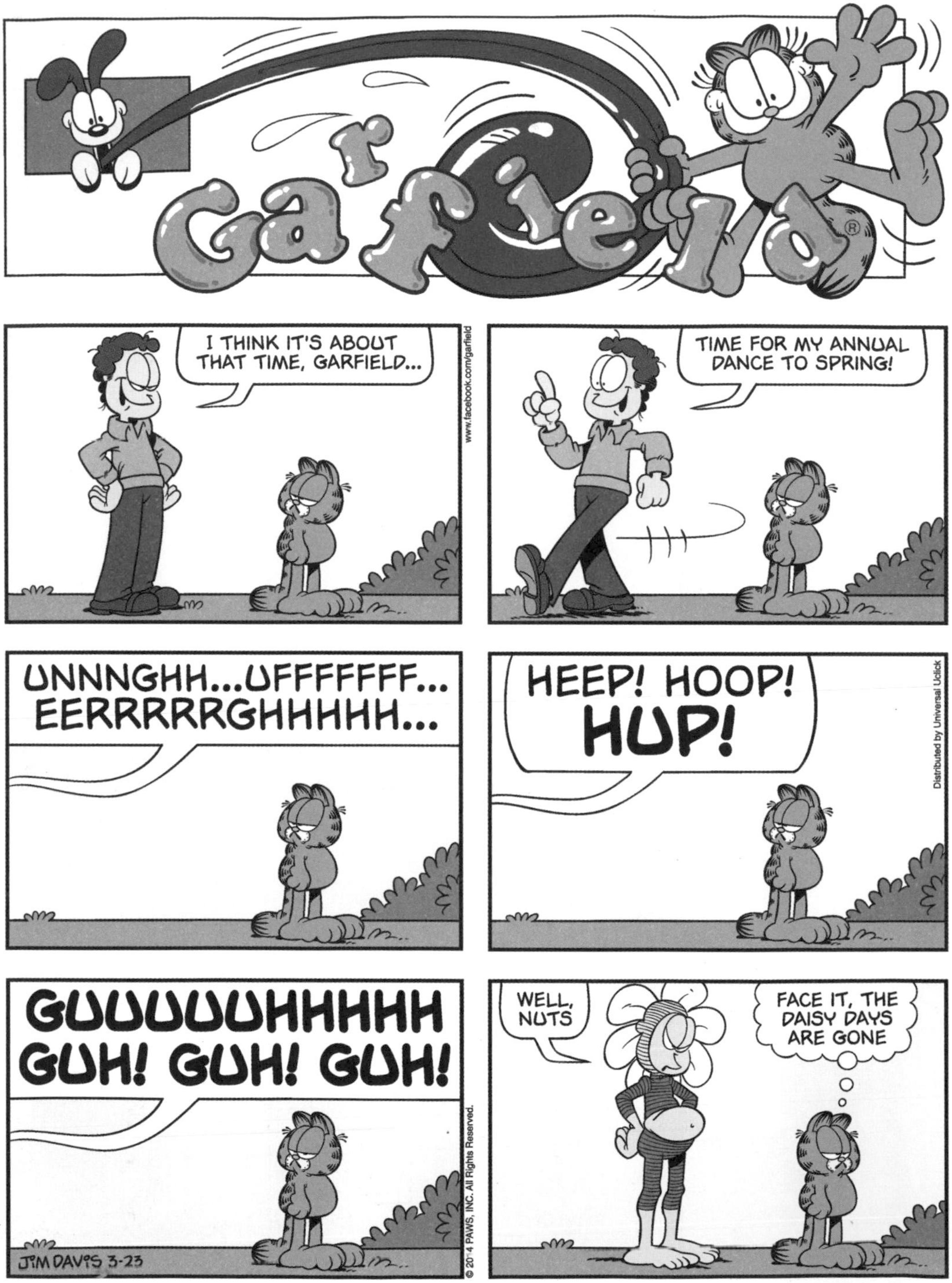
Garfield®
I THINK IT'S ABOUT THAT TIME, GARFIELD...
www.facebook.com/garfield
TIME FOR MY ANNUAL DANCE TO SPRING!
UNNNGHH...UFFFFFFF... EERRRRRGHHHHH...
HEEP! HOOP! HUP!
Distributed by Universal Uclick
GUUUUUHHHHH GUH! GUH! GUH!
JIM DAVIS 3-23
© 2014 PAWS, INC. All Rights Reserved.
WELL, NUTS
FACE IT, THE DAISY DAYS ARE GONE

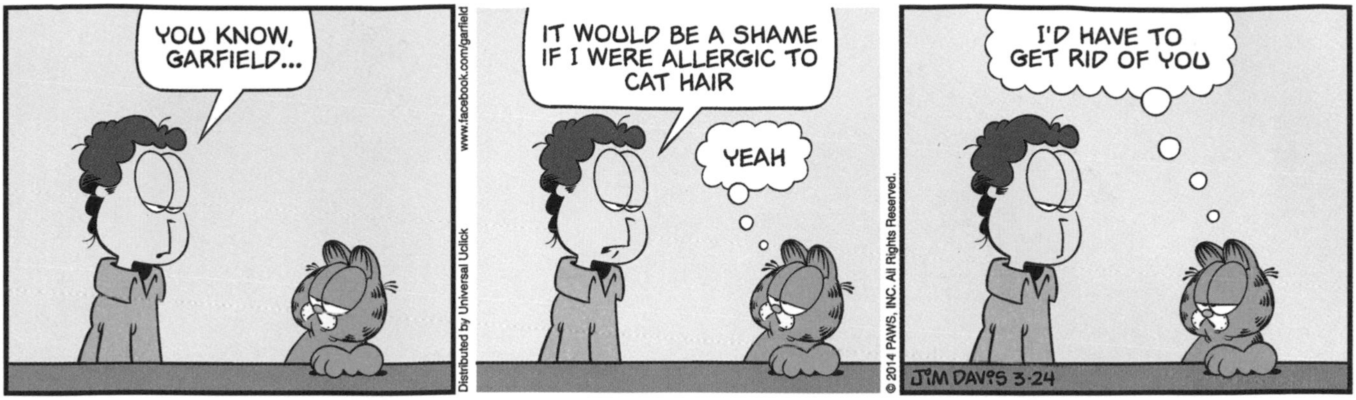
YOU KNOW, GARFIELD...
IT WOULD BE A SHAME IF I WERE ALLERGIC TO CAT HAIR
YEAH
I'D HAVE TO GET RID OF YOU
JIM DAVIS 3-24

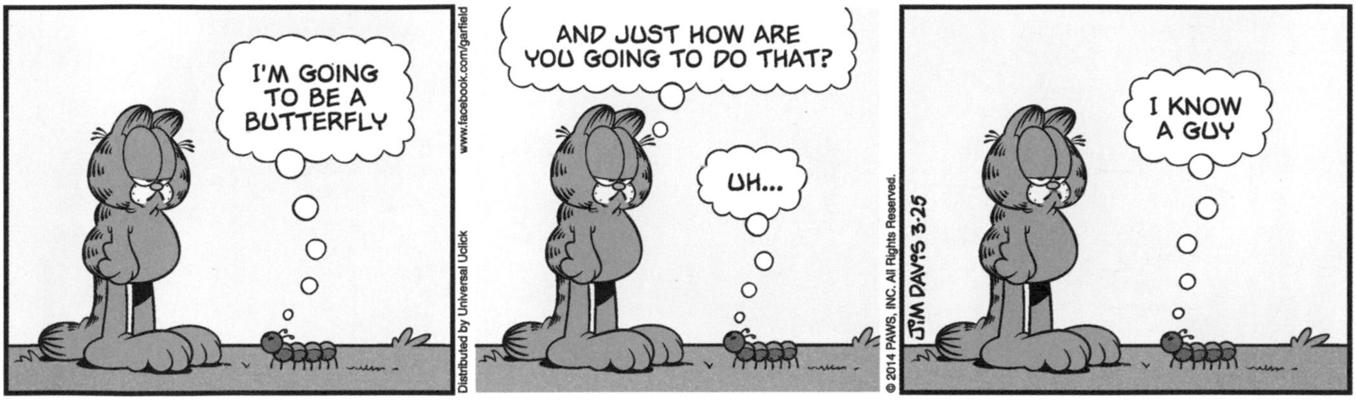
I'M GOING TO BE A BUTTERFLY
AND JUST HOW ARE YOU GOING TO DO THAT?
UH...
I KNOW A GUY
JIM DAVIS 3-25

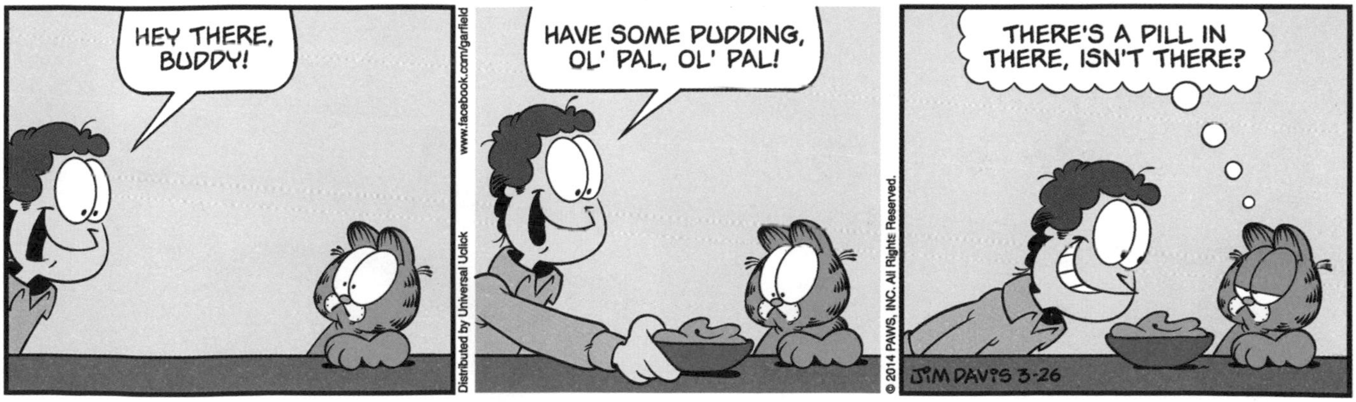
HEY THERE, BUDDY!
HAVE SOME PUDDING, OL' PAL, OL' PAL!
THERE'S A PILL IN THERE, ISN'T THERE?
JIM DAVIS 3-26

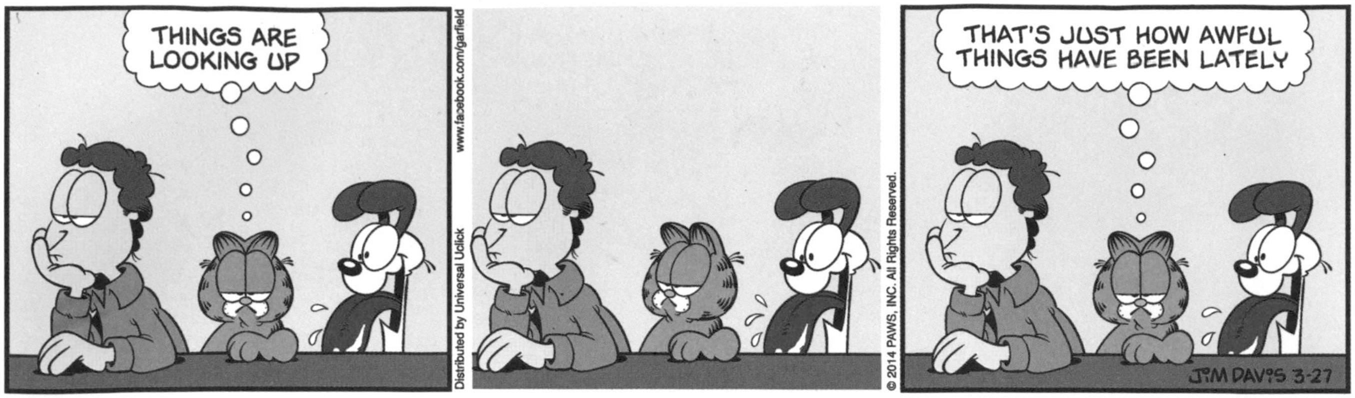
THINGS ARE LOOKING UP
THAT'S JUST HOW AWFUL THINGS HAVE BEEN LATELY
JIM DAVIS 3-27
Distributed by Universal Uclick www.facebook.com/garfield
© 2014 PAWS, INC. All Rights Reserved.

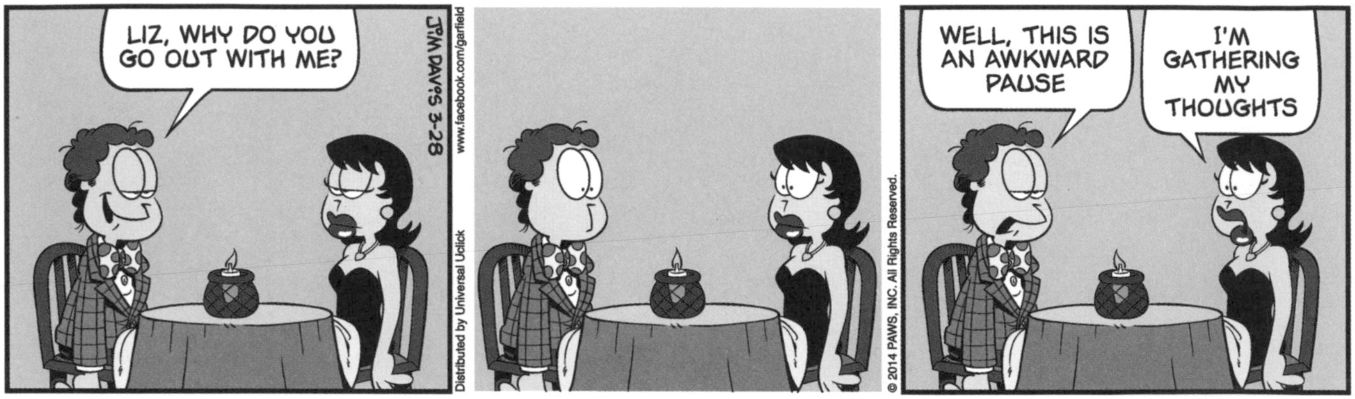
LIZ, WHY DO YOU GO OUT WITH ME?
JIM DAVIS 3-28
WELL, THIS IS AN AWKWARD PAUSE
I'M GATHERING MY THOUGHTS
Distributed by Universal Uclick www.facebook.com/garfield
© 2014 PAWS, INC. All Rights Reserved.

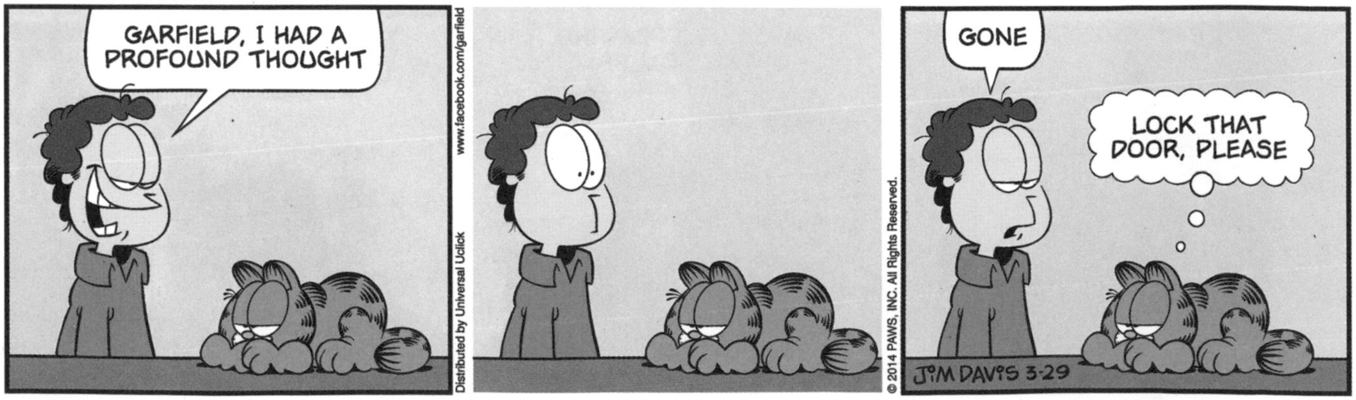
GARFIELD, I HAD A PROFOUND THOUGHT
GONE
LOCK THAT DOOR, PLEASE
JIM DAVIS 3-29
Distributed by Universal Uclick www.facebook.com/garfield
© 2014 PAWS, INC. All Rights Reserved.

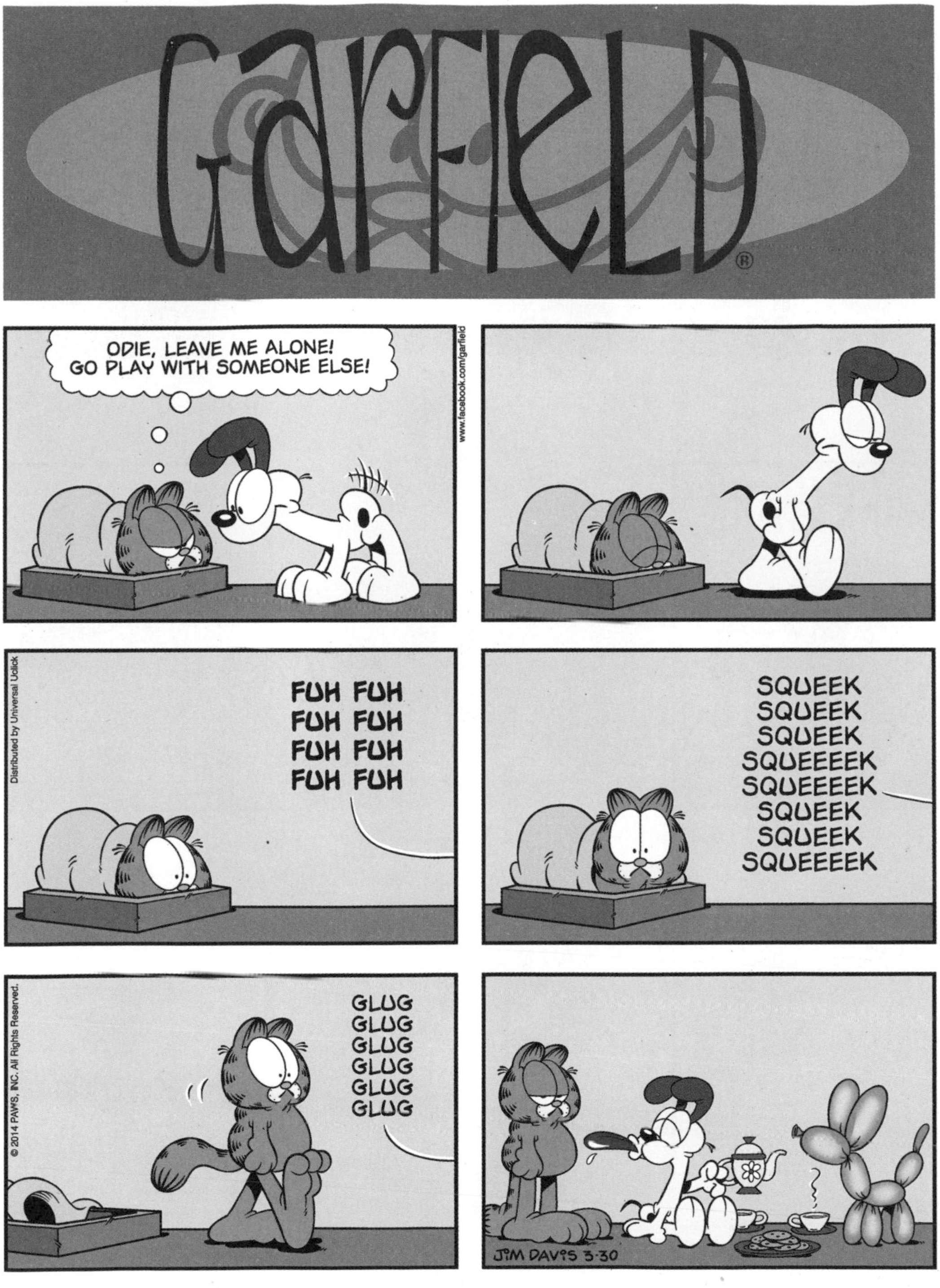
GARFIELD
ODIE, LEAVE ME ALONE! GO PLAY WITH SOMEONE ELSE!
www.facebook.com/garfield
Distributed by Universal Uclick
FUH FUH FUH FUH FUH FUH FUH FUH
SQUEEK SQUEEK SQUEEK SQUEEEEK SQUEEEEK SQUEEK SQUEEK SQUEEEEK
© 2014 PAWS, INC. All Rights Reserved.
GLUG GLUG GLUG GLUG GLUG GLUG
JIM DAVIS 3-30

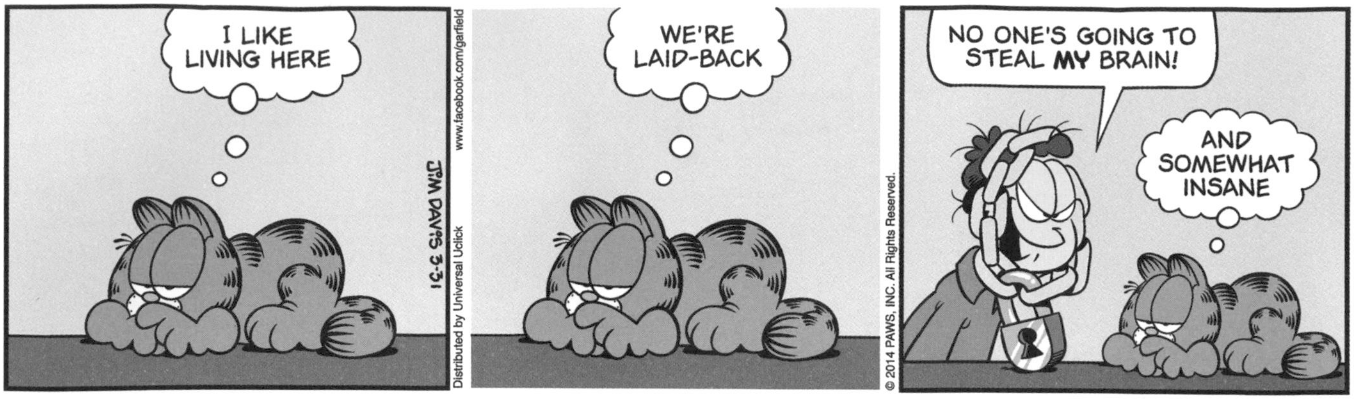
I LIKE LIVING HERE
JIM DAVIS 3-31
WE'RE LAID-BACK
Distributed by Universal Uclick www.facebook.com/garfield
NO ONE'S GOING TO STEAL MY BRAIN!
AND SOMEWHAT INSANE
© 2014 PAWS, INC. All Rights Reserved.

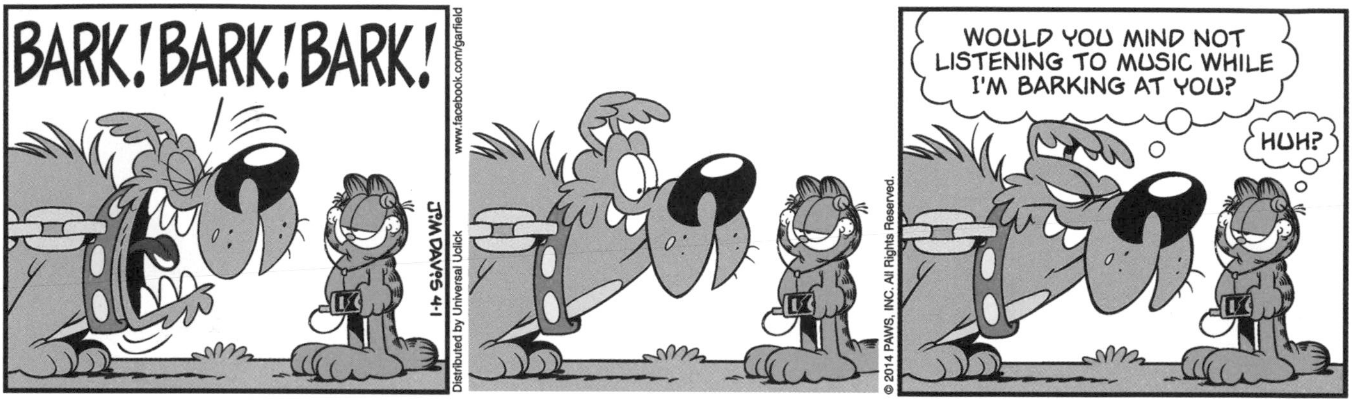
BARK! BARK! BARK!
JIM DAVIS 4-1
Distributed by Universal Uclick www.facebook.com/garfield
WOULD YOU MIND NOT LISTENING TO MUSIC WHILE I'M BARKING AT YOU?
HUH?
© 2014 PAWS, INC. All Rights Reserved.

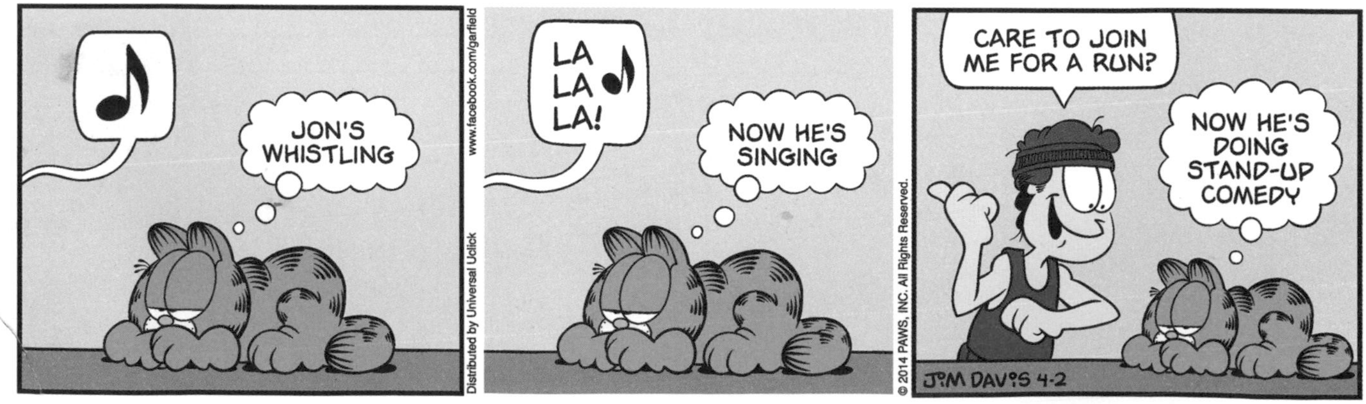
JON'S WHISTLING
Distributed by Universal Uclick www.facebook.com/garfield
LA LA LA!
NOW HE'S SINGING
CARE TO JOIN ME FOR A RUN?
NOW HE'S DOING STAND-UP COMEDY
JIM DAVIS 4-2
© 2014 PAWS, INC. All Rights Reserved.

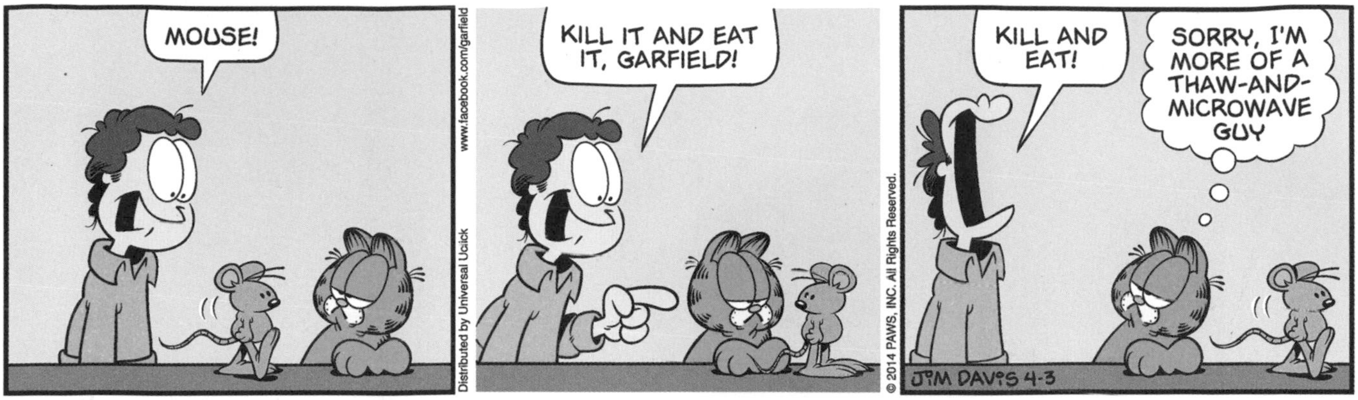
MOUSE!
KILL IT AND EAT IT, GARFIELD!
KILL AND EAT!
SORRY, I'M MORE OF A THAW-AND-MICROWAVE GUY
JIM DAVIS 4-3
Distributed by Universal Uclick www.facebook.com/garfield
© 2014 PAWS, INC. All Rights Reserved.

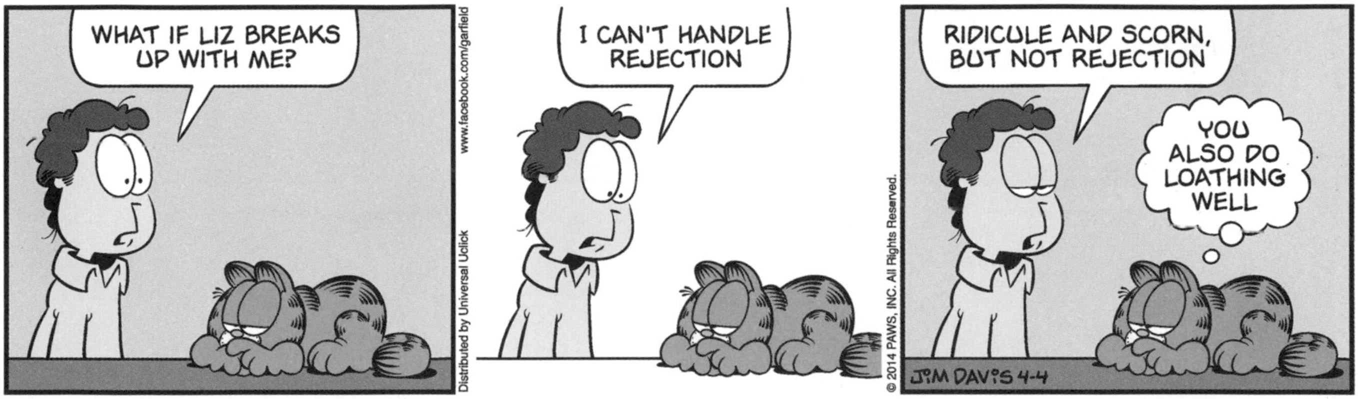
WHAT IF LIZ BREAKS UP WITH ME?
I CAN'T HANDLE REJECTION
RIDICULE AND SCORN, BUT NOT REJECTION
YOU ALSO DO LOATHING WELL
JIM DAVIS 4-4
Distributed by Universal Uclick www.facebook.com/garfield
© 2014 PAWS, INC. All Rights Reserved.

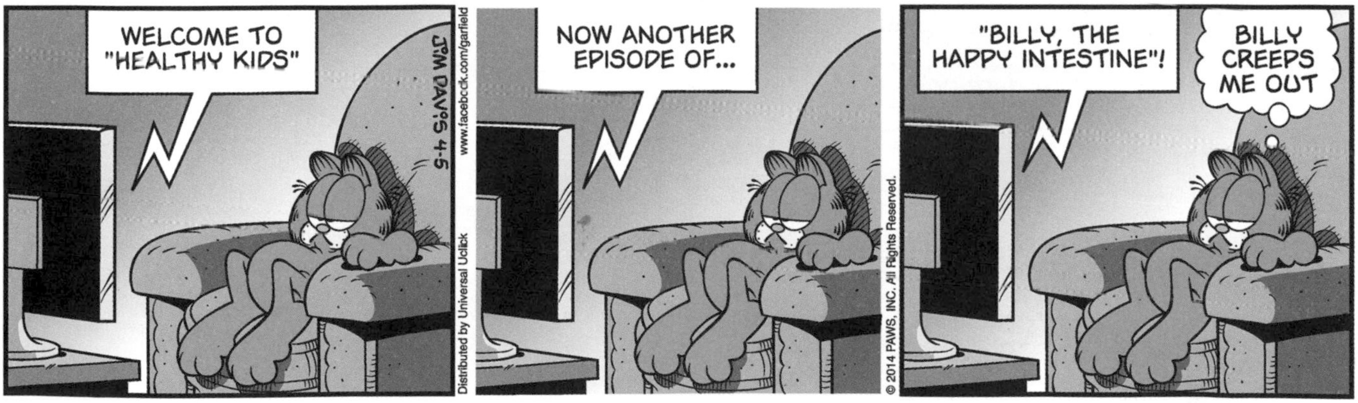
WELCOME TO "HEALTHY KIDS"
NOW ANOTHER EPISODE OF...
"BILLY, THE HAPPY INTESTINE"!
BILLY CREEPS ME OUT
JIM DAVIS 4-5
Distributed by Universal Uclick www.facebook.com/garfield
© 2014 PAWS, INC. All Rights Reserved.

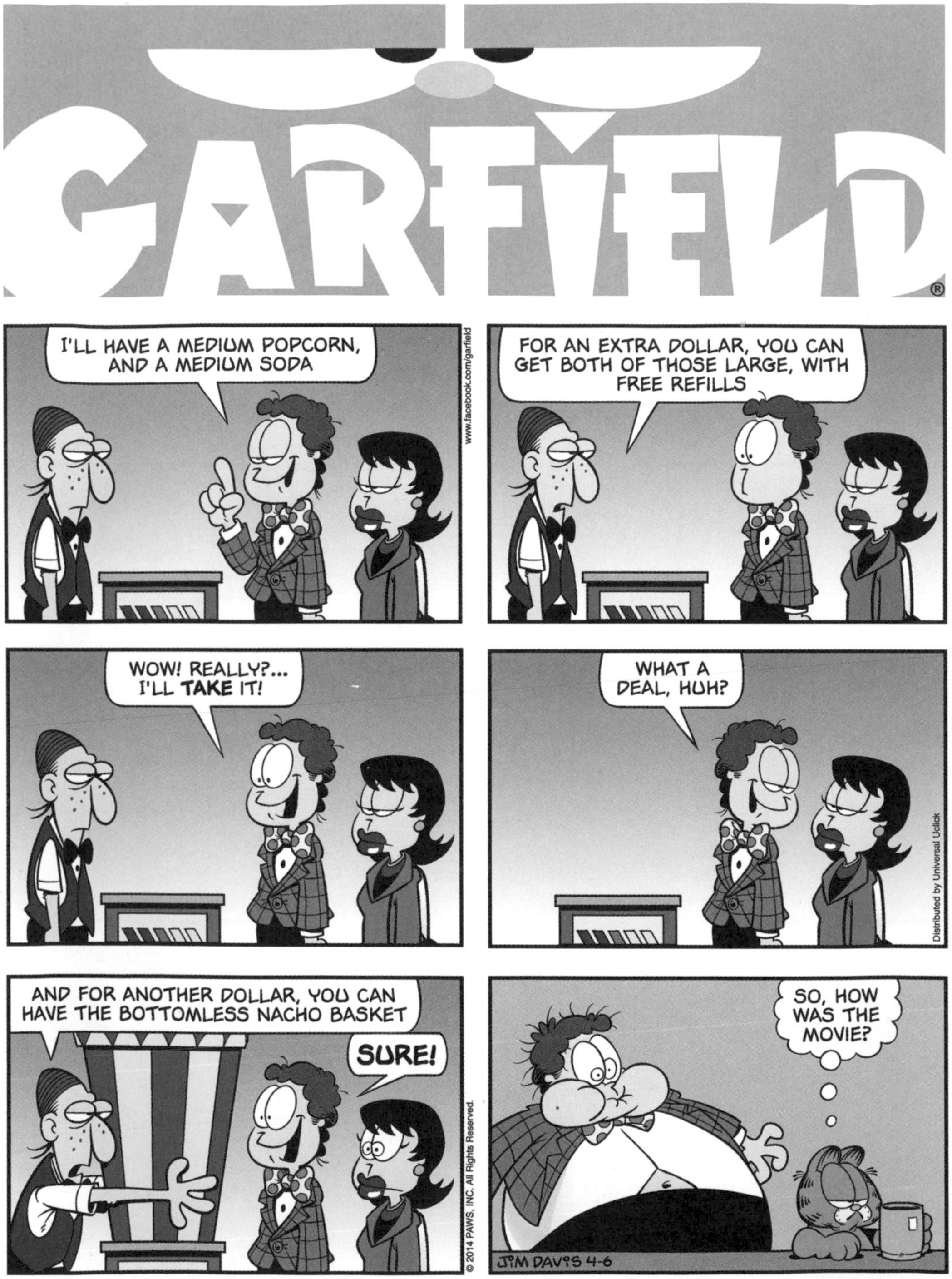
GARFIELD
I'LL HAVE A MEDIUM POPCORN, AND A MEDIUM SODA
www.facebook.com/garfield
FOR AN EXTRA DOLLAR, YOU CAN GET BOTH OF THOSE LARGE, WITH FREE REFILLS
WOW! REALLY?... I'LL TAKE IT!
WHAT A DEAL, HUH?
Distributed by Universal Uclick
AND FOR ANOTHER DOLLAR, YOU CAN HAVE THE BOTTOMLESS NACHO BASKET
SURE!
© 2014 PAWS, INC. All Rights Reserved.
SO, HOW WAS THE MOVIE?
JIM DAVIS 4-6

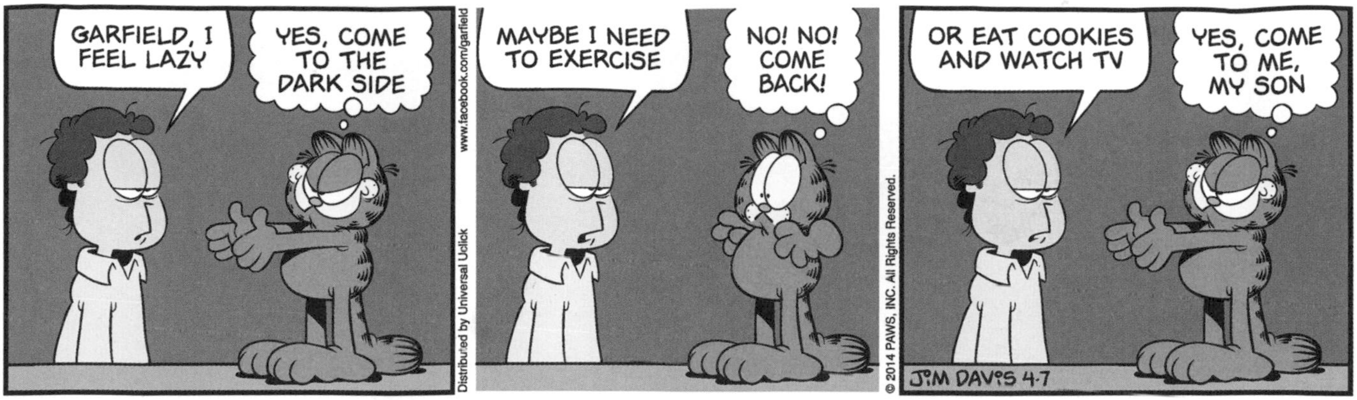
GARFIELD, I FEEL LAZY
YES, COME TO THE DARK SIDE
Distributed by Universal Uclick
www.facebook.com/garfield
MAYBE I NEED TO EXERCISE
NO! NO! COME BACK!
© 2014 PAWS, INC. All Rights Reserved.
OR EAT COOKIES AND WATCH TV
YES, COME TO ME, MY SON
JIM DAVIS 4-7

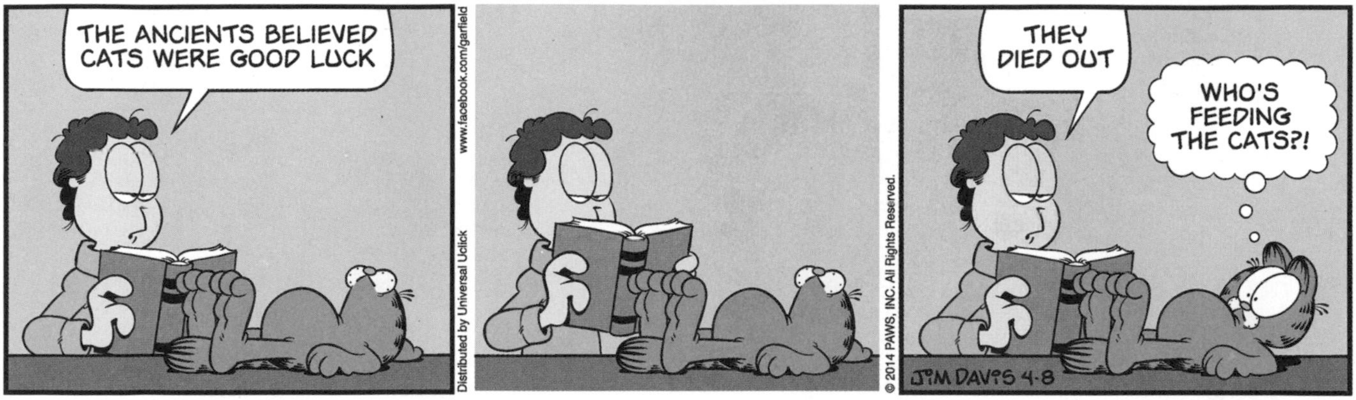
THE ANCIENTS BELIEVED CATS WERE GOOD LUCK
Distributed by Universal Uclick
www.facebook.com/garfield
© 2014 PAWS, INC. All Rights Reserved.
THEY DIED OUT
WHO'S FEEDING THE CATS?!
JIM DAVIS 4-8

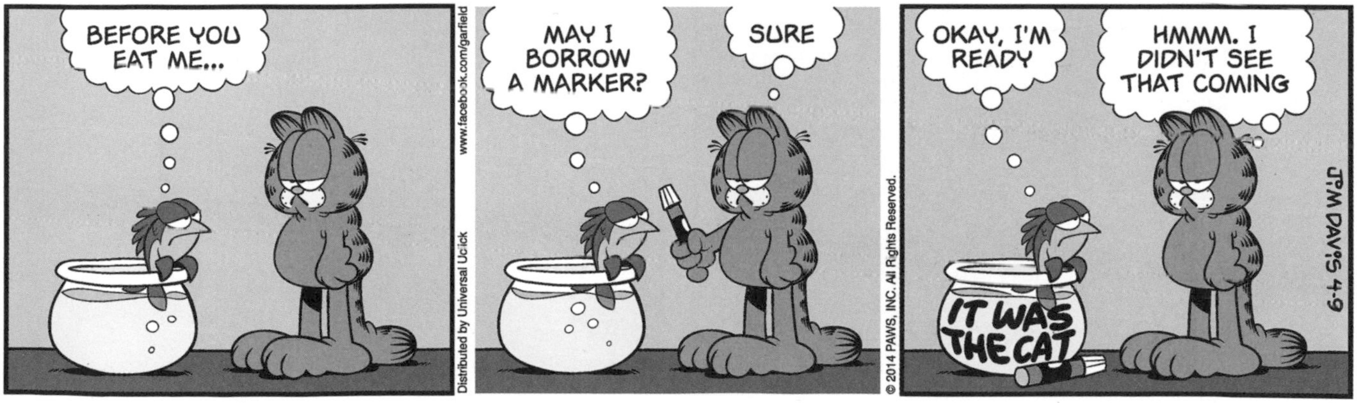
BEFORE YOU EAT ME...
Distributed by Universal Uclick
www.facebook.com/garfield
MAY I BORROW A MARKER?
SURE
© 2014 PAWS, INC. All Rights Reserved.
OKAY, I'M READY
HMMM. I DIDN'T SEE THAT COMING
IT WAS THE CAT
JIM DAVIS 4-9

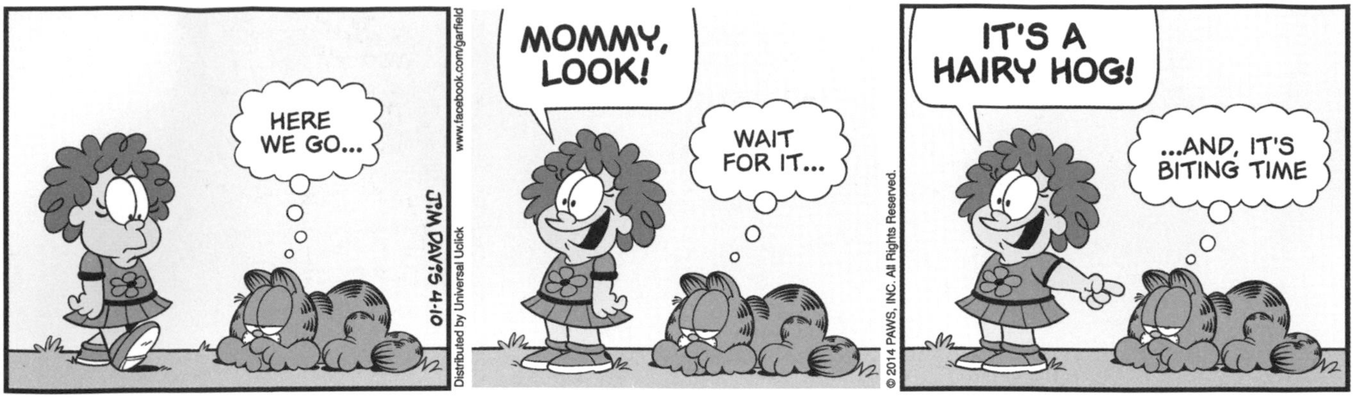
HERE WE GO...
MOMMY, LOOK!
WAIT FOR IT...
IT'S A HAIRY HOG!
...AND, IT'S BITING TIME
JIM DAVIS 4-10
Distributed by Universal Uclick www.facebook.com/garfield
© 2014 PAWS, INC. All Rights Reserved.

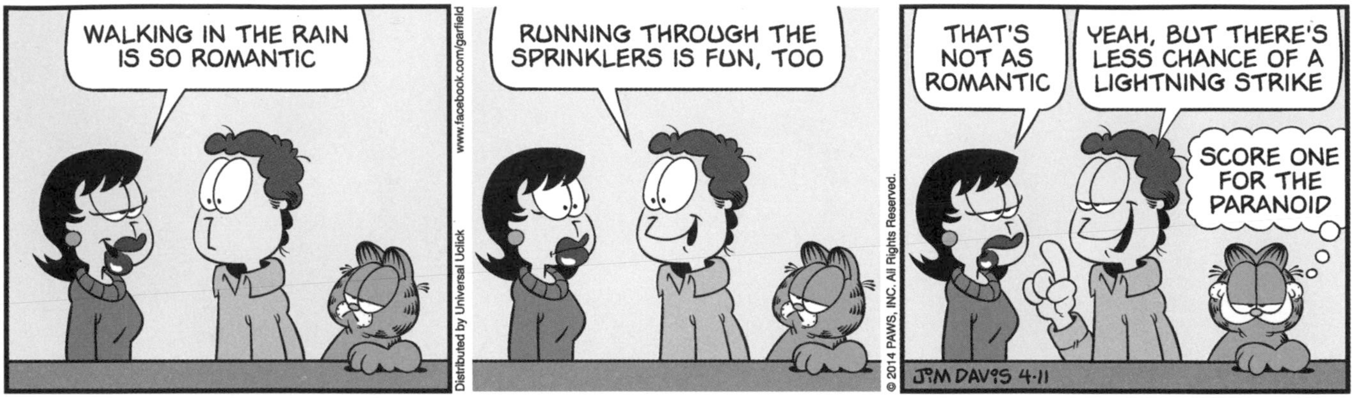
WALKING IN THE RAIN IS SO ROMANTIC
RUNNING THROUGH THE SPRINKLERS IS FUN, TOO
THAT'S NOT AS ROMANTIC
YEAH, BUT THERE'S LESS CHANCE OF A LIGHTNING STRIKE
SCORE ONE FOR THE PARANOID
JIM DAVIS 4-11
Distributed by Universal Uclick www.facebook.com/garfield
© 2014 PAWS, INC. All Rights Reserved.

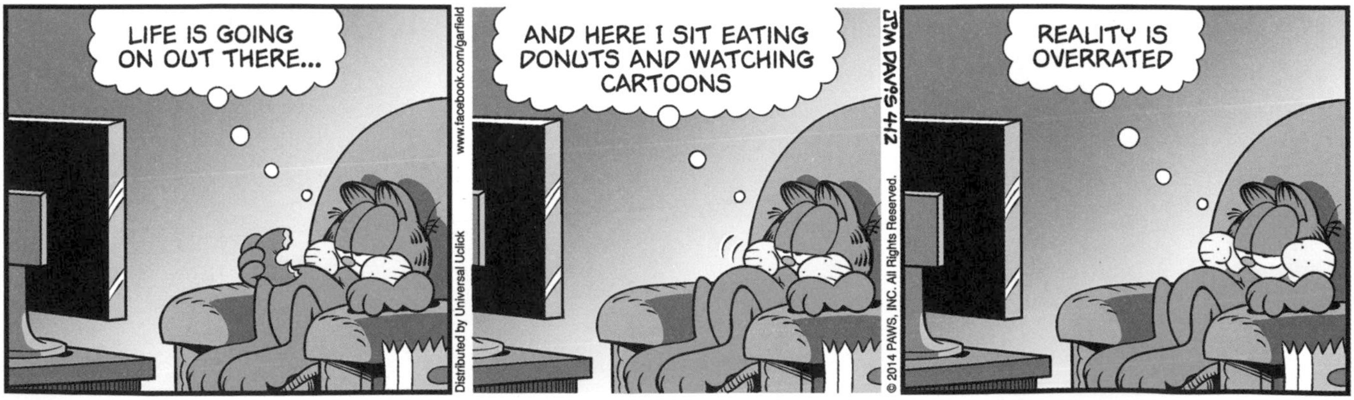
LIFE IS GOING ON OUT THERE...
AND HERE I SIT EATING DONUTS AND WATCHING CARTOONS
REALITY IS OVERRATED
JIM DAVIS 4-12
Distributed by Universal Uclick www.facebook.com/garfield
© 2014 PAWS, INC. All Rights Reserved.

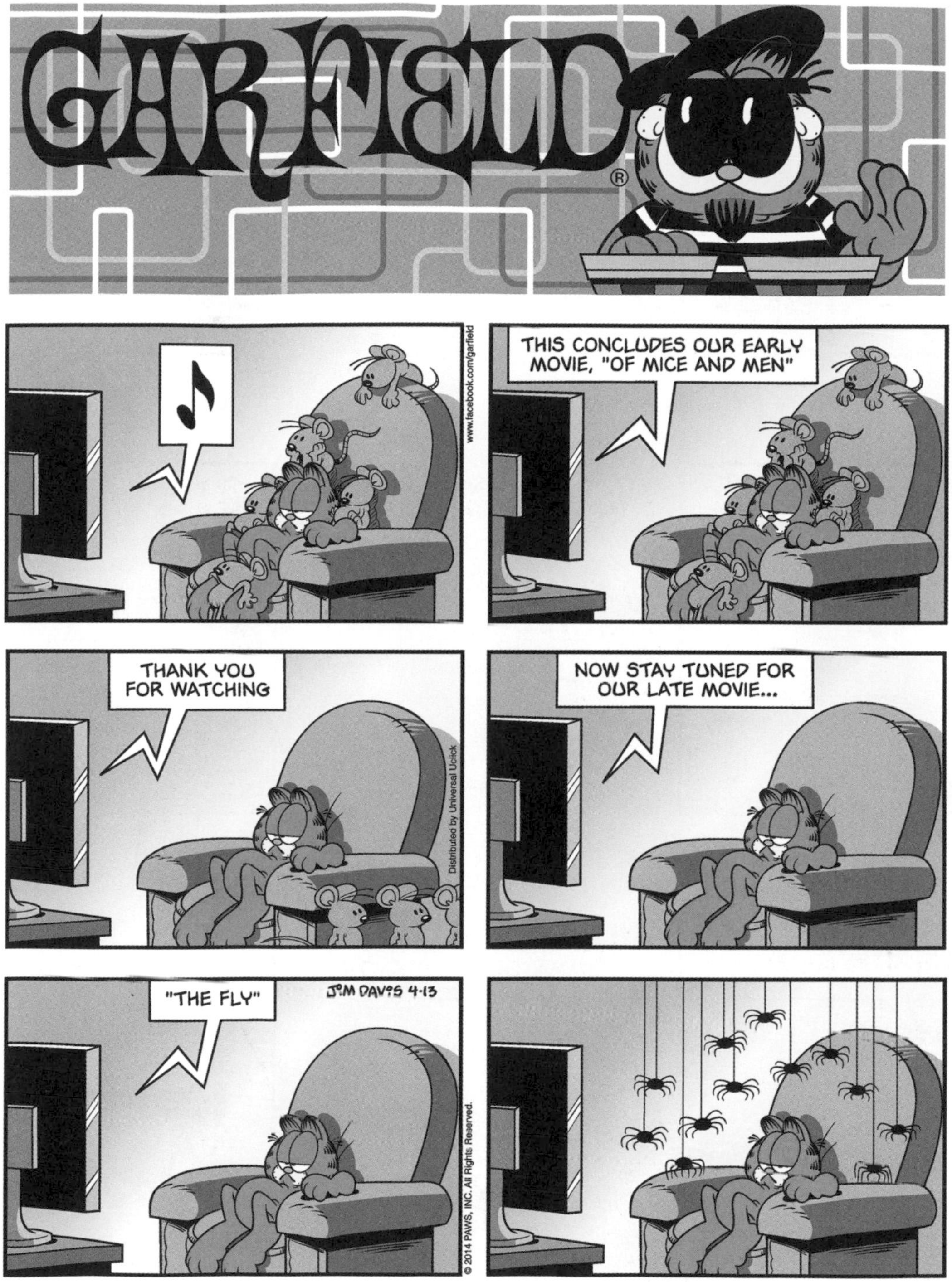
GARFIELD
THIS CONCLUDES OUR EARLY MOVIE, "OF MICE AND MEN"
THANK YOU FOR WATCHING
NOW STAY TUNED FOR OUR LATE MOVIE...
"THE FLY"
JIM DAVIS 4-13
www.facebook.com/garfield
Distributed by Universal Uclick
© 2014 PAWS, INC. All Rights Reserved.

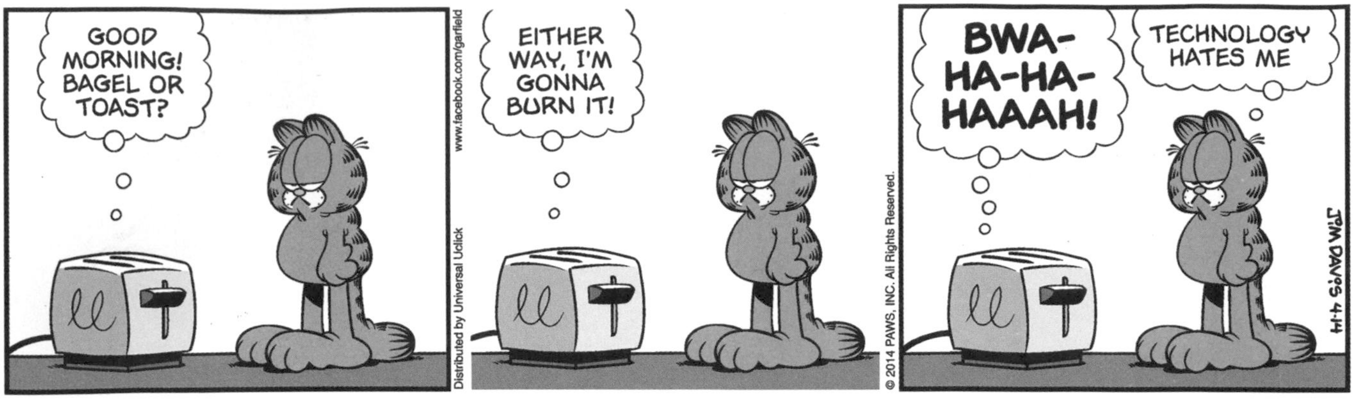
GOOD MORNING! BAGEL OR TOAST?
www.facebook.com/garfield
Distributed by Universal Uclick
EITHER WAY, I'M GONNA BURN IT!
© 2014 PAWS, INC. All Rights Reserved.
BWA-HA-HA-HAAAH!
TECHNOLOGY HATES ME
JIM DAVIS 4-14

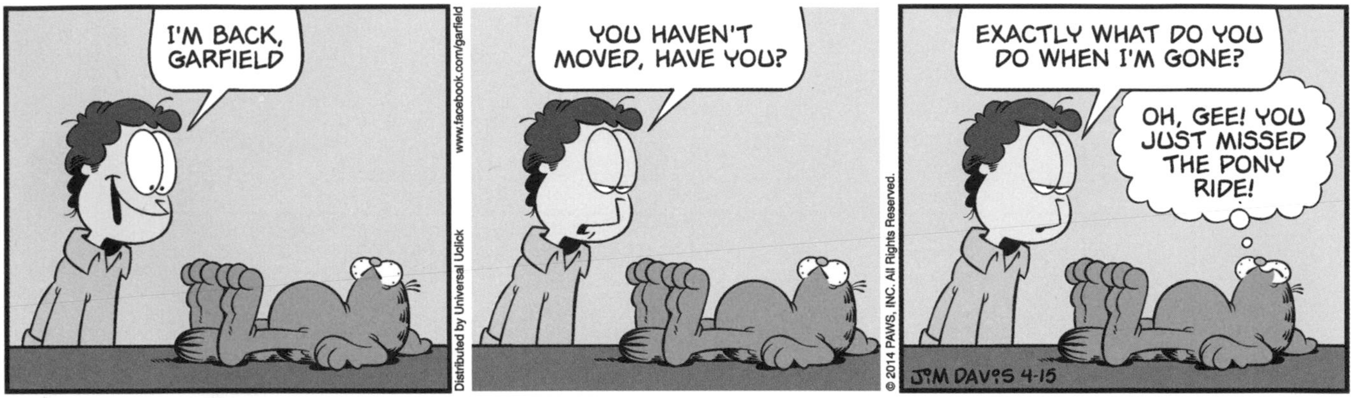
I'M BACK, GARFIELD
www.facebook.com/garfield
Distributed by Universal Uclick
YOU HAVEN'T MOVED, HAVE YOU?
© 2014 PAWS, INC. All Rights Reserved.
EXACTLY WHAT DO YOU DO WHEN I'M GONE?
OH, GEE! YOU JUST MISSED THE PONY RIDE!
JIM DAVIS 4-15

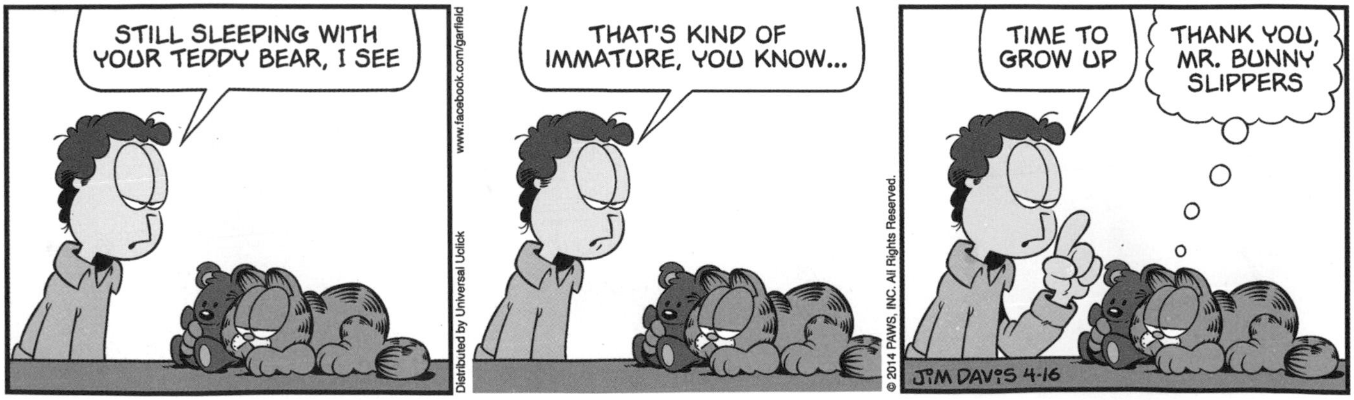
STILL SLEEPING WITH YOUR TEDDY BEAR, I SEE
www.facebook.com/garfield
Distributed by Universal Uclick
THAT'S KIND OF IMMATURE, YOU KNOW...
© 2014 PAWS, INC. All Rights Reserved.
TIME TO GROW UP
THANK YOU, MR. BUNNY SLIPPERS
JIM DAVIS 4-16

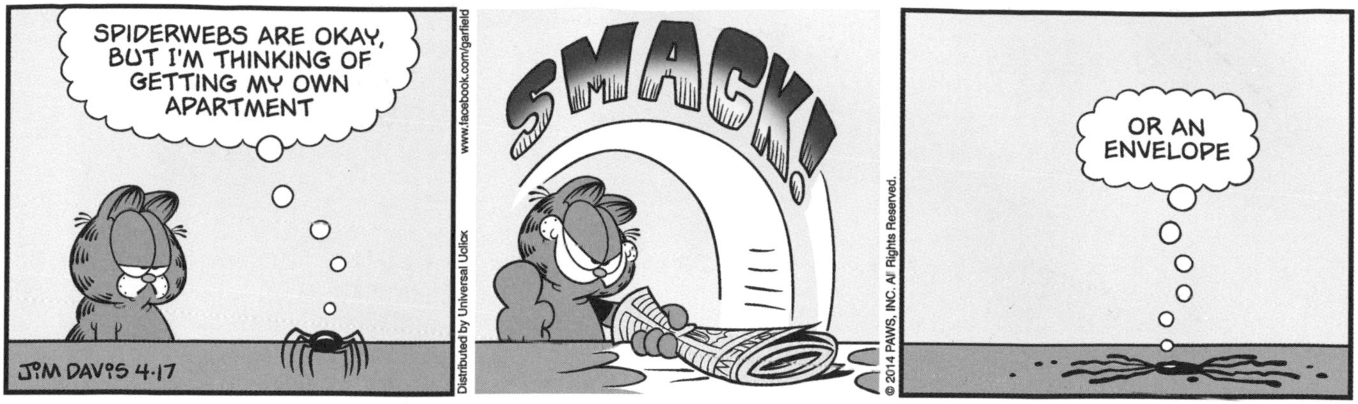
SPIDERWEBS ARE OKAY, BUT I'M THINKING OF GETTING MY OWN APARTMENT
JIM DAVIS 4-17
Distributed by Universal Uclick www.facebook.com/garfield
SMACK!
© 2014 PAWS, INC. All Rights Reserved.
OR AN ENVELOPE

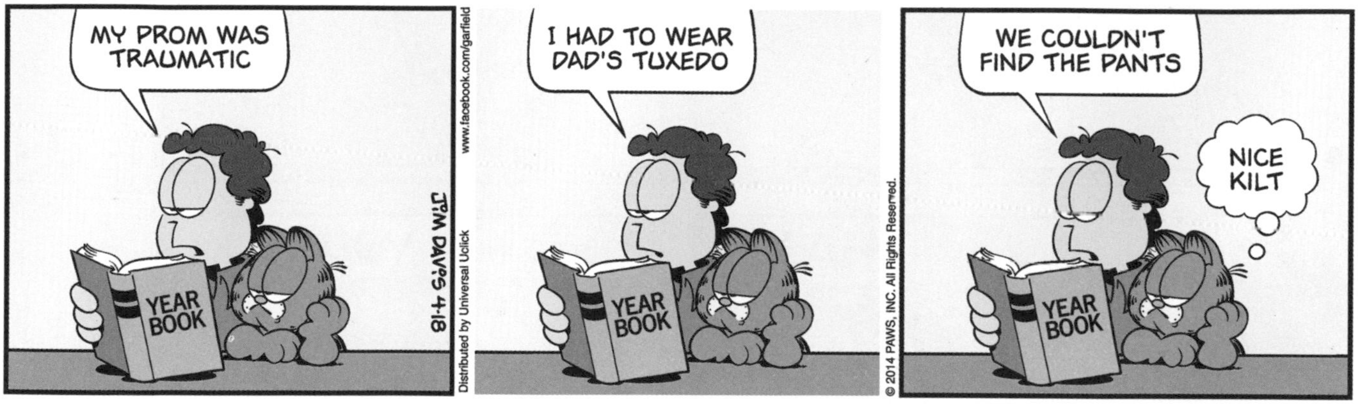
MY PROM WAS TRAUMATIC
YEAR BOOK
JIM DAVIS 4-18
Distributed by Universal Uclick www.facebook.com/garfield
I HAD TO WEAR DAD'S TUXEDO
YEAR BOOK
© 2014 PAWS, INC. All Rights Reserved.
WE COULDN'T FIND THE PANTS
NICE KILT
YEAR BOOK

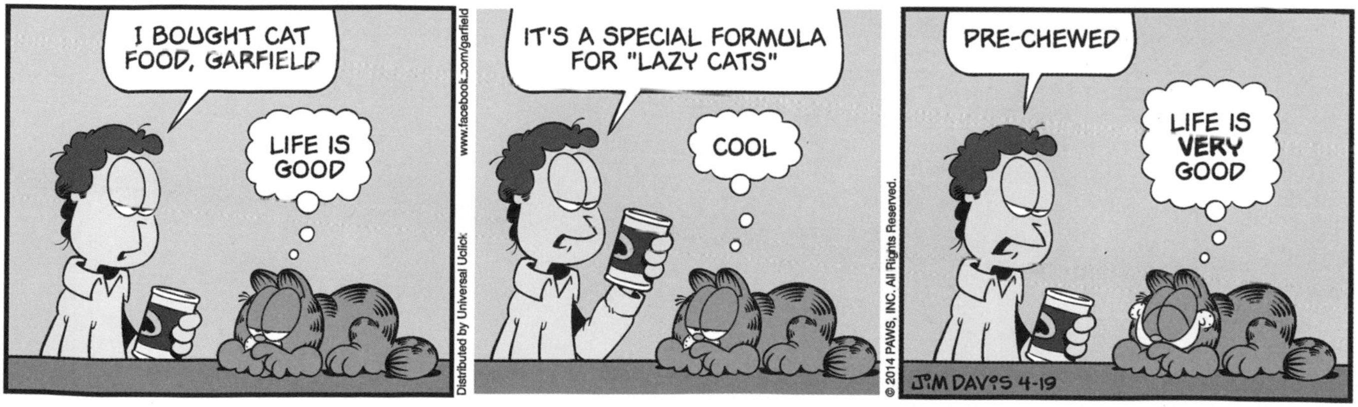
I BOUGHT CAT FOOD, GARFIELD
LIFE IS GOOD
Distributed by Universal Uclick www.facebook.com/garfield
IT'S A SPECIAL FORMULA FOR "LAZY CATS"
COOL
© 2014 PAWS, INC. All Rights Reserved.
PRE-CHEWED
LIFE IS VERY GOOD
JIM DAVIS 4-19

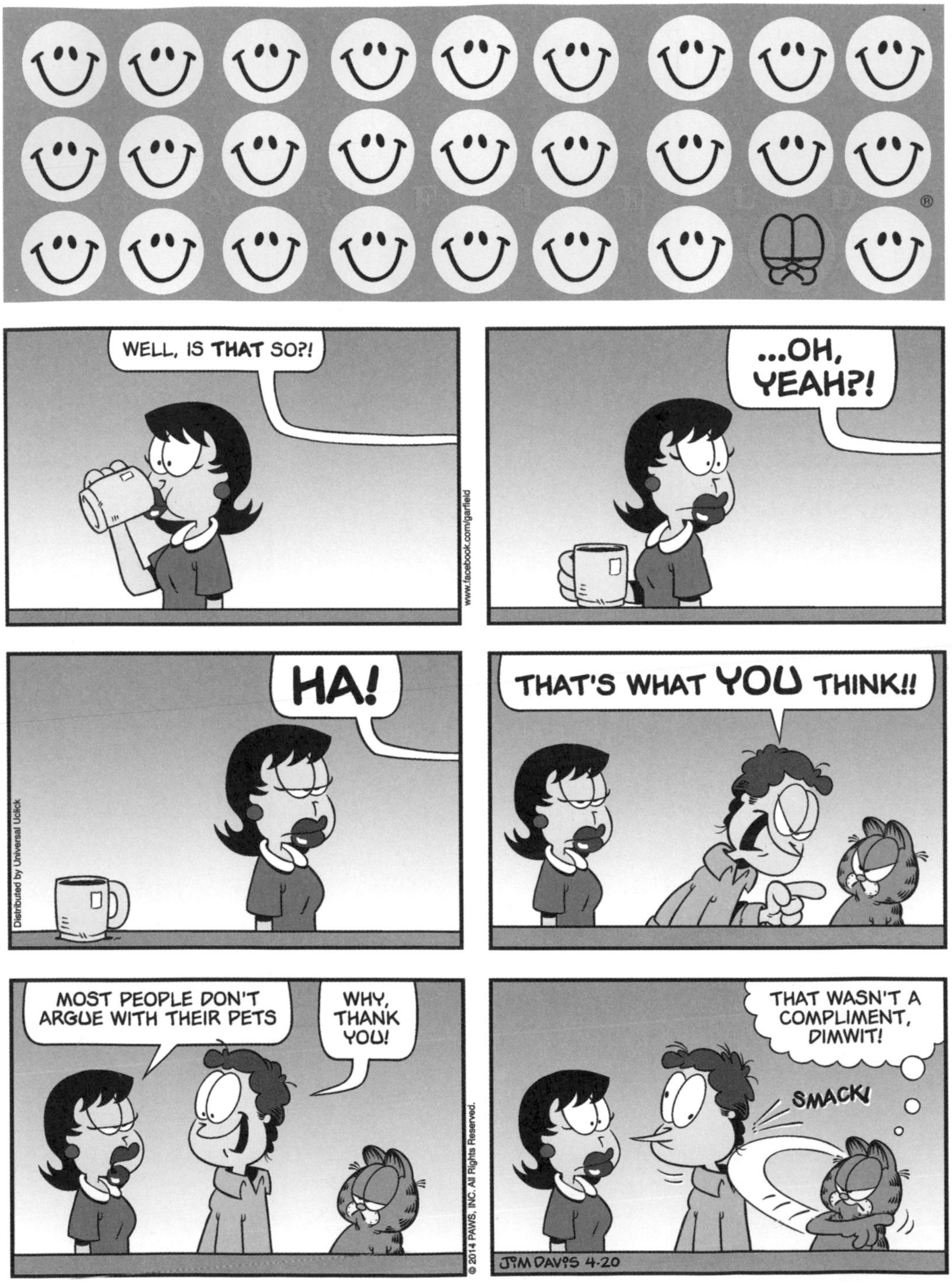
WELL, IS THAT SO?!
...OH, YEAH?!
HA!
THAT'S WHAT YOU THINK!!
MOST PEOPLE DON'T ARGUE WITH THEIR PETS
WHY, THANK YOU!
THAT WASN'T A COMPLIMENT, DIMWIT!
SMACK!
JIM DAVIS 4-20
www.facebook.com/garfield
Distributed by Universal Uclick
© 2014 PAWS, INC. All Rights Reserved.

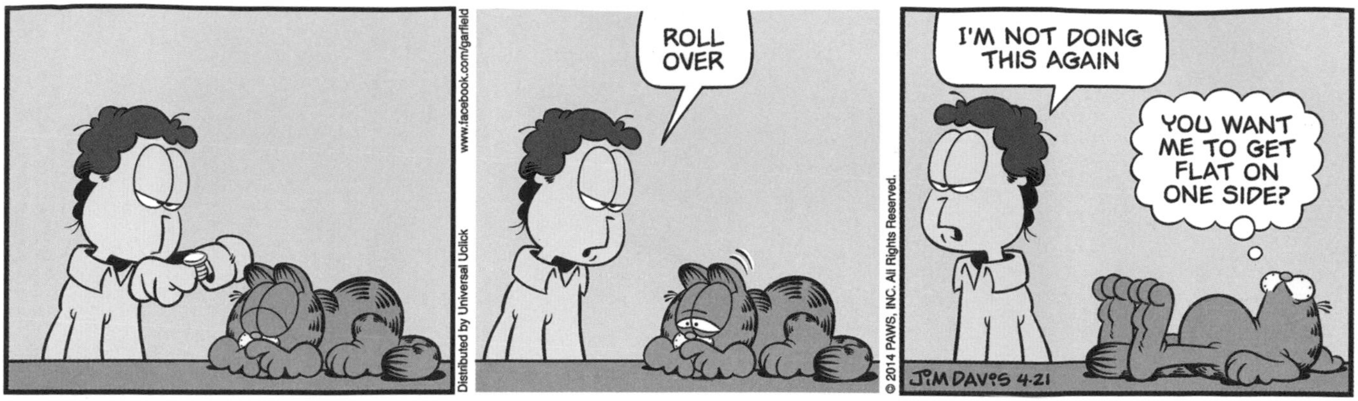
ROLL OVER
I'M NOT DOING THIS AGAIN
YOU WANT ME TO GET FLAT ON ONE SIDE?
JIM DAVIS 4-21
Distributed by Universal Uclick www.facebook.com/garfield
© 2014 PAWS, INC. All Rights Reserved.

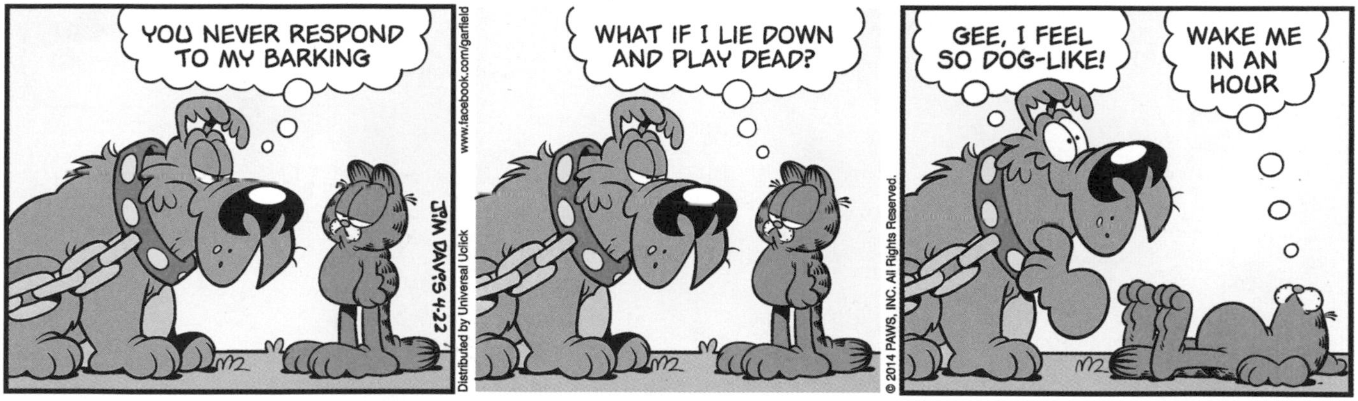
YOU NEVER RESPOND TO MY BARKING
WHAT IF I LIE DOWN AND PLAY DEAD?
GEE, I FEEL SO DOG-LIKE!
WAKE ME IN AN HOUR
JIM DAVIS 4-22
Distributed by Universal Uclick www.facebook.com/garfield
© 2014 PAWS, INC. All Rights Reserved.

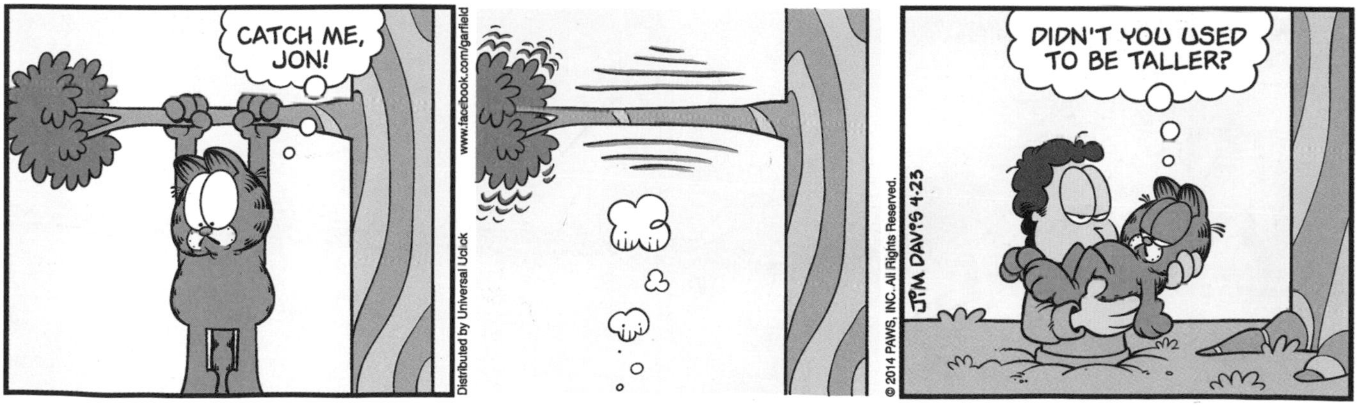
CATCH ME, JON!
DIDN'T YOU USED TO BE TALLER?
JIM DAVIS 4-23
Distributed by Universal Uclick www.facebook.com/garfield
© 2014 PAWS, INC. All Rights Reserved.

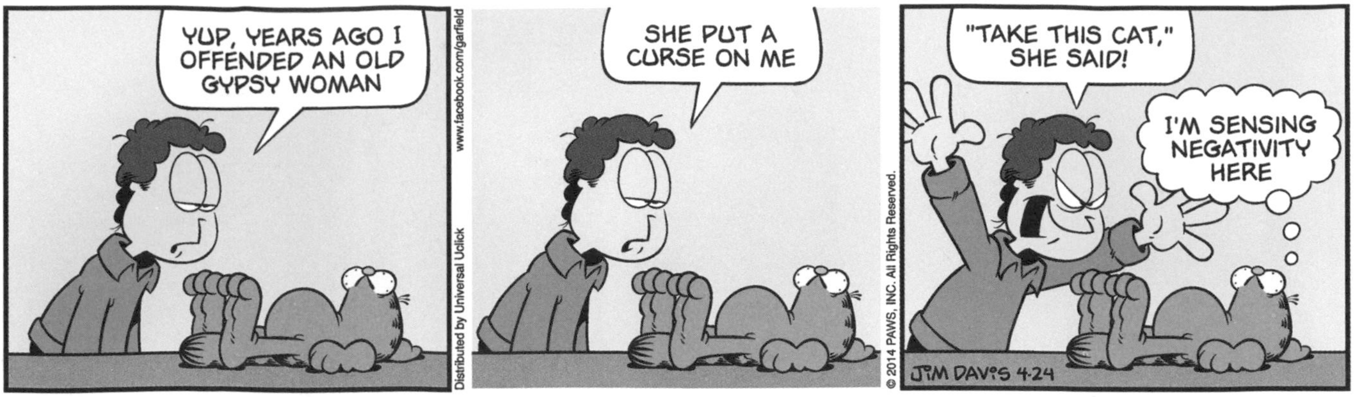
YUP, YEARS AGO I OFFENDED AN OLD GYPSY WOMAN
Distributed by Universal Uclick www.facebook.com/garfield
SHE PUT A CURSE ON ME
"TAKE THIS CAT," SHE SAID!
I'M SENSING NEGATIVITY HERE
© 2014 PAWS, INC. All Rights Reserved.
JIM DAVIS 4-24

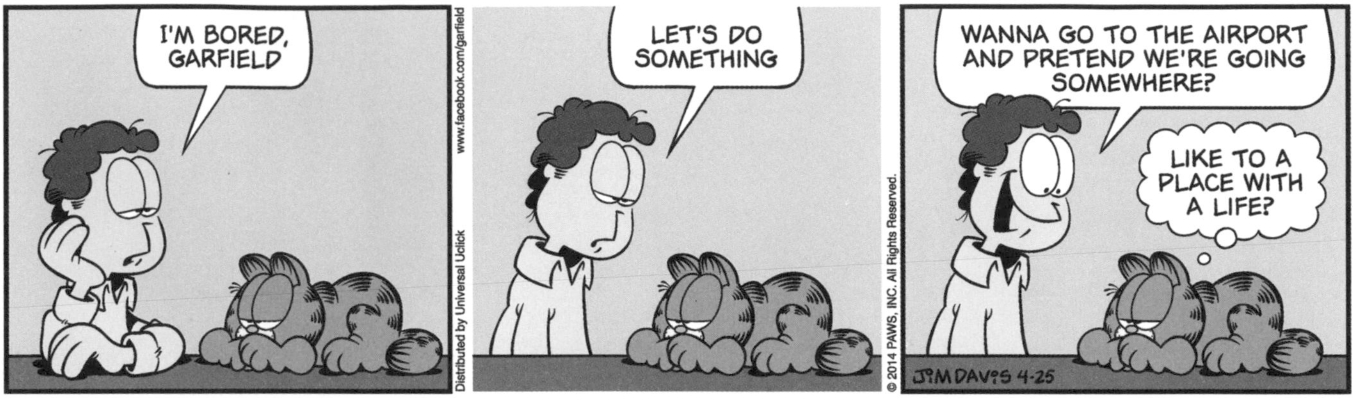
I'M BORED, GARFIELD
Distributed by Universal Uclick www.facebook.com/garfield
LET'S DO SOMETHING
WANNA GO TO THE AIRPORT AND PRETEND WE'RE GOING SOMEWHERE?
LIKE TO A PLACE WITH A LIFE?
© 2014 PAWS, INC. All Rights Reserved.
JIM DAVIS 4-25

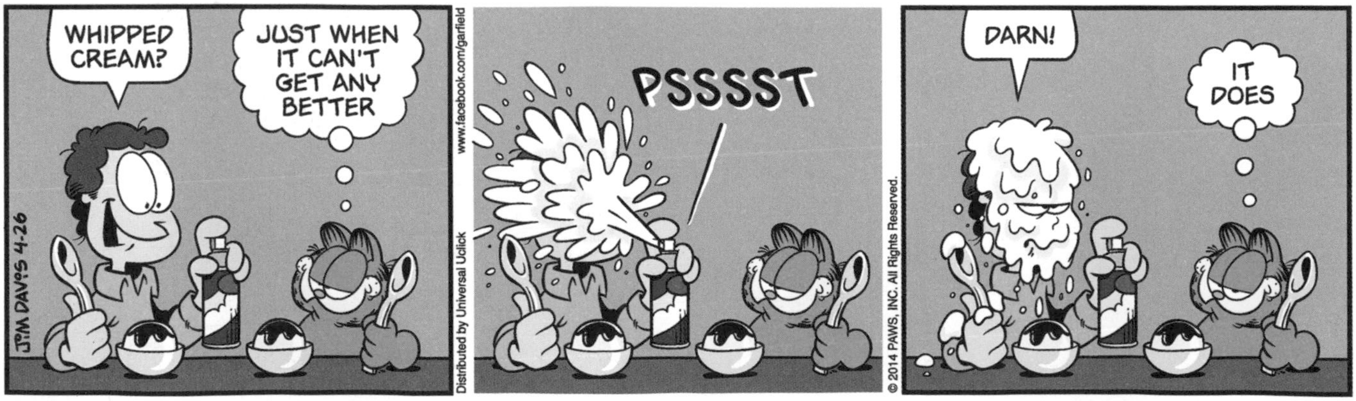
JIM DAVIS 4-26
WHIPPED CREAM?
JUST WHEN IT CAN'T GET ANY BETTER
Distributed by Universal Uclick www.facebook.com/garfield
PSSSST
© 2014 PAWS, INC. All Rights Reserved.
DARN!
IT DOES

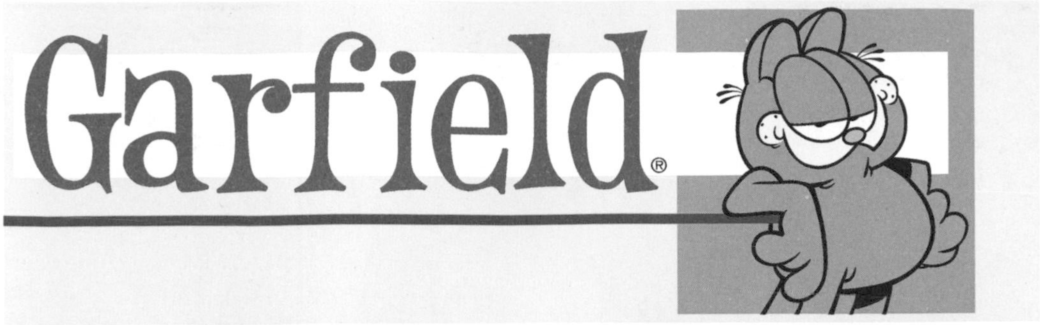
Garfield®

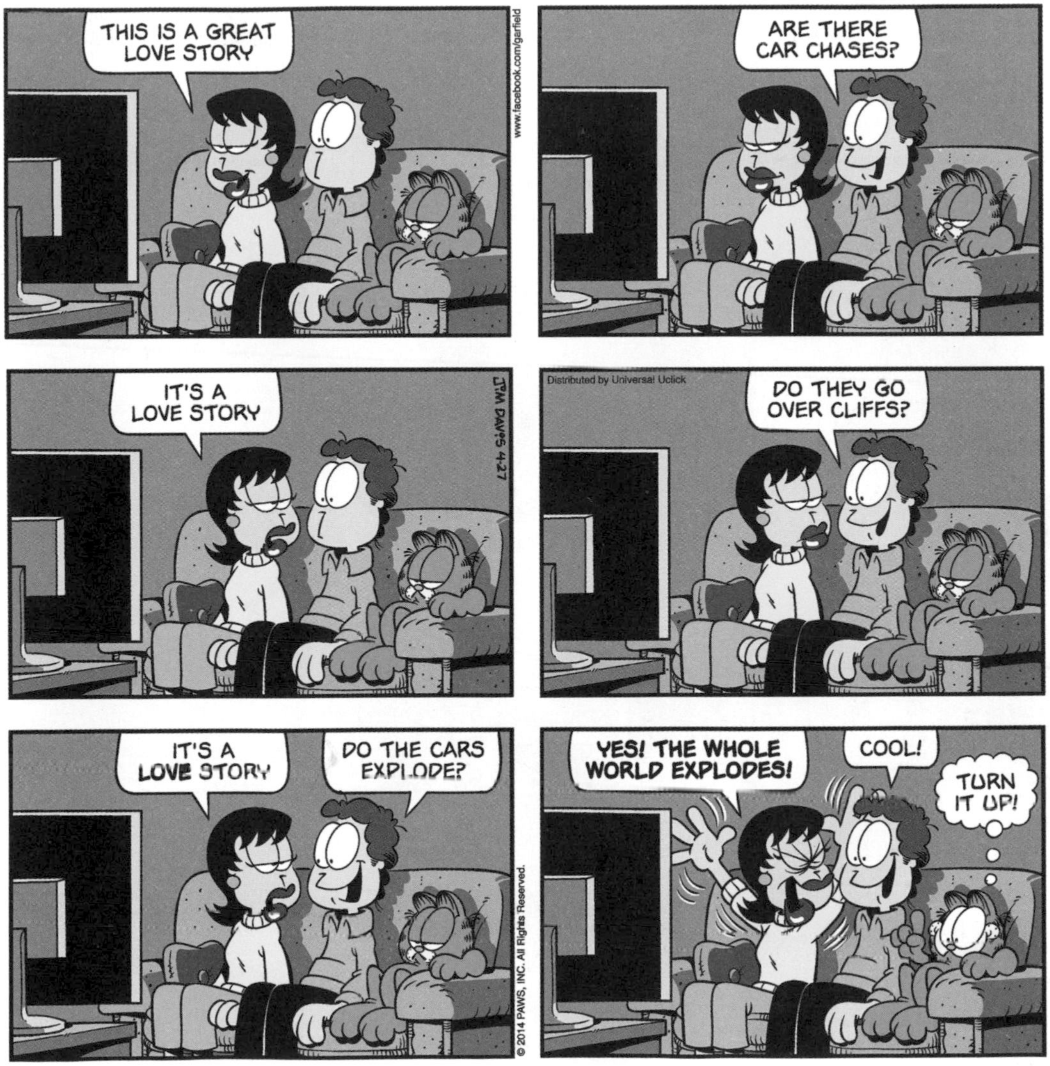
THIS IS A GREAT LOVE STORY
www.facebook.com/garfield
ARE THERE CAR CHASES?
IT'S A LOVE STORY
JIM DAVIS 4-27
Distributed by Universal Uclick
DO THEY GO OVER CLIFFS?
IT'S A LOVE STORY
DO THE CARS EXPLODE?
© 2014 PAWS, INC. All Rights Reserved.
YES! THE WHOLE WORLD EXPLODES!
COOL!
TURN IT UP!

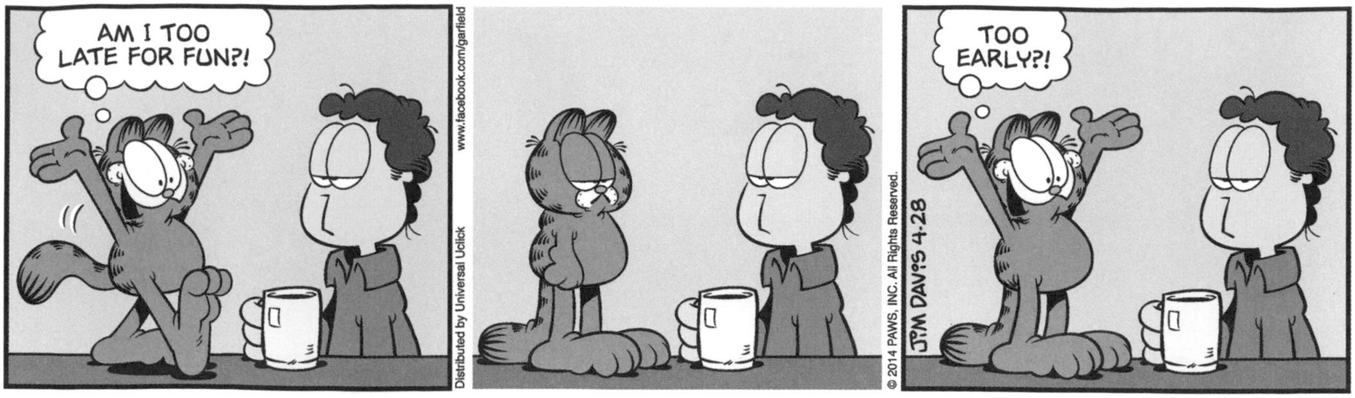
AM I TOO LATE FOR FUN?!
TOO EARLY?!
JIM DAVIS 4-28
Distributed by Universal Uclick www.facebook.com/garfield
© 2014 PAWS, INC. All Rights Reserved.

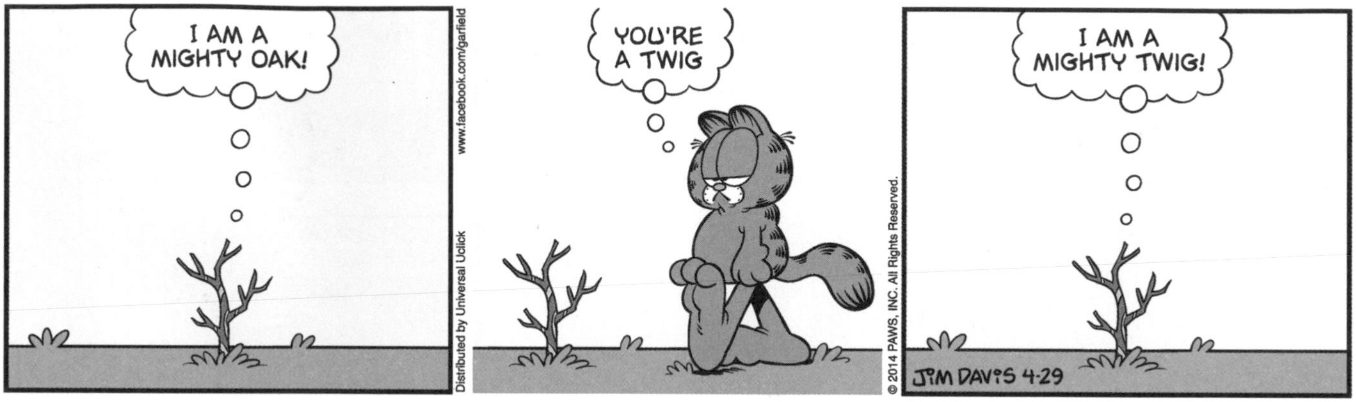
I AM A MIGHTY OAK!
YOU'RE A TWIG
I AM A MIGHTY TWIG!
JIM DAVIS 4-29
Distributed by Universal Uclick www.facebook.com/garfield
© 2014 PAWS, INC. All Rights Reserved.

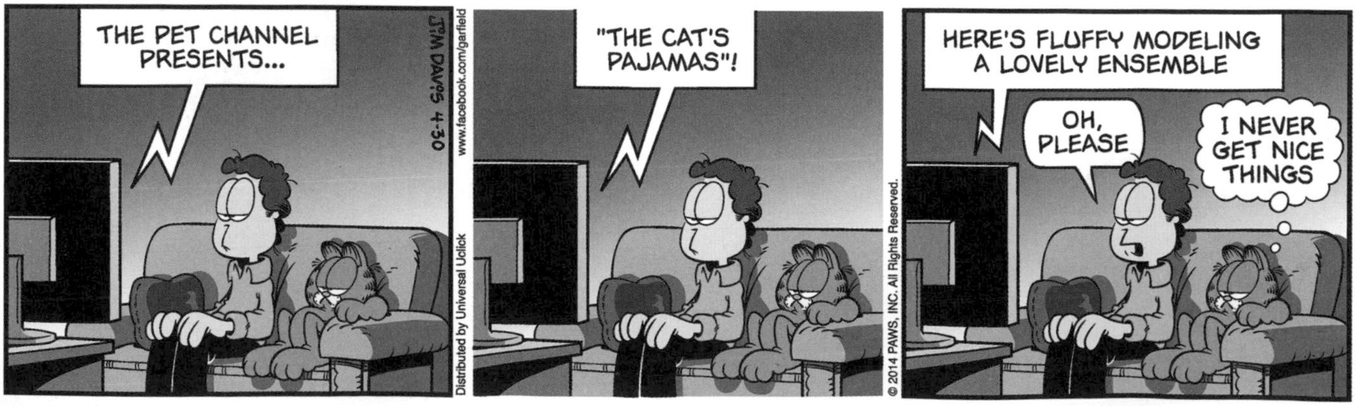
THE PET CHANNEL PRESENTS...
"THE CAT'S PAJAMAS"!
HERE'S FLUFFY MODELING A LOVELY ENSEMBLE
OH, PLEASE
I NEVER GET NICE THINGS
JIM DAVIS 4-30
Distributed by Universal Uclick www.facebook.com/garfield
© 2014 PAWS, INC. All Rights Reserved.

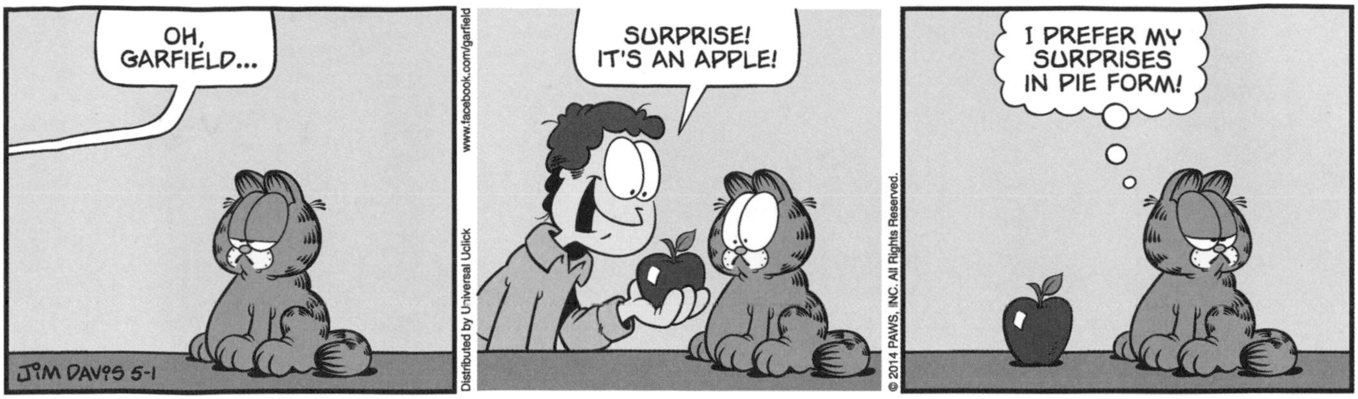
OH, GARFIELD...
JIM DAVIS 5-1
Distributed by Universal Uclick
www.facebook.com/garfield
SURPRISE! IT'S AN APPLE!
© 2014 PAWS, INC. All Rights Reserved.
I PREFER MY SURPRISES IN PIE FORM!

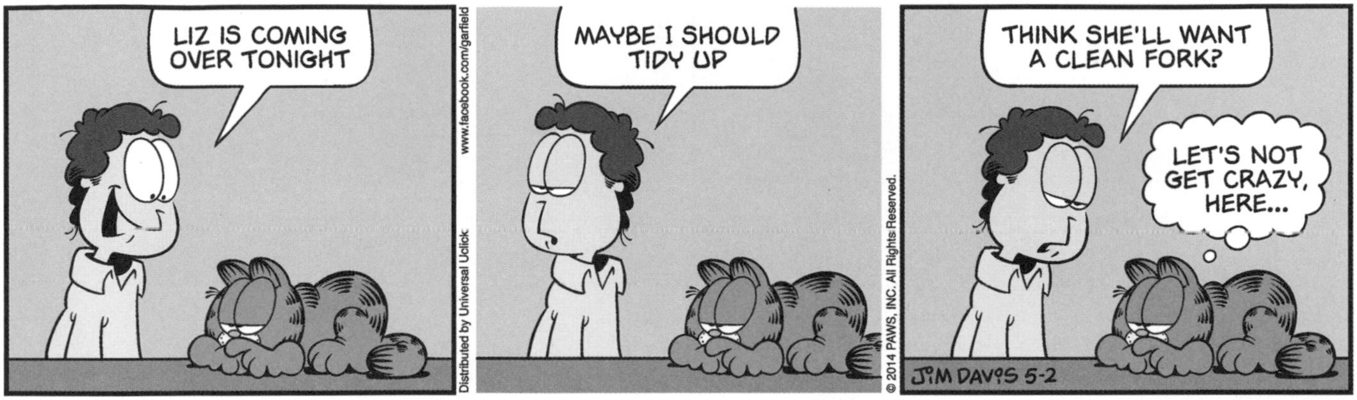
LIZ IS COMING OVER TONIGHT
Distributed by Universal Uclick
www.facebook.com/garfield
MAYBE I SHOULD TIDY UP
© 2014 PAWS, INC. All Rights Reserved.
THINK SHE'LL WANT A CLEAN FORK?
LET'S NOT GET CRAZY, HERE...
JIM DAVIS 5-2

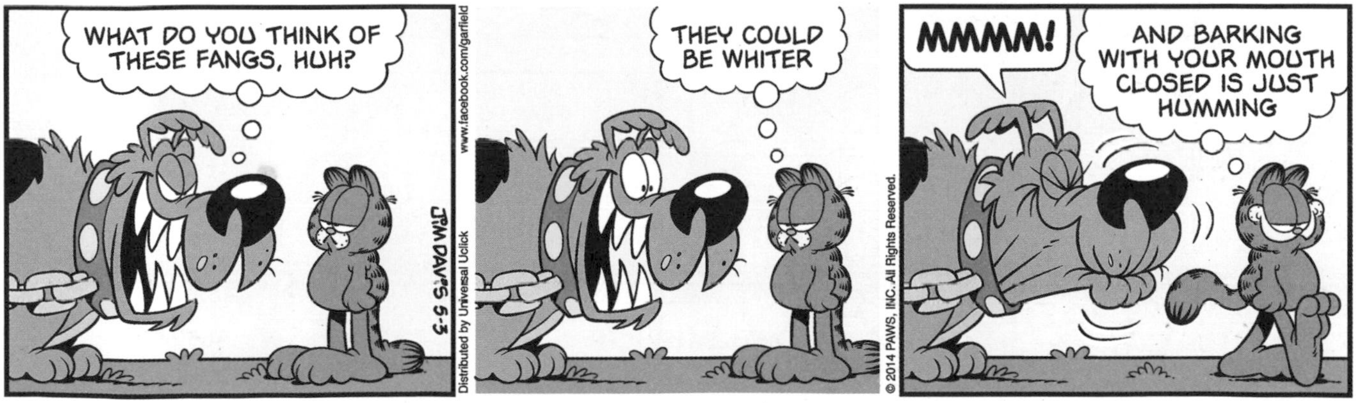
WHAT DO YOU THINK OF THESE FANGS, HUH?
JIM DAVIS 5-3
Distributed by Universal Uclick
www.facebook.com/garfield
THEY COULD BE WHITER
© 2014 PAWS, INC. All Rights Reserved.
MMMM!
AND BARKING WITH YOUR MOUTH CLOSED IS JUST HUMMING

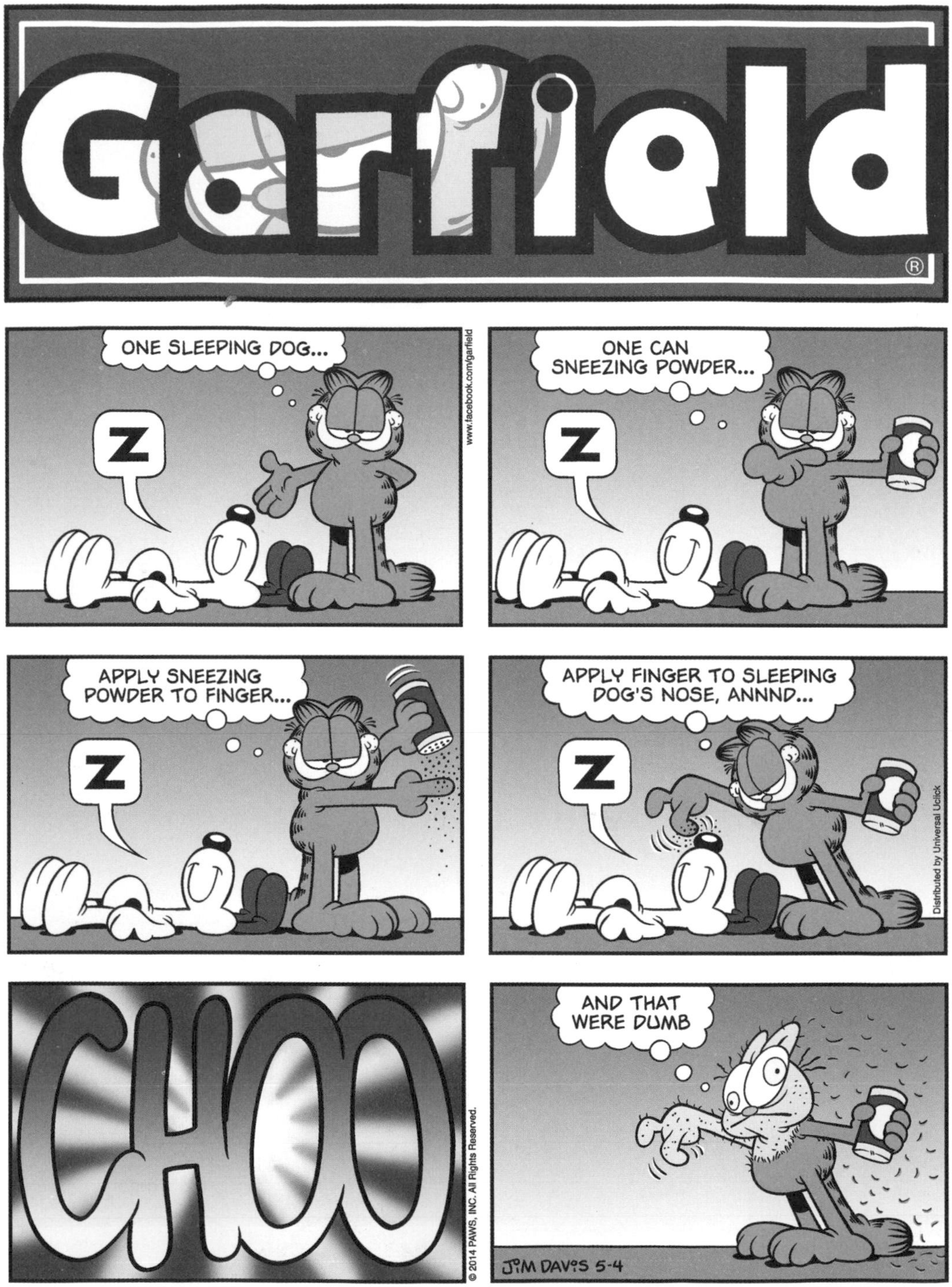
Garfield
ONE SLEEPING DOG...
Z
www.facebook.com/garfield
ONE CAN SNEEZING POWDER...
Z
APPLY SNEEZING POWDER TO FINGER...
Z
APPLY FINGER TO SLEEPING DOG'S NOSE, ANNND...
Z
Distributed by Universal Uclick
CHOO
© 2014 PAWS, INC. All Rights Reserved.
AND THAT WERE DUMB
JIM DAVIS 5-4

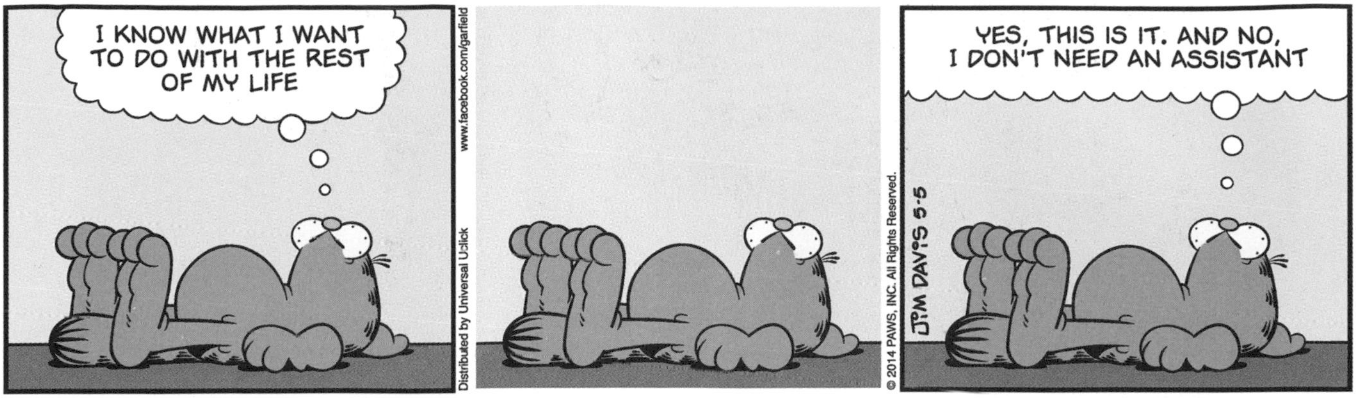
I KNOW WHAT I WANT TO DO WITH THE REST OF MY LIFE
Distributed by Universal Uclick www.facebook.com/garfield
YES, THIS IS IT. AND NO, I DON'T NEED AN ASSISTANT
© 2014 PAWS, INC. All Rights Reserved.
JIM DAVIS 5-5

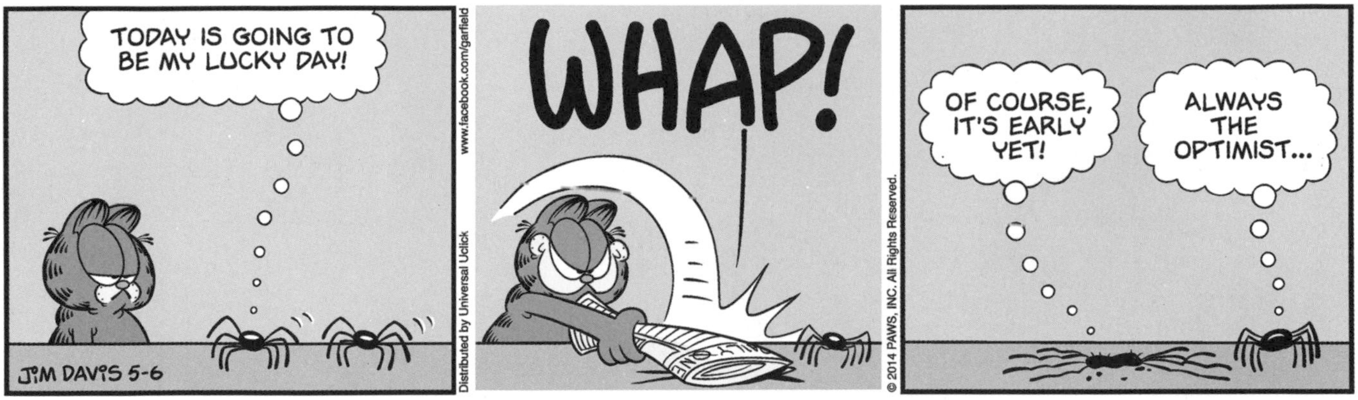
TODAY IS GOING TO BE MY LUCKY DAY!
JIM DAVIS 5-6
Distributed by Universal Uclick www.facebook.com/garfield
WHAP!
OF COURSE, IT'S EARLY YET!
ALWAYS THE OPTIMIST...
© 2014 PAWS, INC. All Rights Reserved.

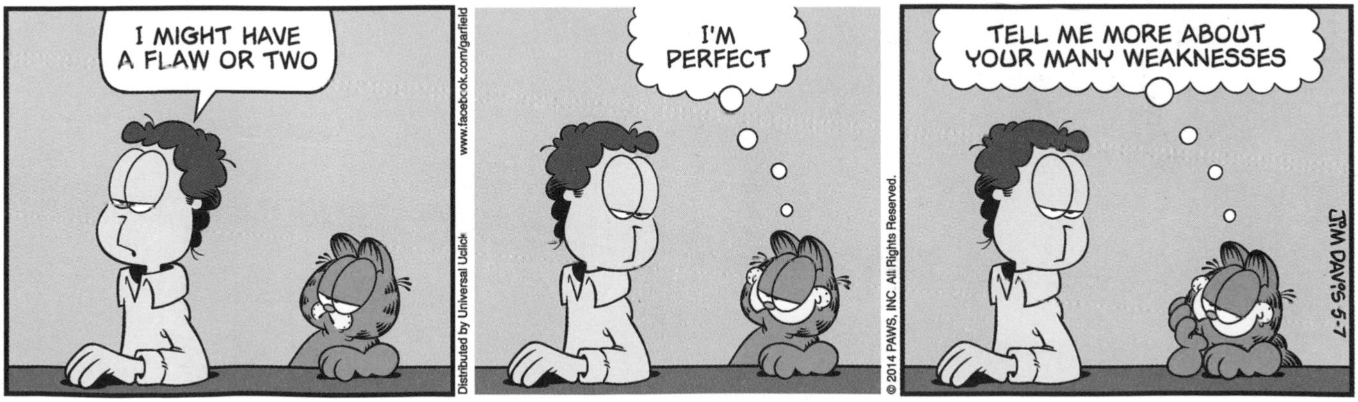
I MIGHT HAVE A FLAW OR TWO
Distributed by Universal Uclick www.facebook.com/garfield
I'M PERFECT
© 2014 PAWS, INC. All Rights Reserved.
TELL ME MORE ABOUT YOUR MANY WEAKNESSES
JIM DAVIS 5-7

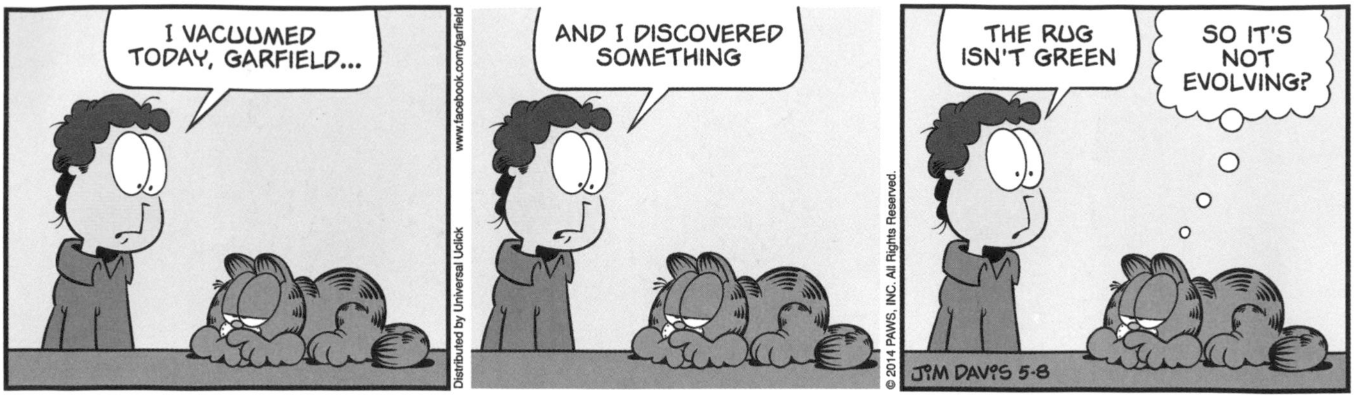
I VACUUMED TODAY, GARFIELD...
AND I DISCOVERED SOMETHING
THE RUG ISN'T GREEN
SO IT'S NOT EVOLVING?
Distributed by Universal Uclick www.facebook.com/garfield
© 2014 PAWS, INC. All Rights Reserved.
JIM DAVIS 5-8

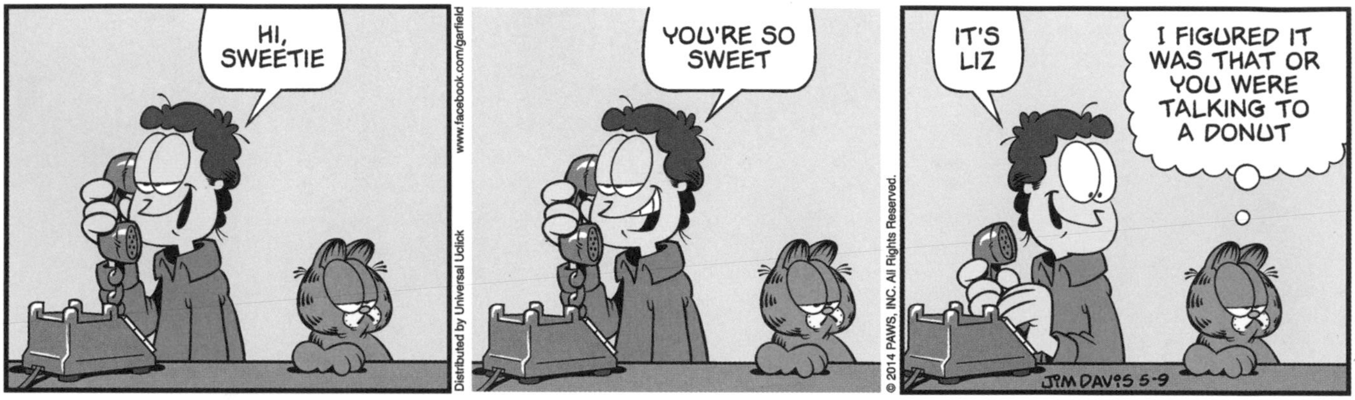
HI, SWEETIE
YOU'RE SO SWEET
IT'S LIZ
I FIGURED IT WAS THAT OR YOU WERE TALKING TO A DONUT
Distributed by Universal Uclick www.facebook.com/garfield
© 2014 PAWS, INC. All Rights Reserved.
JIM DAVIS 5-9

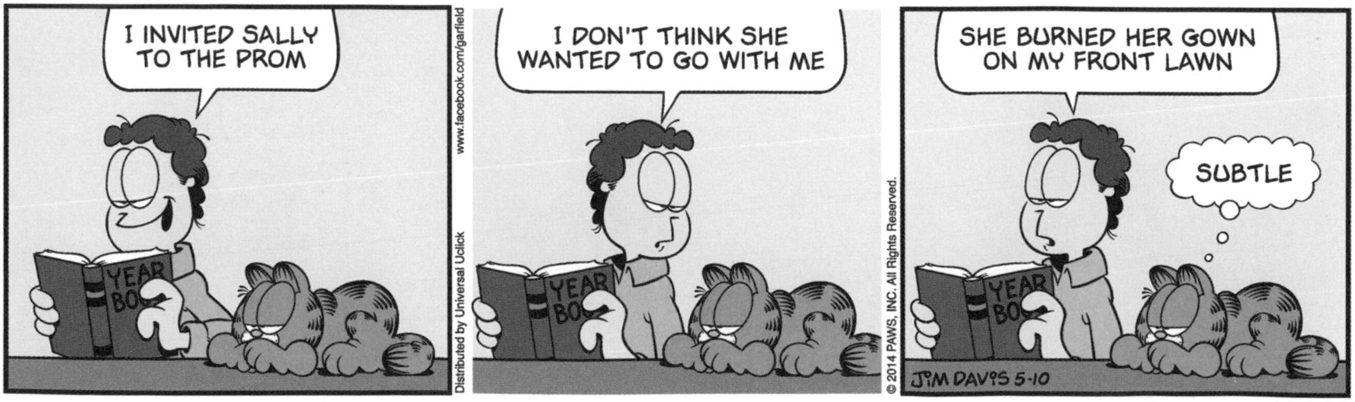
I INVITED SALLY TO THE PROM
I DON'T THINK SHE WANTED TO GO WITH ME
SHE BURNED HER GOWN ON MY FRONT LAWN
SUBTLE
Distributed by Universal Uclick www.facebook.com/garfield
© 2014 PAWS, INC. All Rights Reserved.
JIM DAVIS 5-10

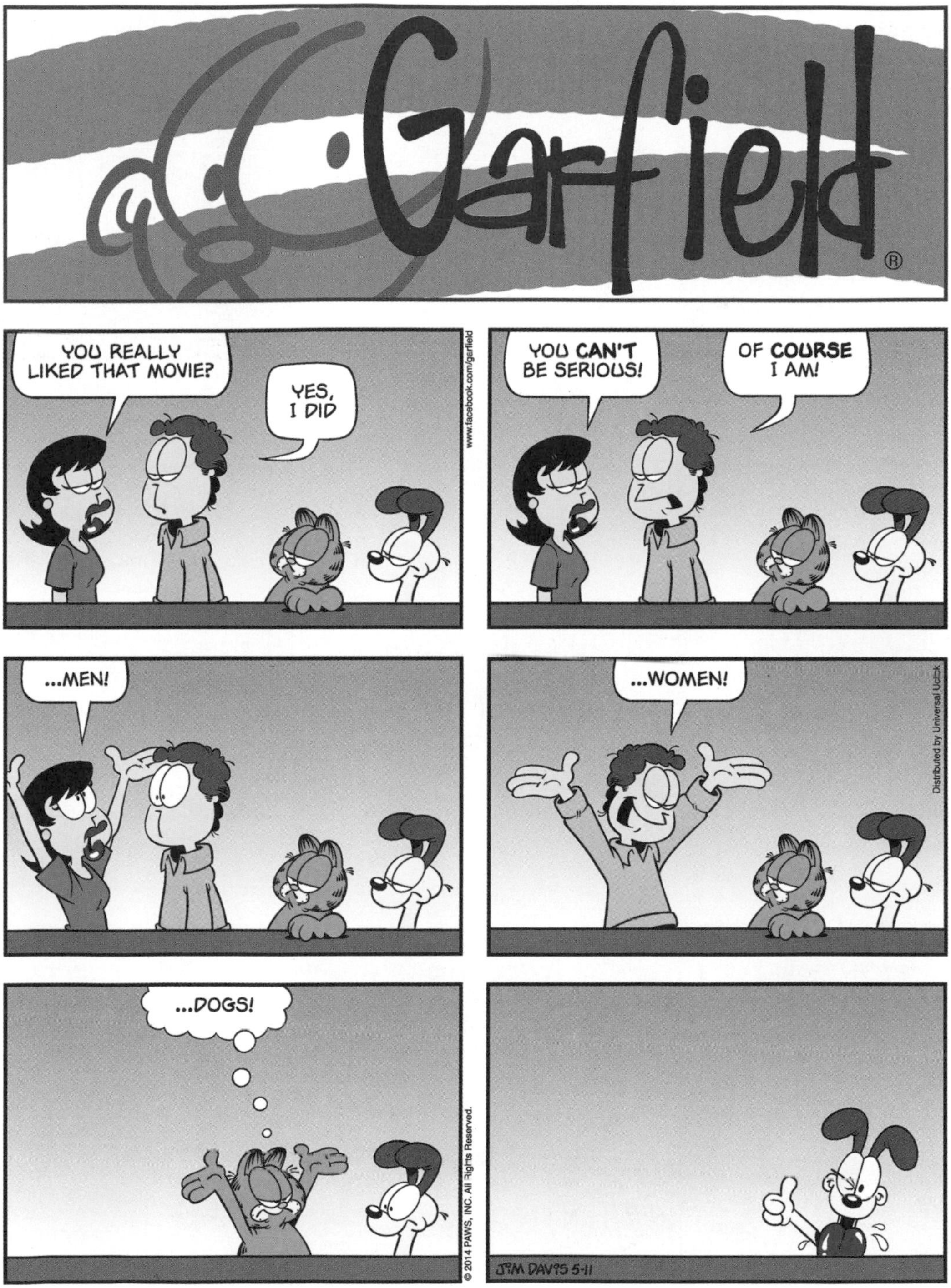
Garfield®
YOU REALLY LIKED THAT MOVIE?
YES, I DID
www.facebook.com/garfield
YOU CAN'T BE SERIOUS!
OF COURSE I AM!
...MEN!
...WOMEN!
Distributed by Universal Uclick
...DOGS!
© 2014 PAWS, INC. All Rights Reserved.
JIM DAVIS 5-11

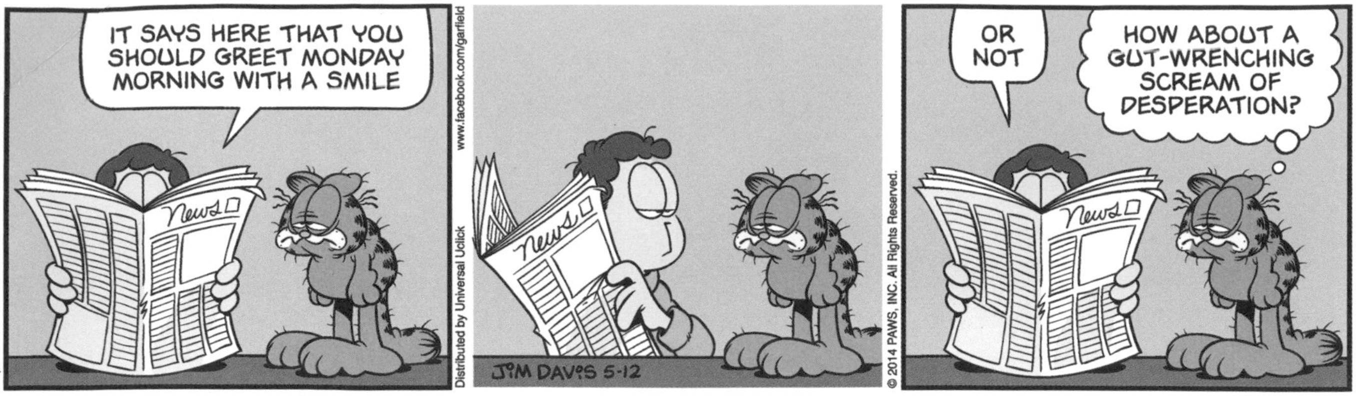
IT SAYS HERE THAT YOU SHOULD GREET MONDAY MORNING WITH A SMILE
OR NOT
HOW ABOUT A GUT-WRENCHING SCREAM OF DESPERATION?
JIM DAVIS 5-12
Distributed by Universal Uclick www.facebook.com/garfield
© 2014 PAWS, INC. All Rights Reserved.

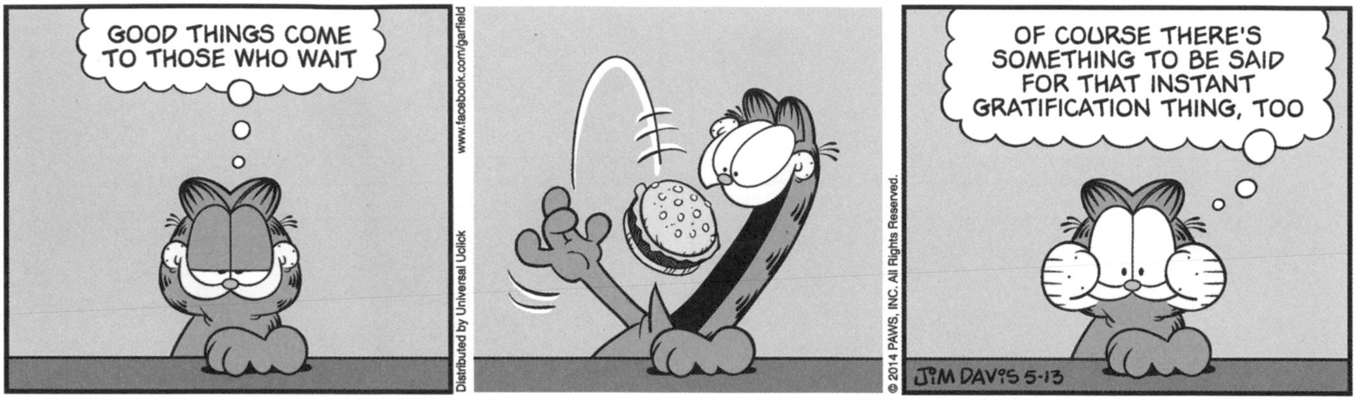
GOOD THINGS COME TO THOSE WHO WAIT
OF COURSE THERE'S SOMETHING TO BE SAID FOR THAT INSTANT GRATIFICATION THING, TOO
JIM DAVIS 5-13
Distributed by Universal Uclick www.facebook.com/garfield
© 2014 PAWS, INC. All Rights Reserved.

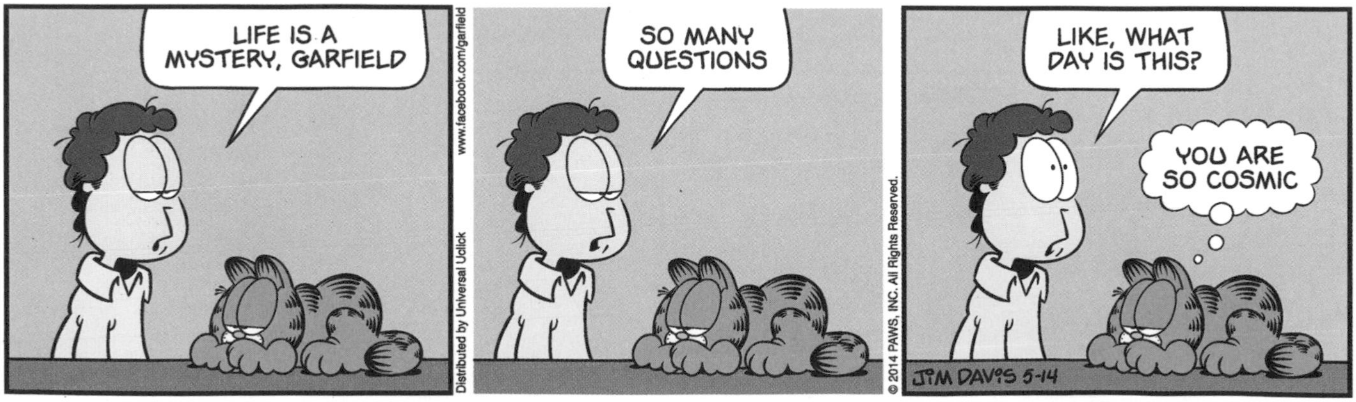
LIFE IS A MYSTERY, GARFIELD
SO MANY QUESTIONS
LIKE, WHAT DAY IS THIS?
YOU ARE SO COSMIC
JIM DAVIS 5-14
Distributed by Universal Uclick www.facebook.com/garfield
© 2014 PAWS, INC. All Rights Reserved.

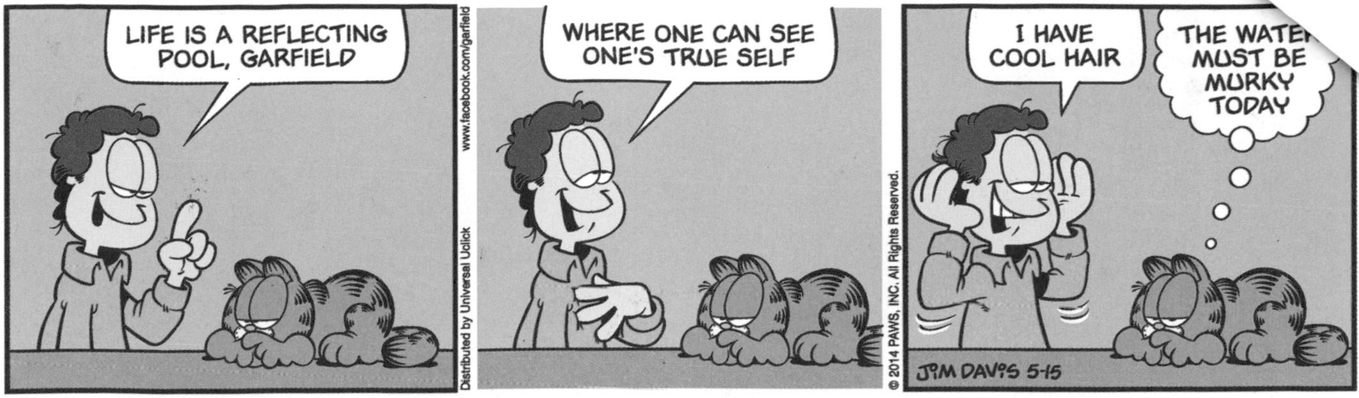
LIFE IS A REFLECTING POOL, GARFIELD
Distributed by Universal Uclick
www.facebook.com/garfield
WHERE ONE CAN SEE ONE'S TRUE SELF
© 2014 PAWS, INC. All Rights Reserved.
I HAVE COOL HAIR
THE WATE MUST BE MURKY TODAY
JIM DAVIS 5-15

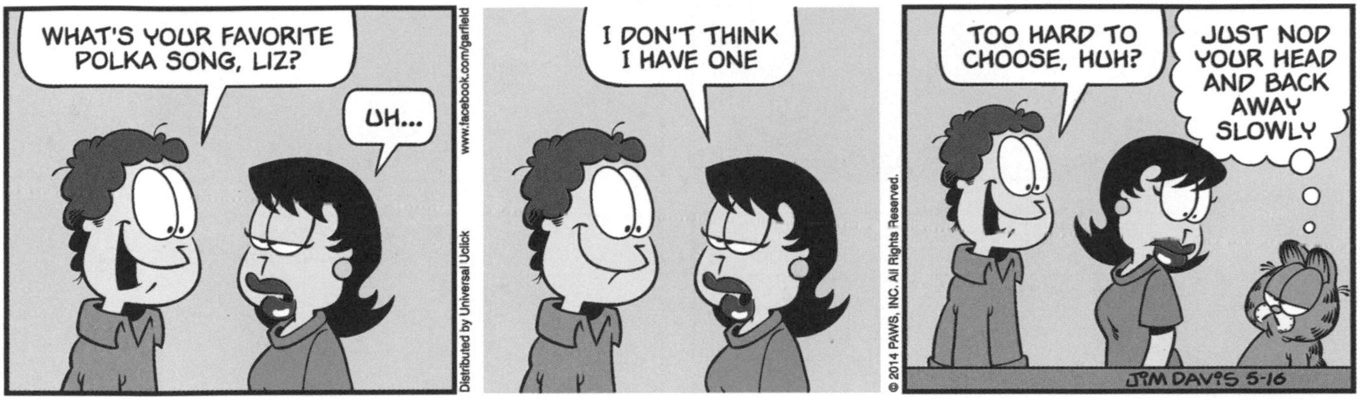
WHAT'S YOUR FAVORITE POLKA SONG, LIZ?
UH...
Distributed by Universal Uclick
www.facebook.com/garfield
I DON'T THINK I HAVE ONE
© 2014 PAWS, INC. All Rights Reserved.
TOO HARD TO CHOOSE, HUH?
JUST NOD YOUR HEAD AND BACK AWAY SLOWLY
JIM DAVIS 5-16

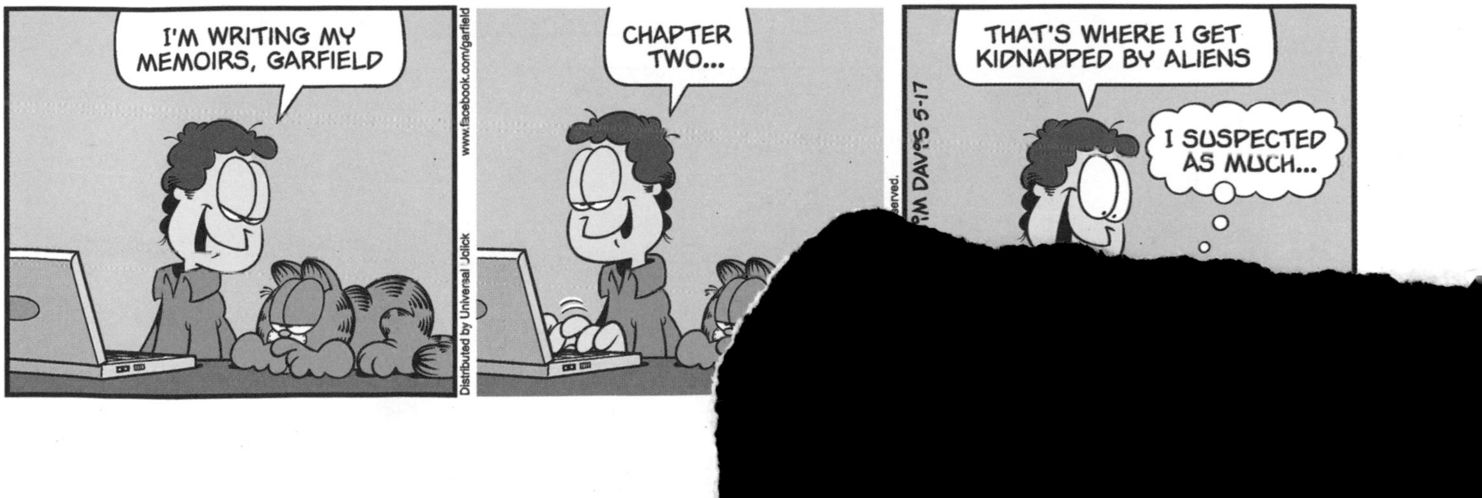
I'M WRITING MY MEMOIRS, GARFIELD
www.facebook.com/garfield
CHAPTER TWO...
THAT'S WHERE I GET KIDNAPPED BY ALIENS
I SUSPECTED AS MUCH...
DAVIS 5-17

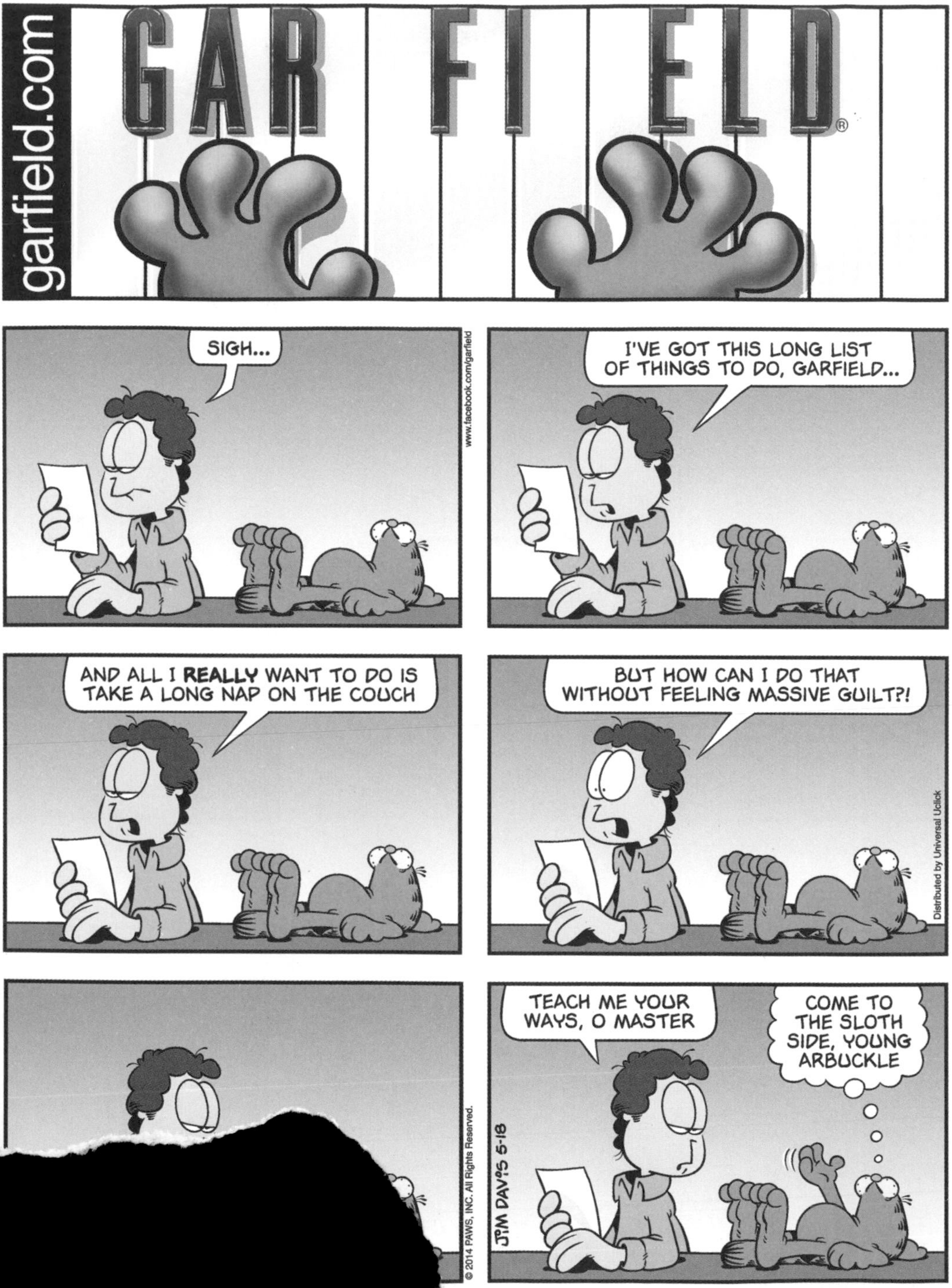
garfield.com
GARFIELD®
SIGH...
www.facebook.com/garfield
I'VE GOT THIS LONG LIST OF THINGS TO DO, GARFIELD...
AND ALL I REALLY WANT TO DO IS TAKE A LONG NAP ON THE COUCH
BUT HOW CAN I DO THAT WITHOUT FEELING MASSIVE GUILT?!
Distributed by Universal Uclick
© 2014 PAWS, INC. All Rights Reserved.
JIM DAVIS 5-18
TEACH ME YOUR WAYS, O MASTER
COME TO THE SLOTH SIDE, YOUNG ARBUCKLE

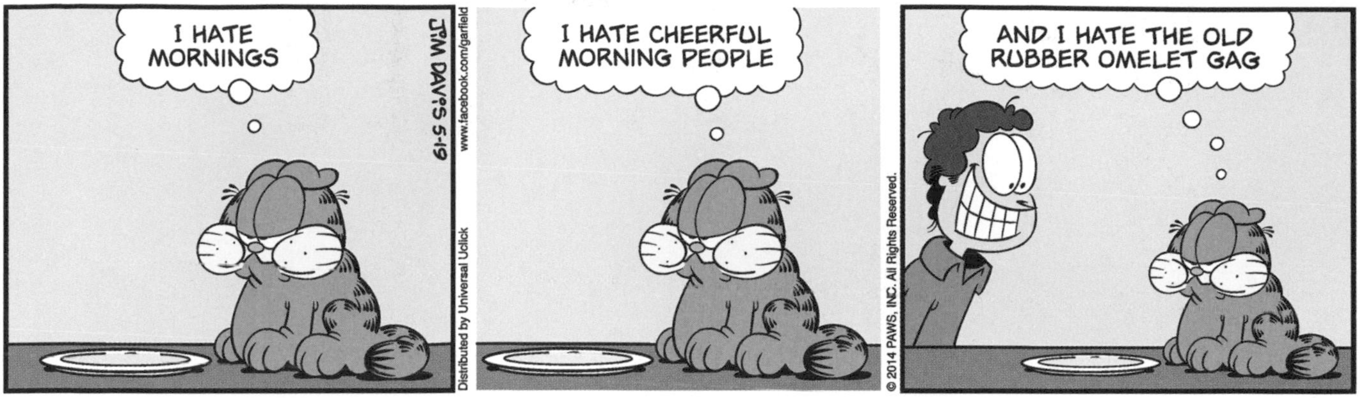
I HATE MORNINGS
JIM DAVIS 5-19
www.facebook.com/garfield
Distributed by Universal Uclick
I HATE CHEERFUL MORNING PEOPLE
© 2014 PAWS, INC. All Rights Reserved.
AND I HATE THE OLD RUBBER OMELET GAG

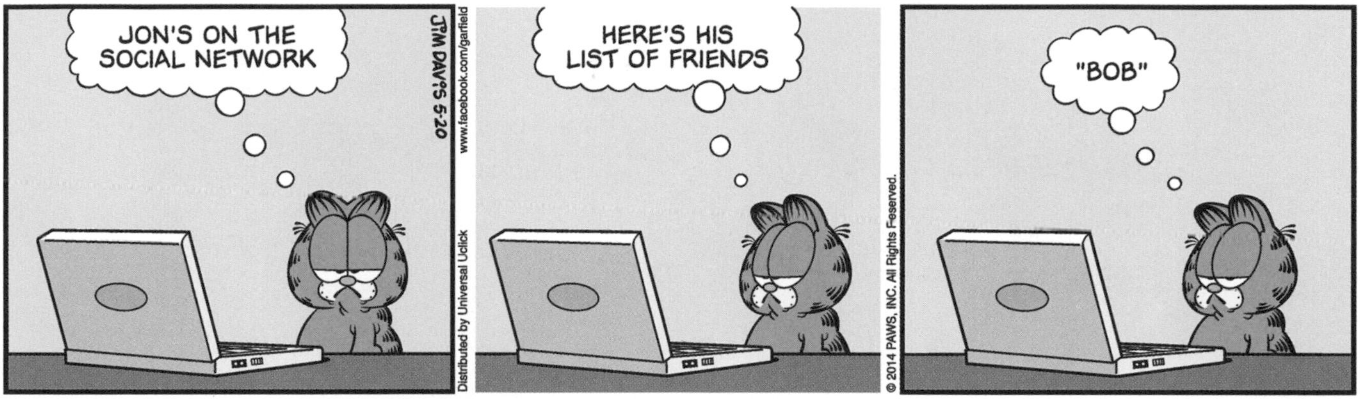
JON'S ON THE SOCIAL NETWORK
JIM DAVIS 5-20
www.facebook.com/garfield
Distributed by Universal Uclick
HERE'S HIS LIST OF FRIENDS
© 2014 PAWS, INC. All Rights Reserved.
"BOB"

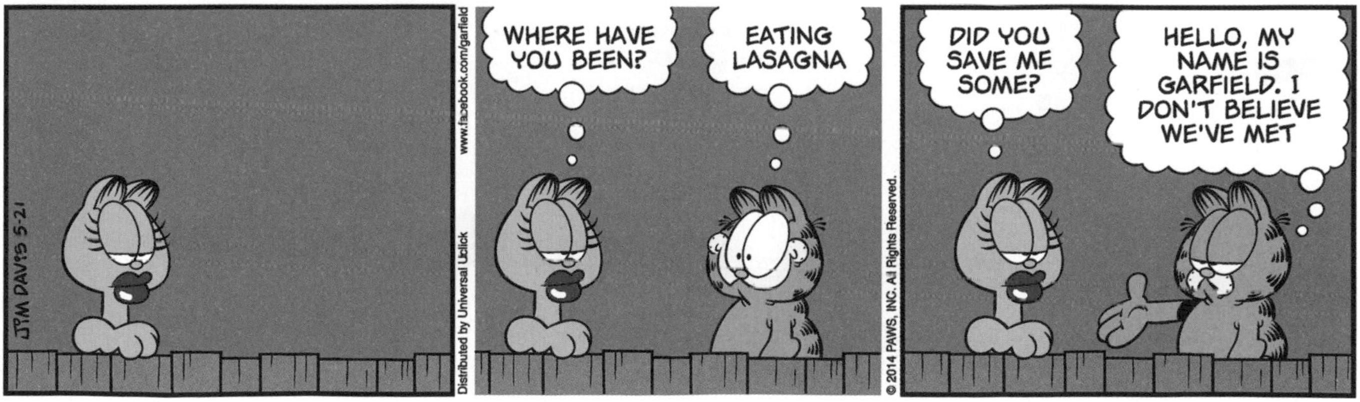
JIM DAVIS 5-21
www.facebook.com/garfield
Distributed by Universal Uclick
WHERE HAVE YOU BEEN?
EATING LASAGNA
© 2014 PAWS, INC. All Rights Reserved.
DID YOU SAVE ME SOME?
HELLO, MY NAME IS GARFIELD. I DON'T BELIEVE WE'VE MET

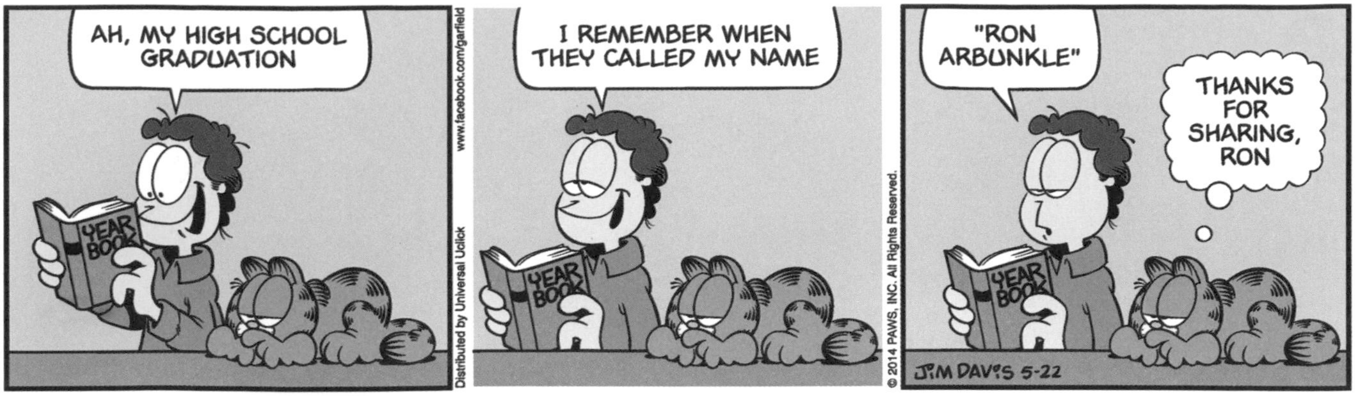
AH, MY HIGH SCHOOL GRADUATION
YEAR BOOK
www.facebook.com/garfield
Distributed by Universal Uclick
I REMEMBER WHEN THEY CALLED MY NAME
YEAR BOOK
© 2014 PAWS, INC. All Rights Reserved.
"RON ARBUNKLE"
THANKS FOR SHARING, RON
YEAR BOOK
JIM DAVIS 5-22

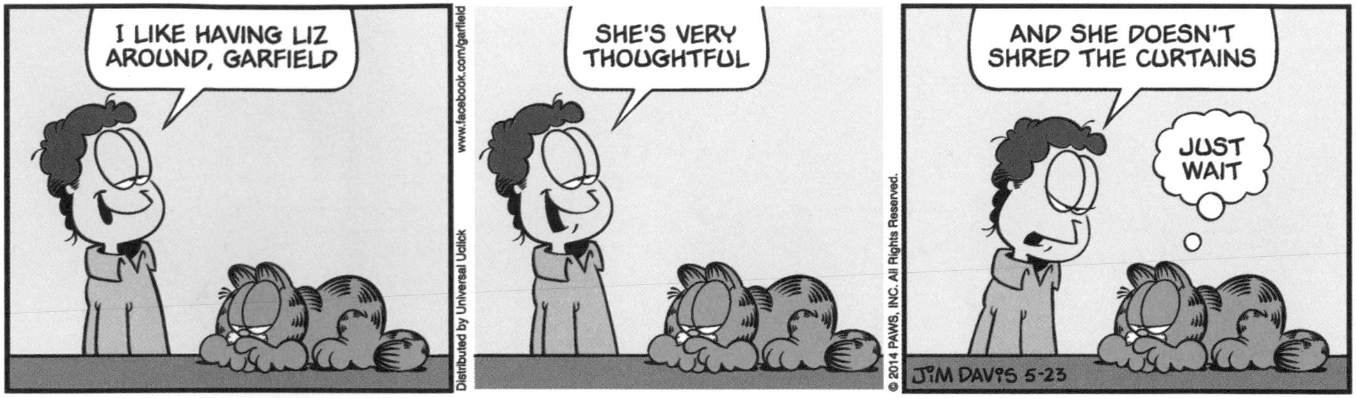
I LIKE HAVING LIZ AROUND, GARFIELD
www.facebook.com/garfield
Distributed by Universal Uclick
SHE'S VERY THOUGHTFUL
© 2014 PAWS, INC. All Rights Reserved.
AND SHE DOESN'T SHRED THE CURTAINS
JUST WAIT
JIM DAVIS 5-23

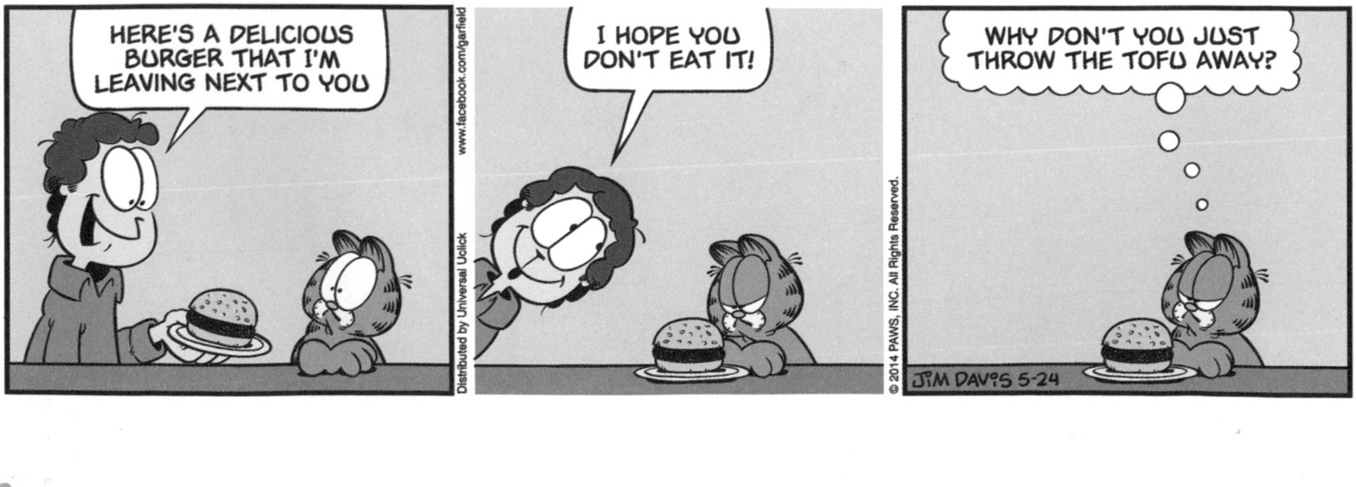
HERE'S A DELICIOUS BURGER THAT I'M LEAVING NEXT TO YOU
www.facebook.com/garfield
Distributed by Universal Uclick
I HOPE YOU DON'T EAT IT!
© 2014 PAWS, INC. All Rights Reserved.
WHY DON'T YOU JUST THROW THE TOFU AWAY?
JIM DAVIS 5-24

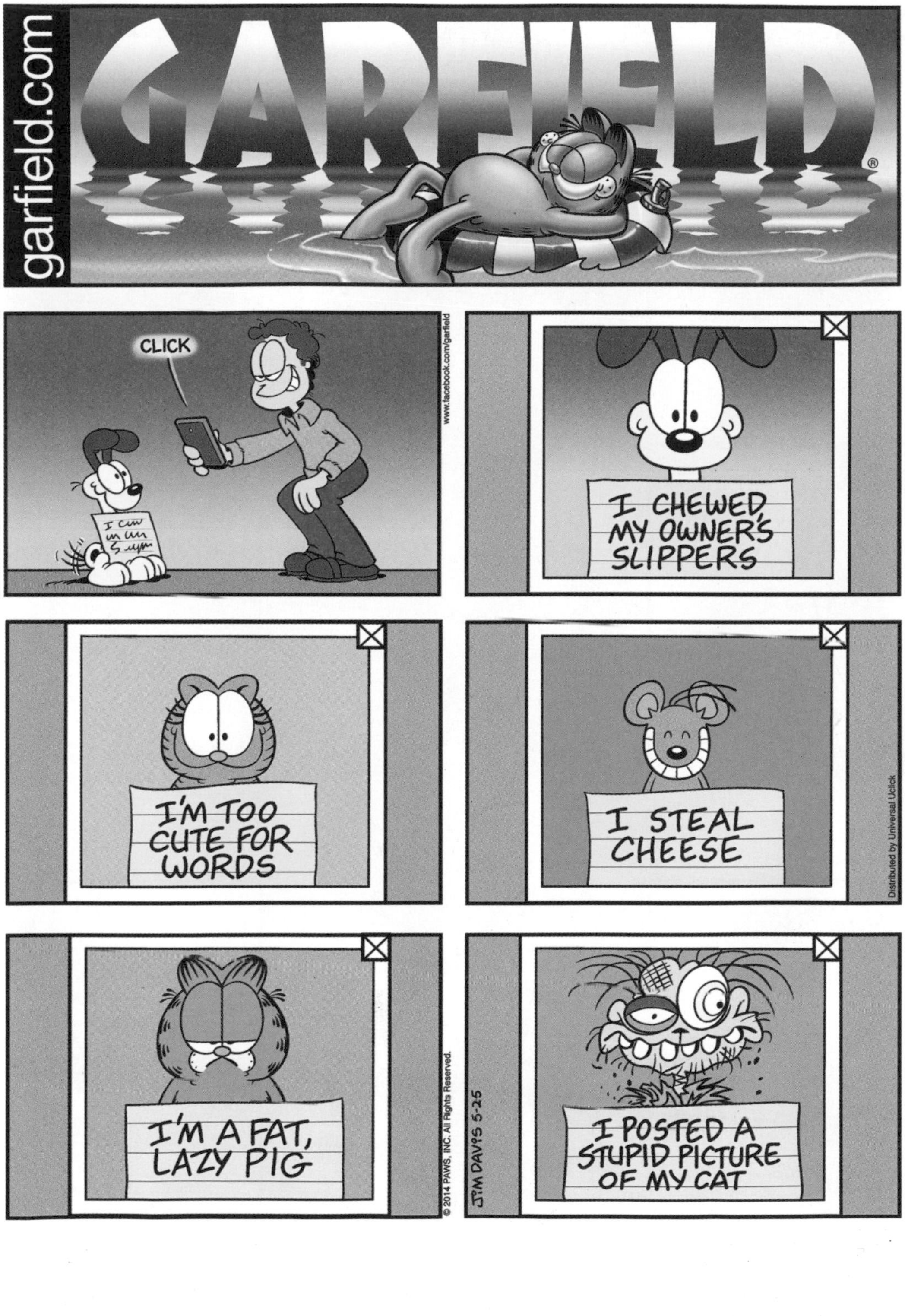
garfield.com
GARFIELD®
www.facebook.com/garfield
CLICK
I CHEWED MY OWNER'S SLIPPERS
I'M TOO CUTE FOR WORDS
I STEAL CHEESE
Distributed by Universal Uclick
I'M A FAT, LAZY PIG
© 2014 PAWS, INC. All Rights Reserved.
JIM DAVIS 5-25
I POSTED A STUPID PICTURE OF MY CAT

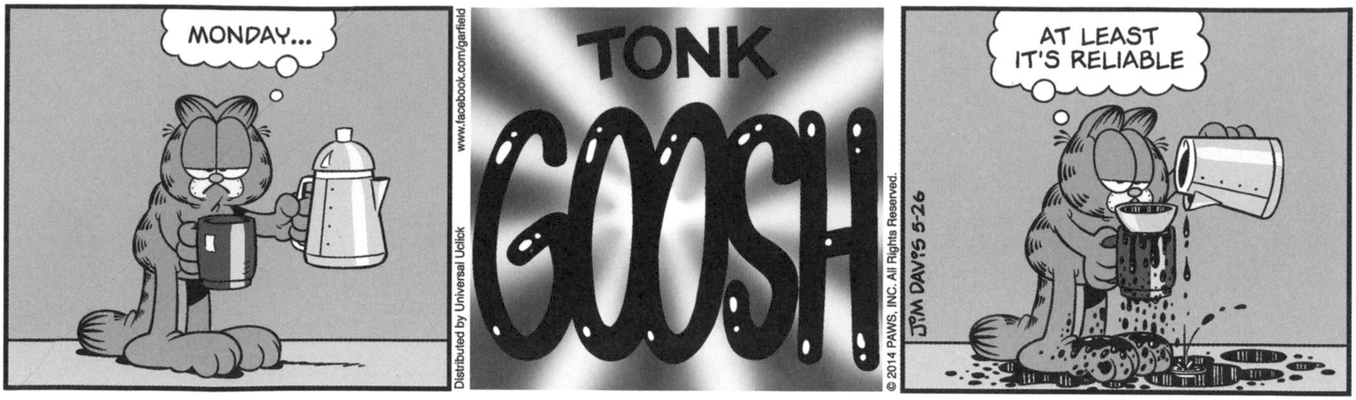
MONDAY...
Distributed by Universal Uclick
www.facebook.com/garfield
TONK
GOOSH
© 2014 PAWS, INC. All Rights Reserved.
JIM DAVIS 5-26
AT LEAST IT'S RELIABLE

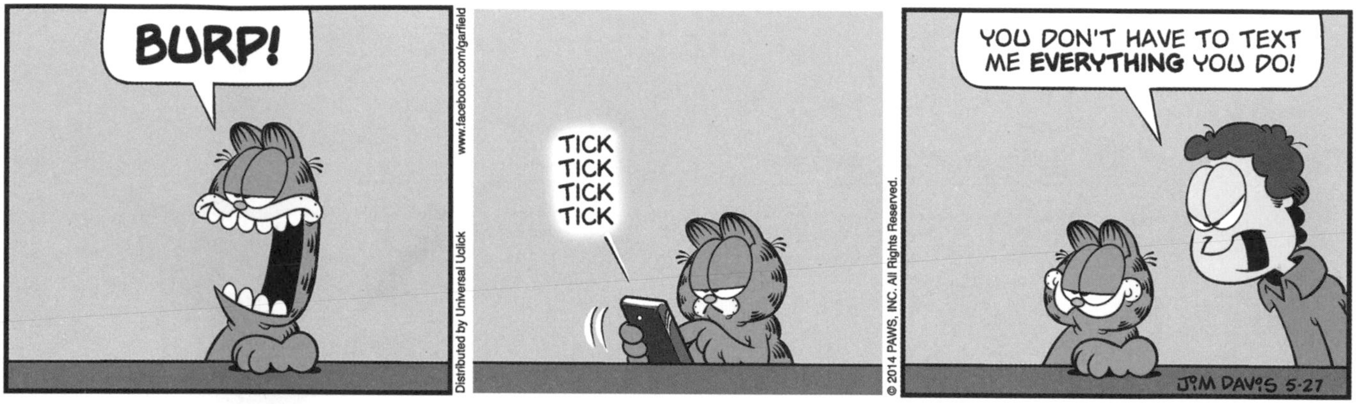
BURP!
Distributed by Universal Uclick
www.facebook.com/garfield
TICK TICK TICK TICK
© 2014 PAWS, INC. All Rights Reserved.
YOU DON'T HAVE TO TEXT ME **EVERYTHING** YOU DO!
JIM DAVIS 5-27

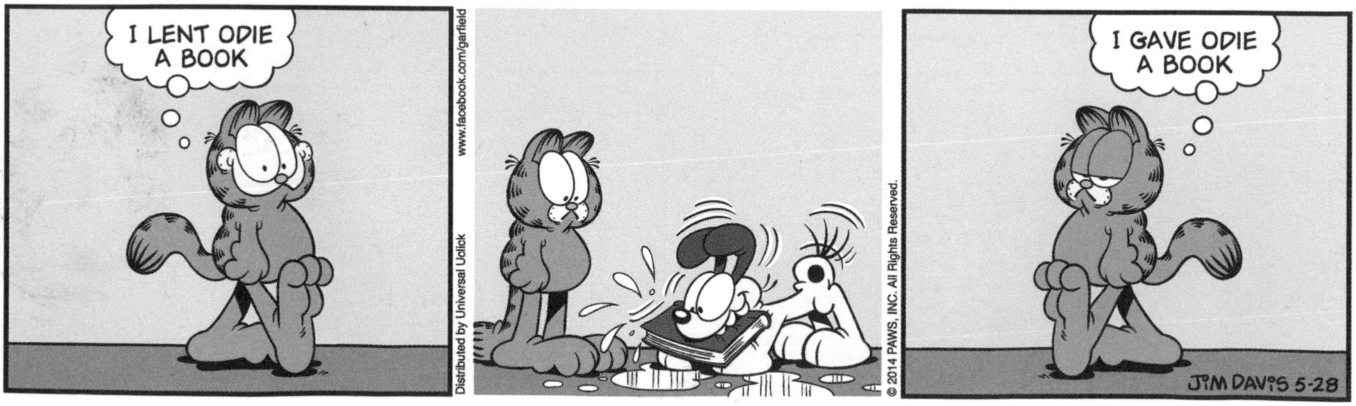
I LENT ODIE A BOOK
Distributed by Universal Uclick
www.facebook.com/garfield
© 2014 PAWS, INC. All Rights Reserved.
I GAVE ODIE A BOOK
JIM DAVIS 5-28

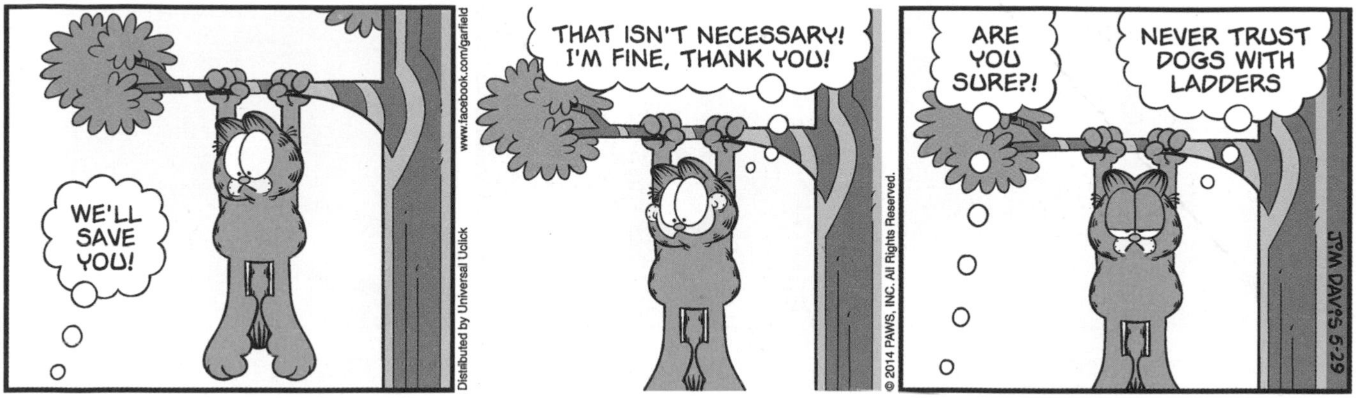
WE'LL SAVE YOU!
THAT ISN'T NECESSARY! I'M FINE, THANK YOU!
ARE YOU SURE?!
NEVER TRUST DOGS WITH LADDERS
JIM DAVIS 5-29
Distributed by Universal Uclick www.facebook.com/garfield
© 2014 PAWS, INC. All Rights Reserved.

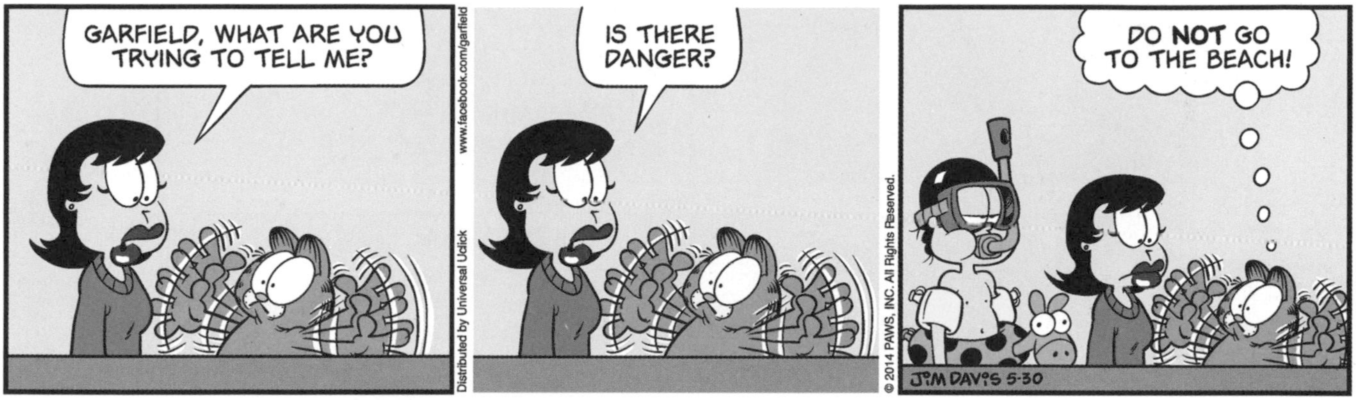
GARFIELD, WHAT ARE YOU TRYING TO TELL ME?
IS THERE DANGER?
DO NOT GO TO THE BEACH!
JIM DAVIS 5-30
Distributed by Universal Uclick www.facebook.com/garfield
© 2014 PAWS, INC. All Rights Reserved.

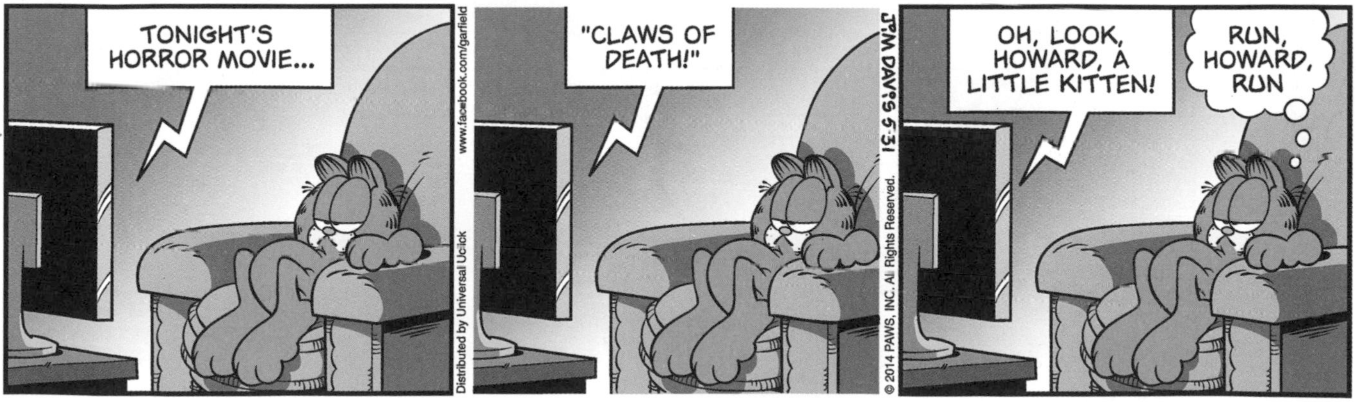
TONIGHT'S HORROR MOVIE...
"CLAWS OF DEATH!"
OH, LOOK, HOWARD, A LITTLE KITTEN!
RUN, HOWARD, RUN
JIM DAVIS 5-31
Distributed by Universal Uclick www.facebook.com/garfield
© 2014 PAWS, INC. All Rights Reserved.

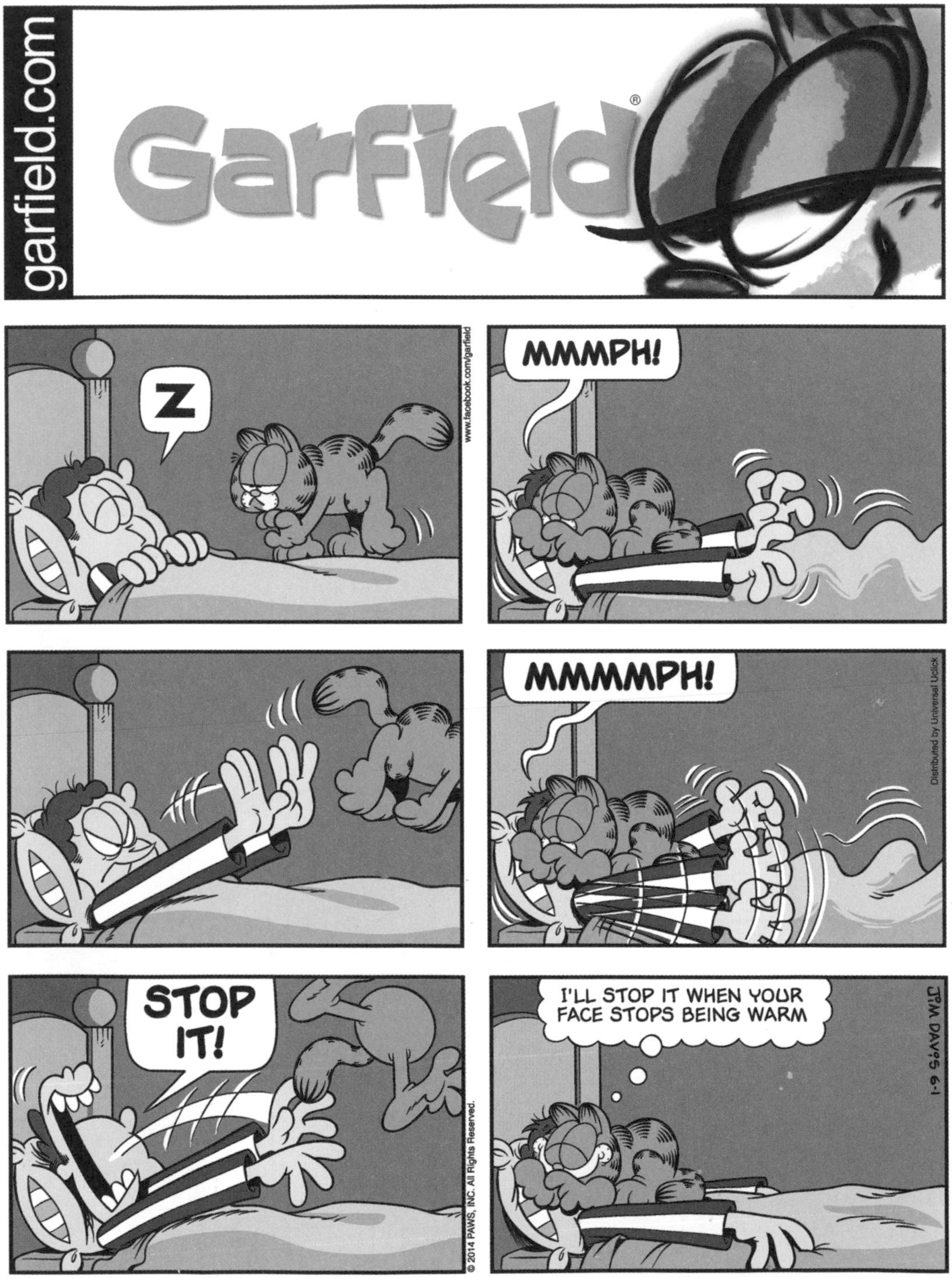
garfield.com
Garfield
Z
www.facebook.com/garfield
MMMPH!
MMMMPH!
Distributed by Universal Uclick
STOP IT!
© 2014 PAWS, INC. All Rights Reserved.
I'LL STOP IT WHEN YOUR FACE STOPS BEING WARM
JIM DAVIS 6-1

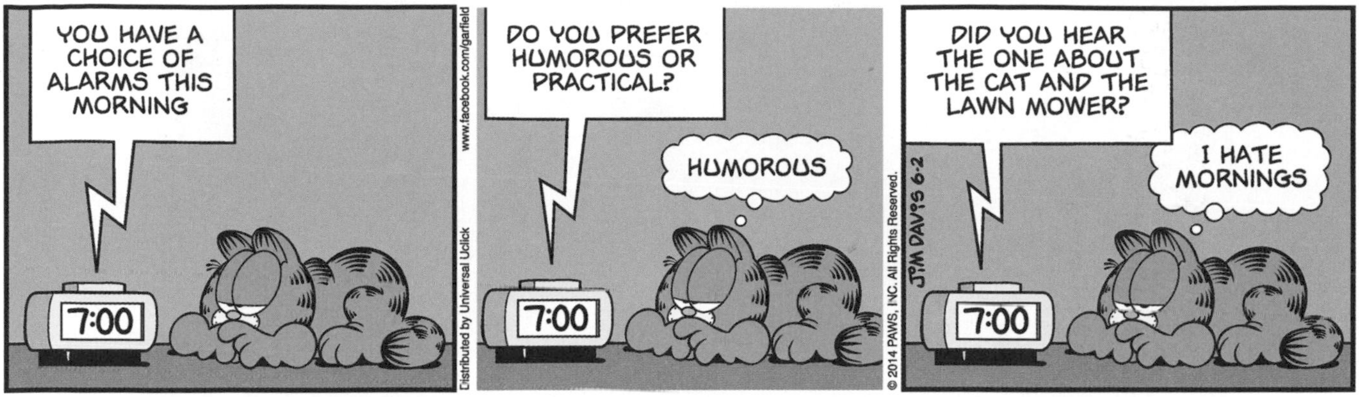
YOU HAVE A CHOICE OF ALARMS THIS MORNING
7:00
Distributed by Universal Uclick www.facebook.com/garfield
DO YOU PREFER HUMOROUS OR PRACTICAL?
HUMOROUS
7:00
© 2014 PAWS, INC. All Rights Reserved.
JIM DAVIS 6-2
DID YOU HEAR THE ONE ABOUT THE CAT AND THE LAWN MOWER?
I HATE MORNINGS
7:00

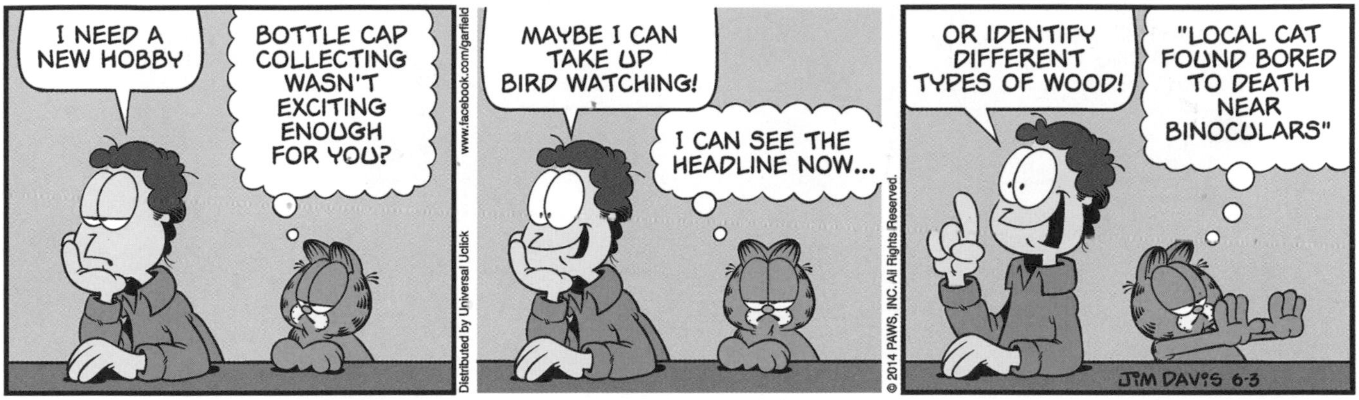
I NEED A NEW HOBBY
BOTTLE CAP COLLECTING WASN'T EXCITING ENOUGH FOR YOU?
Distributed by Universal Uclick www.facebook.com/garfield
MAYBE I CAN TAKE UP BIRD WATCHING!
I CAN SEE THE HEADLINE NOW...
© 2014 PAWS, INC. All Rights Reserved.
OR IDENTIFY DIFFERENT TYPES OF WOOD!
"LOCAL CAT FOUND BORED TO DEATH NEAR BINOCULARS"
JIM DAVIS 6-3

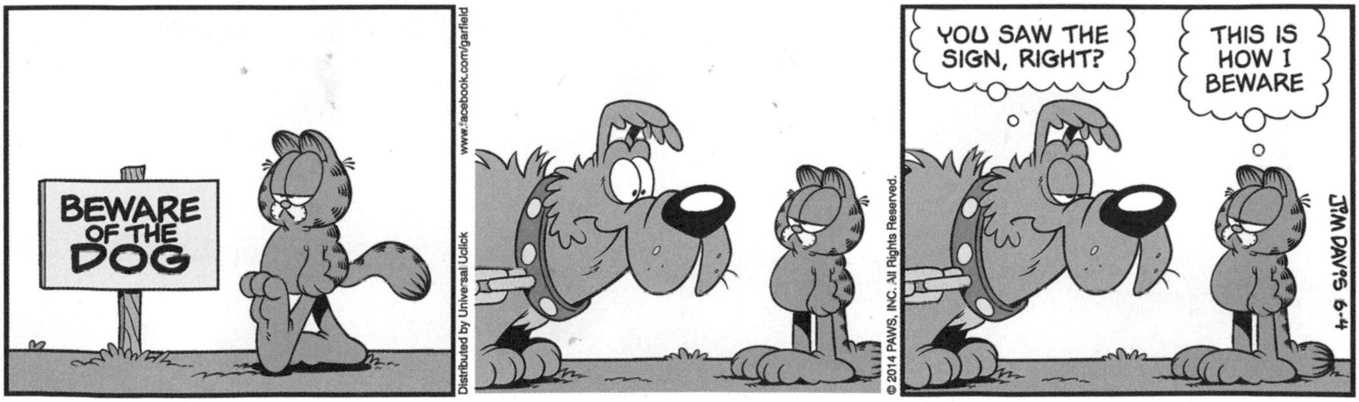
BEWARE OF THE DOG
Distributed by Universal Uclick www.facebook.com/garfield
© 2014 PAWS, INC. All Rights Reserved.
YOU SAW THE SIGN, RIGHT?
THIS IS HOW I BEWARE
JIM DAVIS 6-4

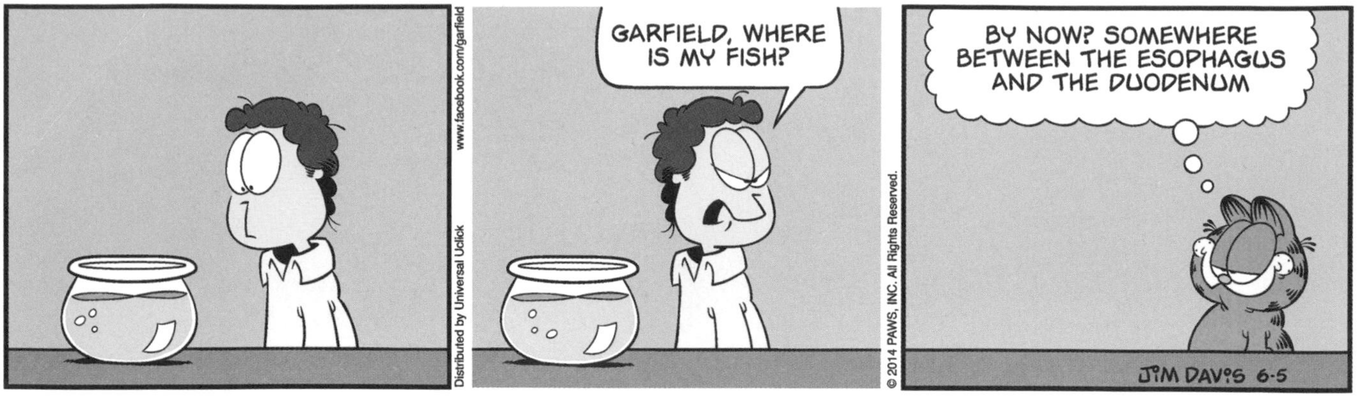
GARFIELD, WHERE IS MY FISH?
BY NOW? SOMEWHERE BETWEEN THE ESOPHAGUS AND THE DUODENUM
JIM DAVIS 6-5
Distributed by Universal Uclick www.facebook.com/garfield
© 2014 PAWS, INC. All Rights Reserved.

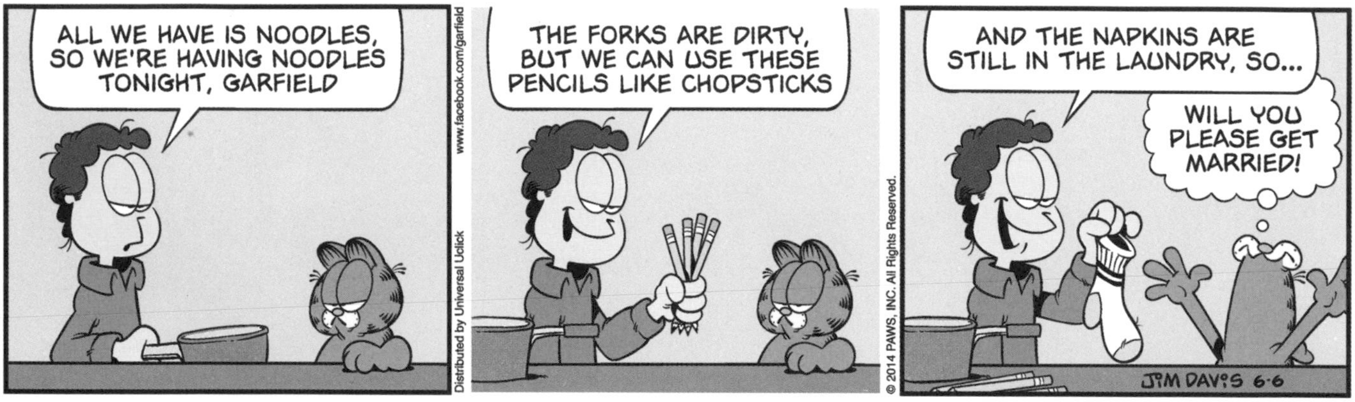
ALL WE HAVE IS NOODLES, SO WE'RE HAVING NOODLES TONIGHT, GARFIELD
THE FORKS ARE DIRTY, BUT WE CAN USE THESE PENCILS LIKE CHOPSTICKS
AND THE NAPKINS ARE STILL IN THE LAUNDRY, SO...
WILL YOU PLEASE GET MARRIED!
JIM DAVIS 6-6
Distributed by Universal Uclick www.facebook.com/garfield
© 2014 PAWS, INC. All Rights Reserved.

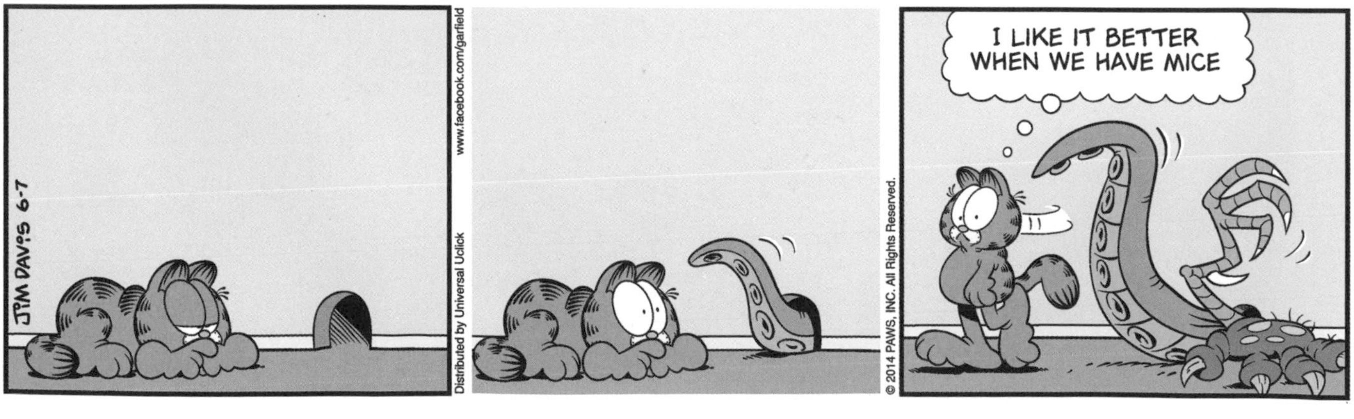
JIM DAVIS 6-7
I LIKE IT BETTER WHEN WE HAVE MICE
Distributed by Universal Uclick www.facebook.com/garfield
© 2014 PAWS, INC. All Rights Reserved.

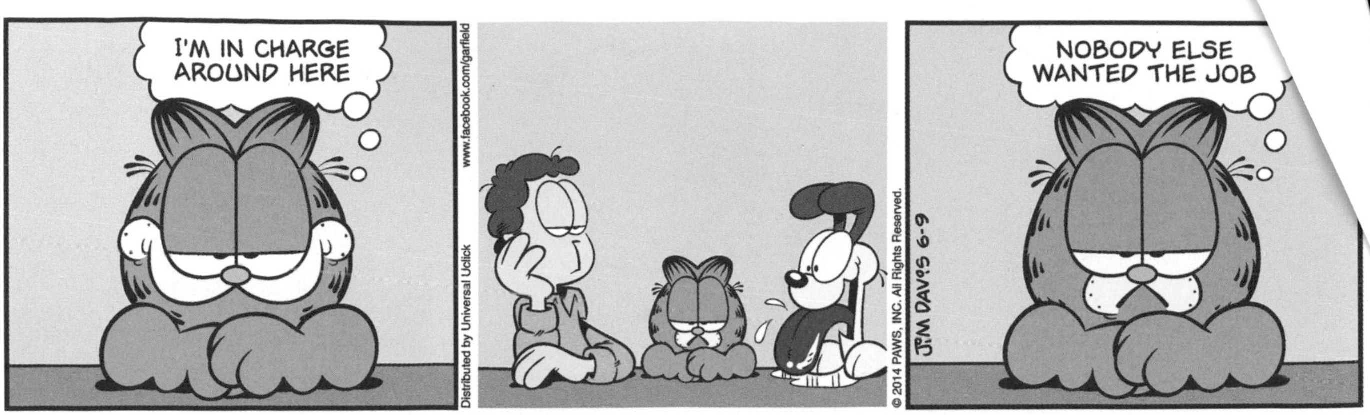
I'M IN CHARGE AROUND HERE
Distributed by Universal Uclick www.facebook.com/garfield
© 2014 PAWS, INC. All Rights Reserved.
JIM DAVIS 6-9
NOBODY ELSE WANTED THE JOB

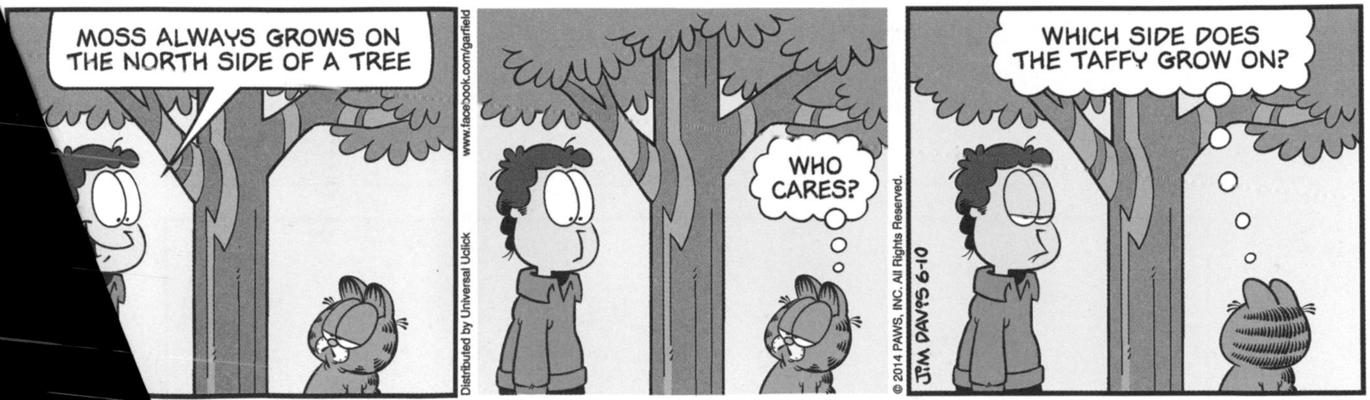
MOSS ALWAYS GROWS ON THE NORTH SIDE OF A TREE
Distributed by Universal Uclick www.facebook.com/garfield
WHO CARES?
© 2014 PAWS, INC. All Rights Reserved.
JIM DAVIS 6-10
WHICH SIDE DOES THE TAFFY GROW ON?

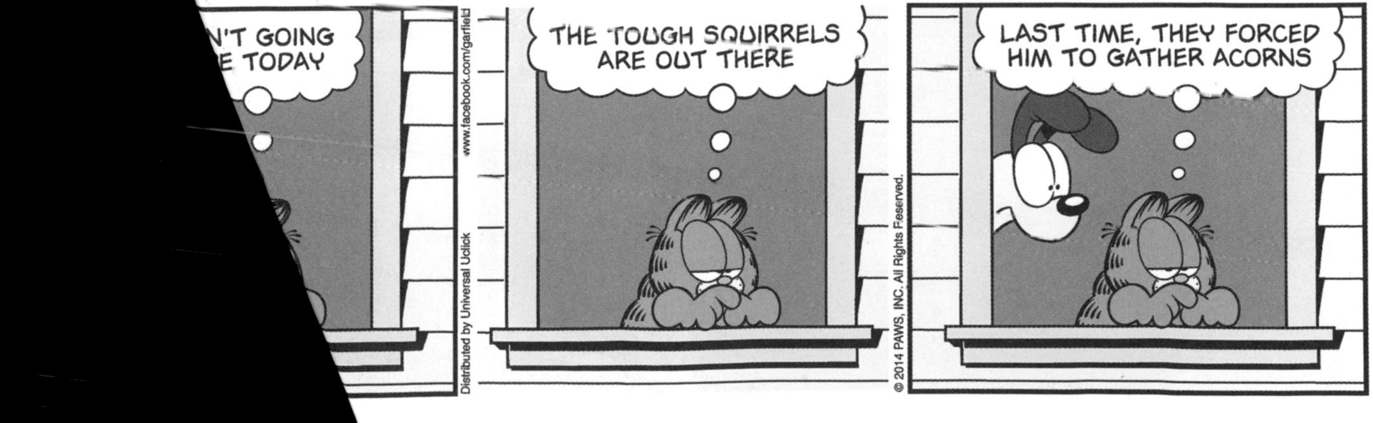
GOING
TODAY
Distributed by Universal Uclick www.facebook.com/garfield
THE TOUGH SQUIRRELS ARE OUT THERE
© 2014 PAWS, INC. All Rights Reserved.
LAST TIME, THEY FORCED HIM TO GATHER ACORNS

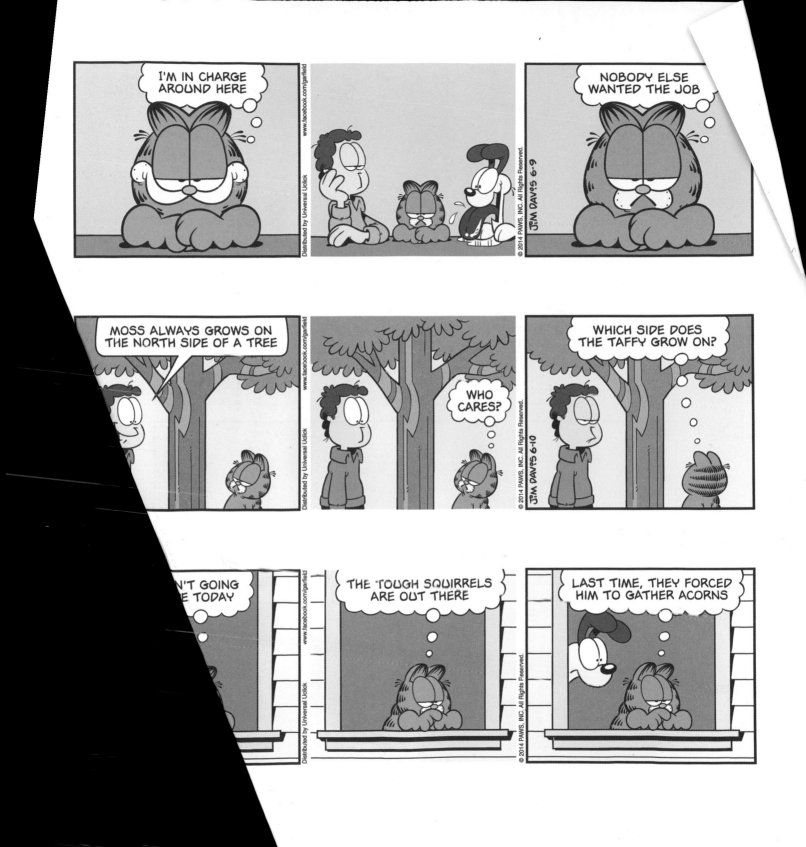

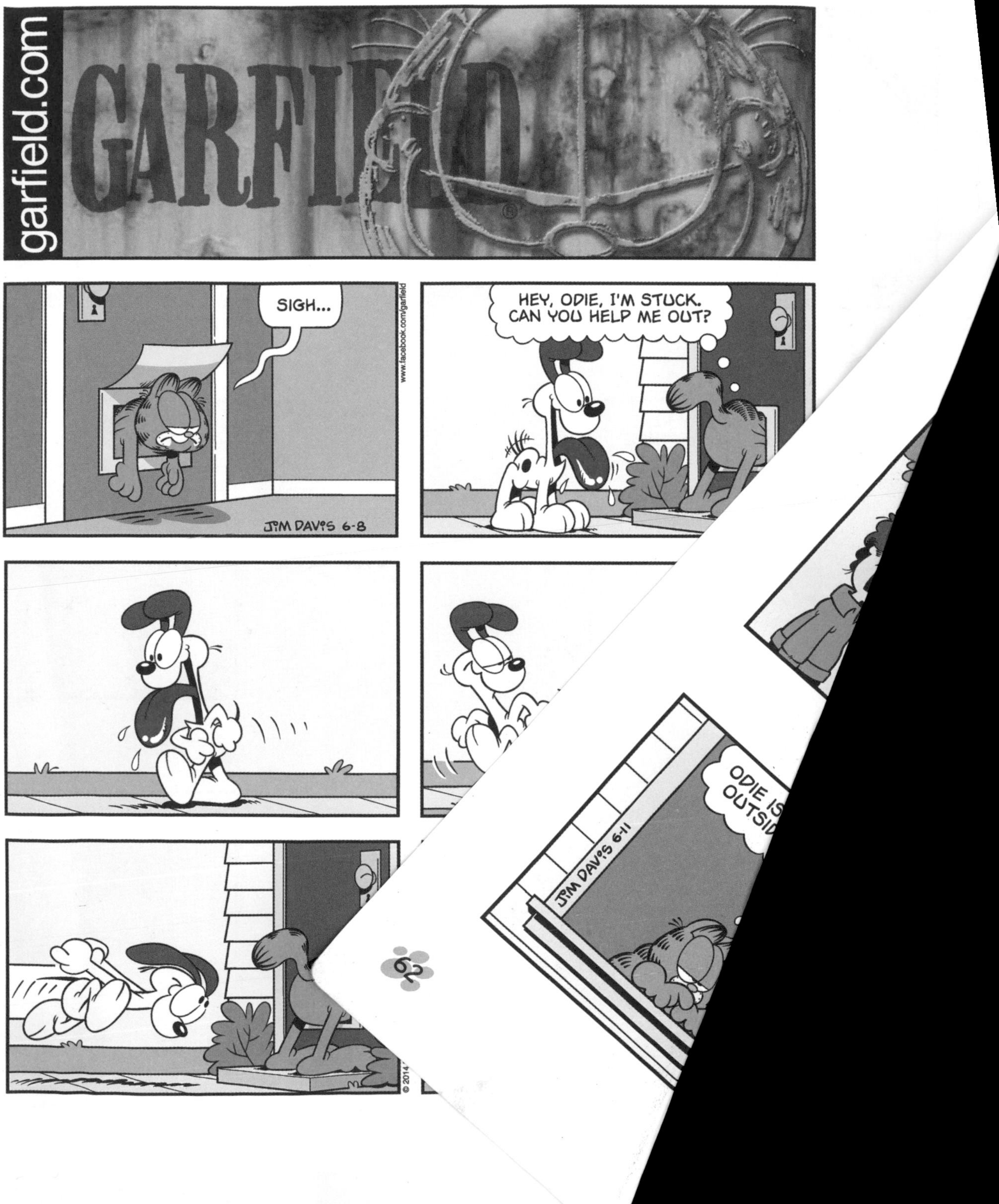
garfield.com
GARFIELD
SIGH...
JIM DAVIS 6-8
www.facebook.com/garfield
HEY, ODIE, I'M STUCK. CAN YOU HELP ME OUT?
JIM DAVIS 6-11

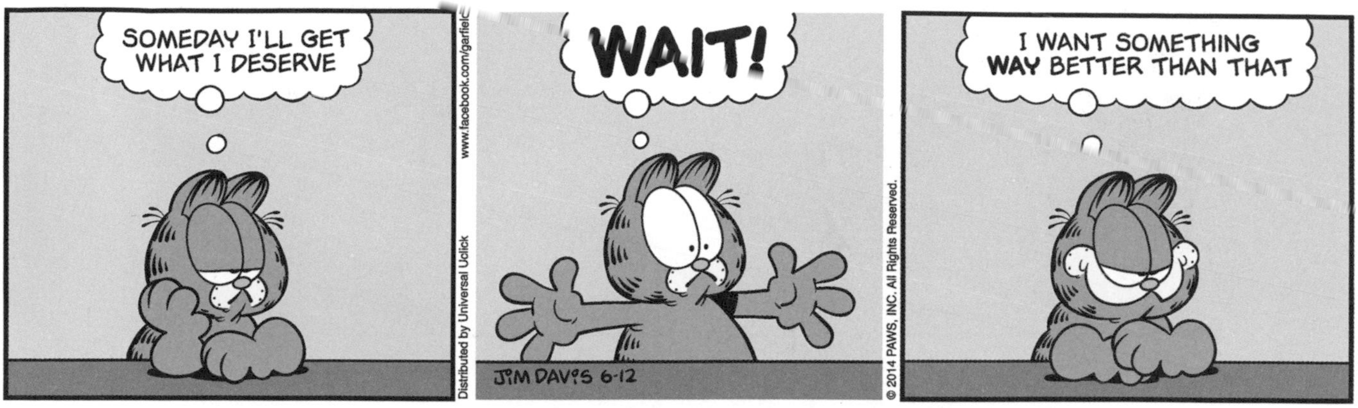
SOMEDAY I'LL GET WHAT I DESERVE
WAIT!
I WANT SOMETHING WAY BETTER THAN THAT
JIM DAVIS 6-12
Distributed by Universal Uclick
www.facebook.com/garfield
© 2014 PAWS, INC. All Rights Reserved.

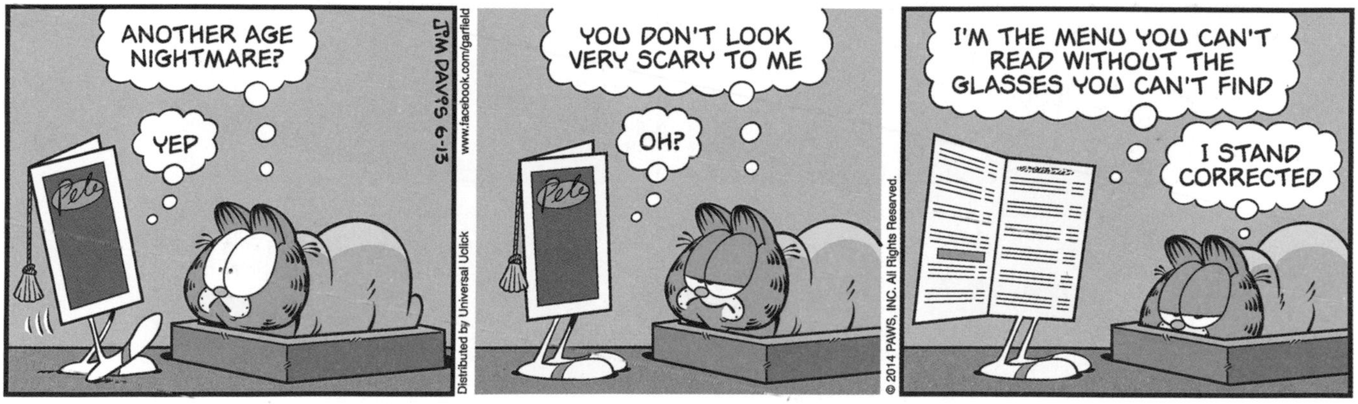
ANOTHER AGE NIGHTMARE?
YEP
YOU DON'T LOOK VERY SCARY TO ME
OH?
I'M THE MENU YOU CAN'T READ WITHOUT THE GLASSES YOU CAN'T FIND
I STAND CORRECTED
JIM DAVIS 6-13
Distributed by Universal Uclick
www.facebook.com/garfield
© 2014 PAWS, INC. All Rights Reserved.

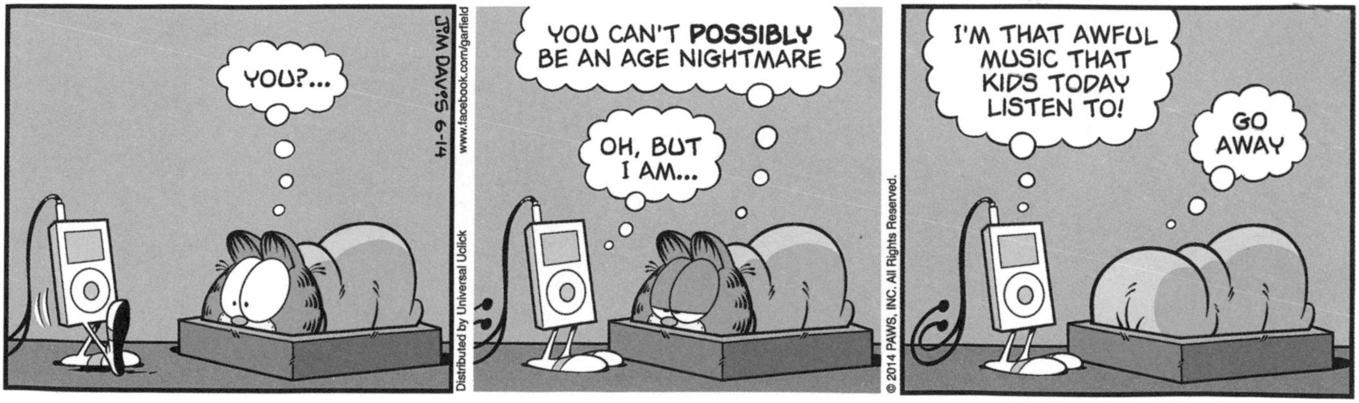
YOU?...
YOU CAN'T POSSIBLY BE AN AGE NIGHTMARE
OH, BUT I AM...
I'M THAT AWFUL MUSIC THAT KIDS TODAY LISTEN TO!
GO AWAY
JIM DAVIS 6-14
Distributed by Universal Uclick
www.facebook.com/garfield
© 2014 PAWS, INC. All Rights Reserved.

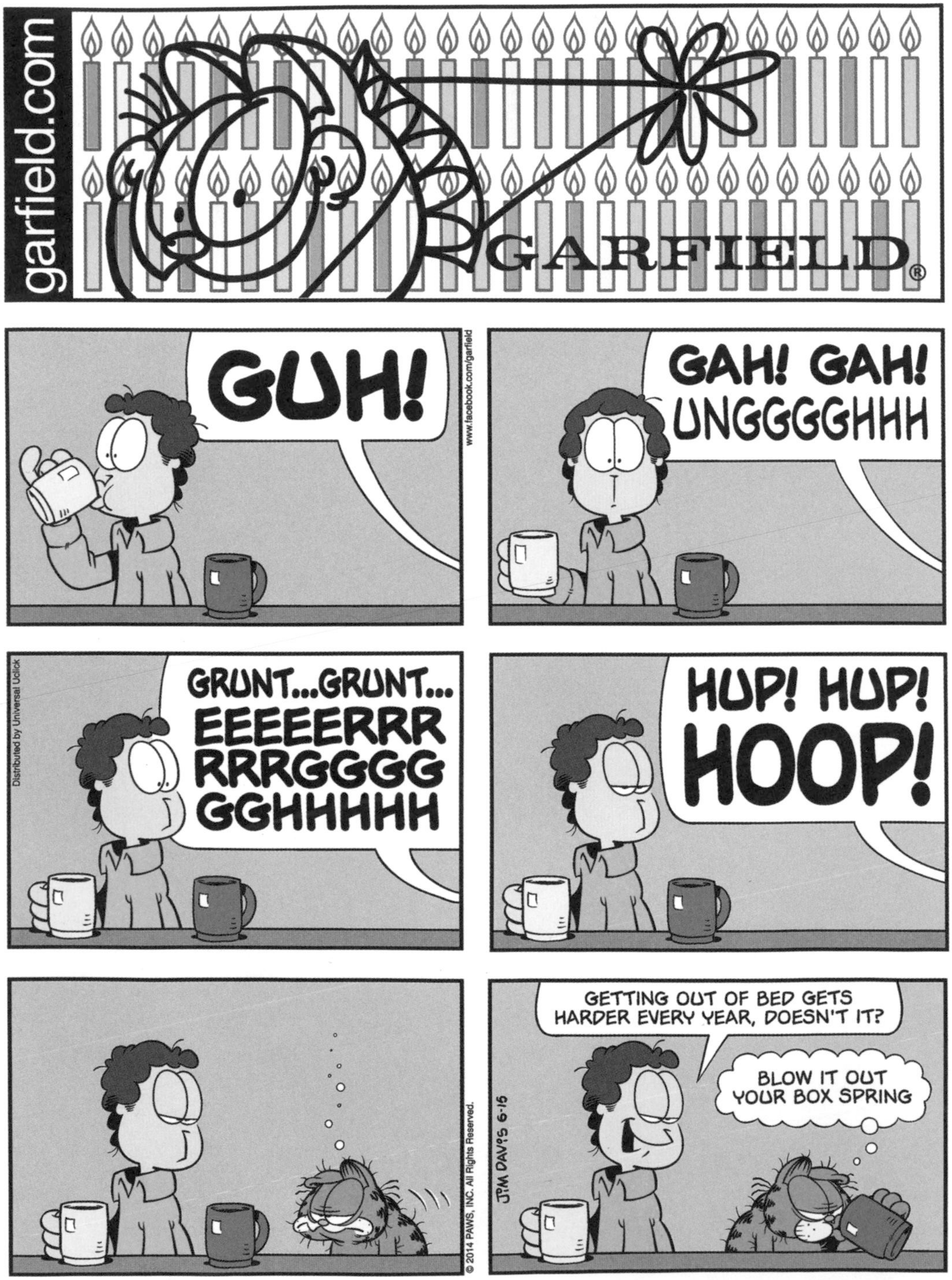
garfield.com
GARFIELD®
GUH!
www.facebook.com/garfield
GAH! GAH! UNGGGGHHH
Distributed by Universal Uclick
GRUNT...GRUNT... EEEEEERRR RRRGGGG GGHHHHH
HUP! HUP! HOOP!
© 2014 PAWS, INC. All Rights Reserved.
JIM DAVIS 6-15
GETTING OUT OF BED GETS HARDER EVERY YEAR, DOESN'T IT?
BLOW IT OUT YOUR BOX SPRING

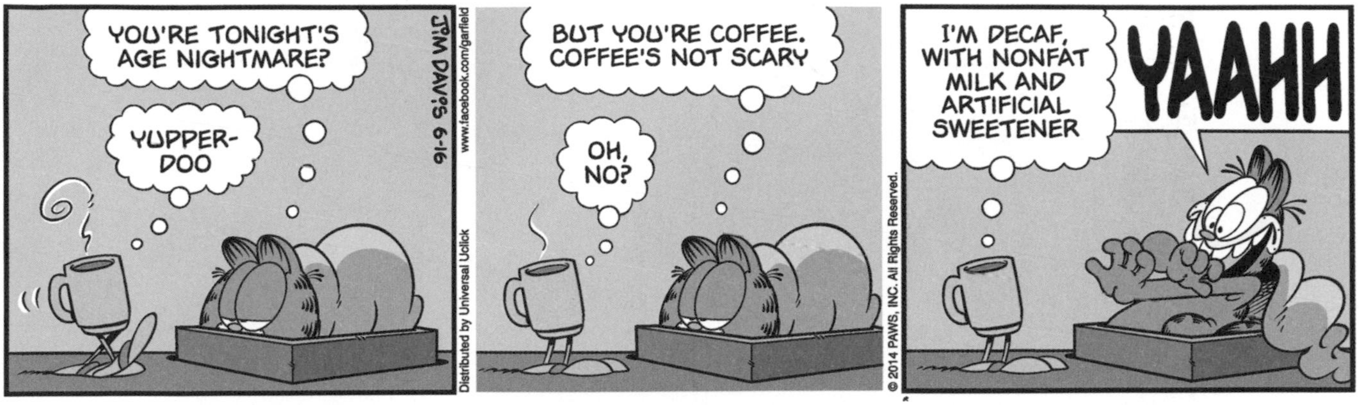
YOU'RE TONIGHT'S AGE NIGHTMARE?
YUPPER-DOO
JIM DAVIS 6-16
www.facebook.com/garfield
Distributed by Universal Uclick
BUT YOU'RE COFFEE. COFFEE'S NOT SCARY
OH, NO?
© 2014 PAWS, INC. All Rights Reserved.
I'M DECAF, WITH NONFAT MILK AND ARTIFICIAL SWEETENER
YAAHH

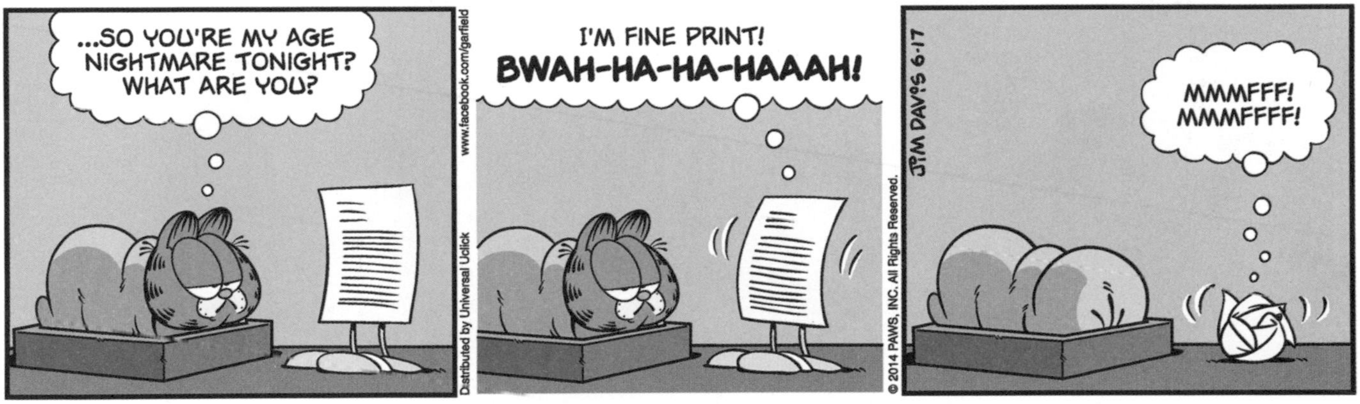
...SO YOU'RE MY AGE NIGHTMARE TONIGHT? WHAT ARE YOU?
www.facebook.com/garfield
Distributed by Universal Uclick
I'M FINE PRINT!
BWAH-HA-HA-HAAAH!
© 2014 PAWS, INC. All Rights Reserved.
JIM DAVIS 6-17
MMMFFF! MMMFFFF!

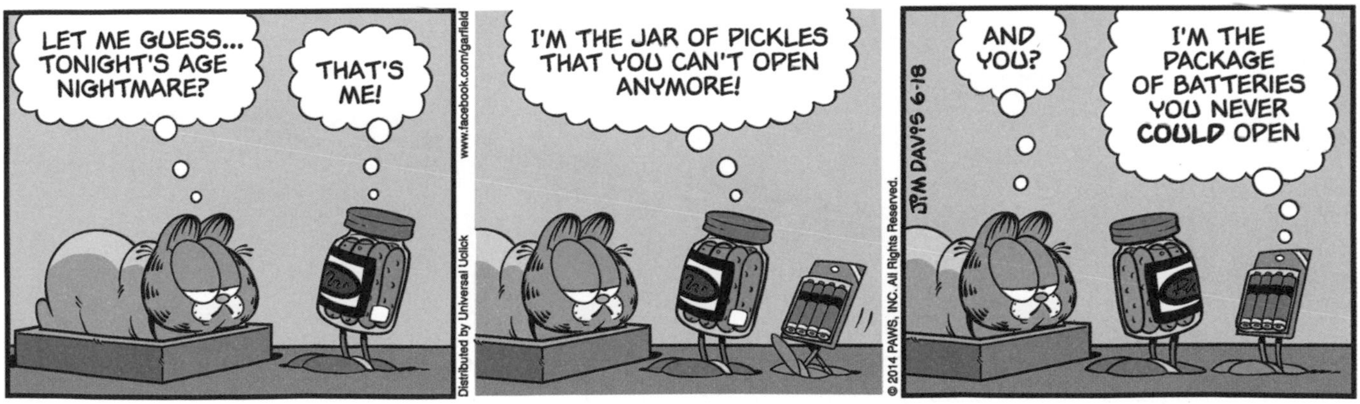
LET ME GUESS... TONIGHT'S AGE NIGHTMARE?
THAT'S ME!
www.facebook.com/garfield
Distributed by Universal Uclick
I'M THE JAR OF PICKLES THAT YOU CAN'T OPEN ANYMORE!
© 2014 PAWS, INC. All Rights Reserved.
JIM DAVIS 6-18
AND YOU?
I'M THE PACKAGE OF BATTERIES YOU NEVER **COULD** OPEN

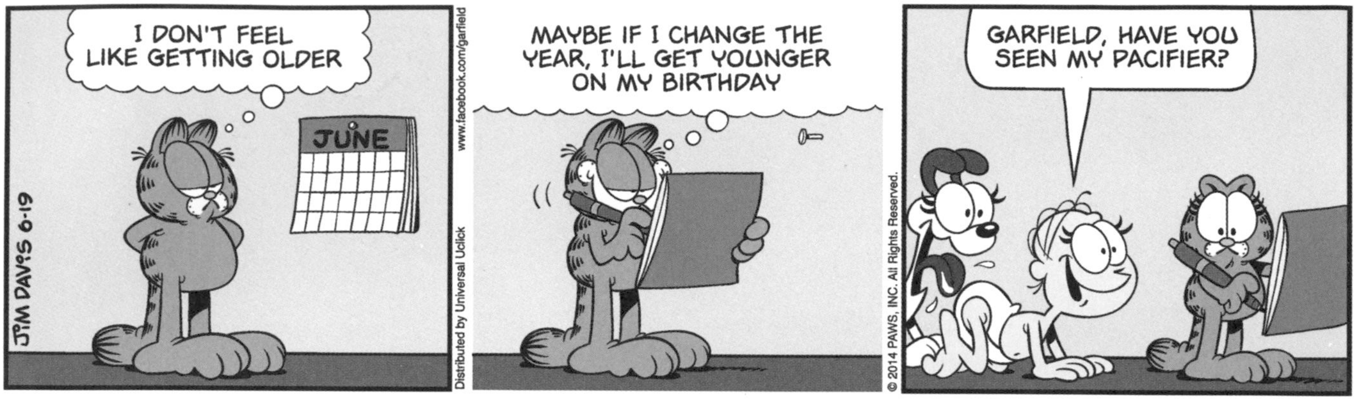
I DON'T FEEL LIKE GETTING OLDER
JUNE
JIM DAVIS 6-19
Distributed by Universal Uclick www.facebook.com/garfield
MAYBE IF I CHANGE THE YEAR, I'LL GET YOUNGER ON MY BIRTHDAY
© 2014 PAWS, INC. All Rights Reserved.
GARFIELD, HAVE YOU SEEN MY PACIFIER?

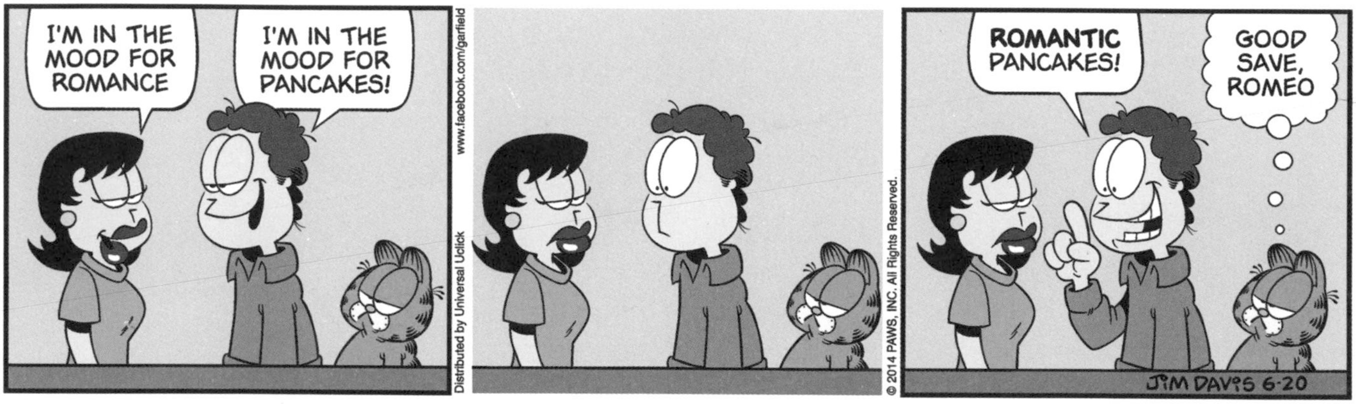
I'M IN THE MOOD FOR ROMANCE
I'M IN THE MOOD FOR PANCAKES!
Distributed by Universal Uclick www.facebook.com/garfield
© 2014 PAWS, INC. All Rights Reserved.
ROMANTIC PANCAKES!
GOOD SAVE, ROMEO
JIM DAVIS 6-20

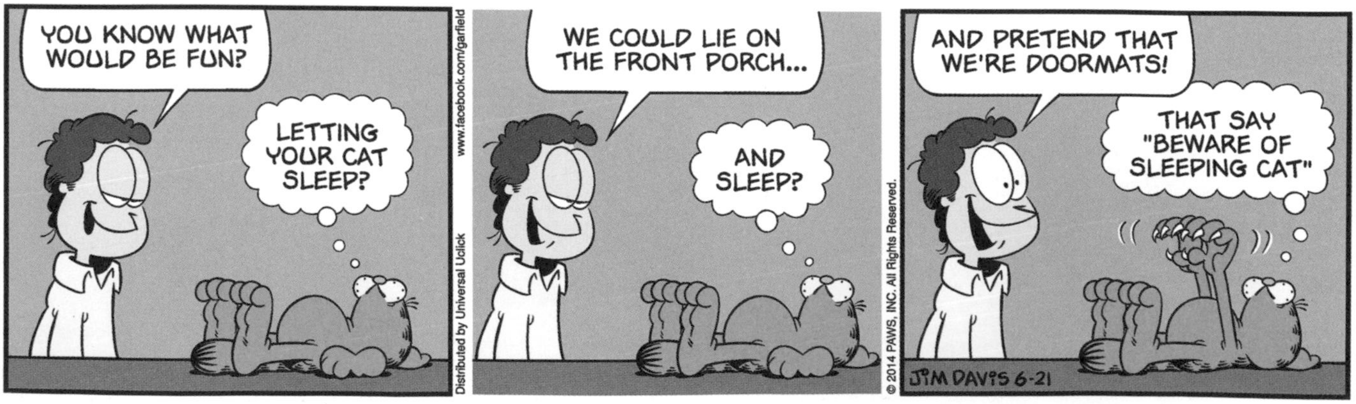
YOU KNOW WHAT WOULD BE FUN?
LETTING YOUR CAT SLEEP?
Distributed by Universal Uclick www.facebook.com/garfield
WE COULD LIE ON THE FRONT PORCH...
AND SLEEP?
© 2014 PAWS, INC. All Rights Reserved.
AND PRETEND THAT WE'RE DOORMATS!
THAT SAY "BEWARE OF SLEEPING CAT"
JIM DAVIS 6-21

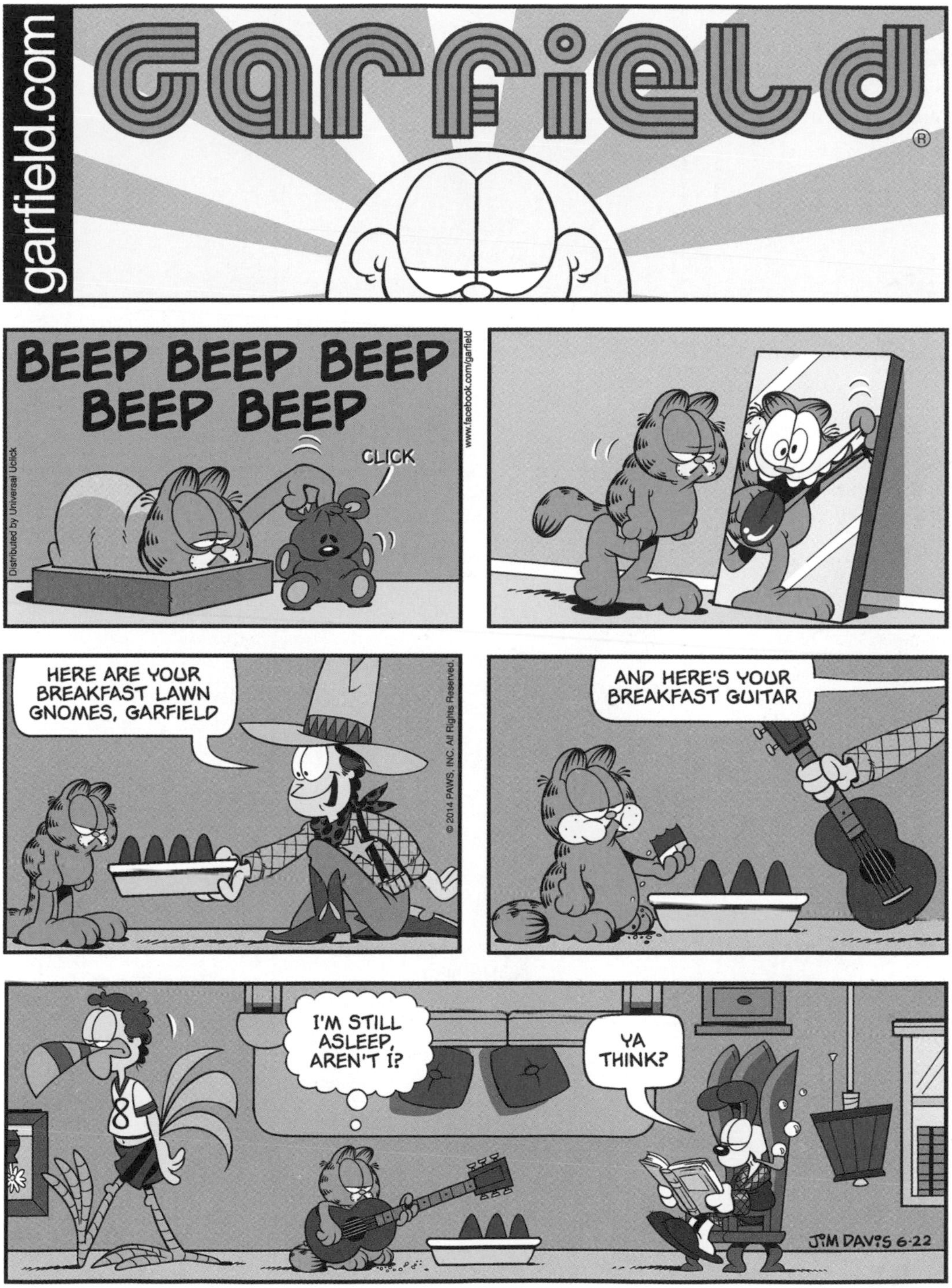
garfield.com
GARFIELD
Distributed by Universal Uclick
BEEP BEEP BEEP BEEP BEEP
CLICK
www.facebook.com/garfield
HERE ARE YOUR BREAKFAST LAWN GNOMES, GARFIELD
© 2014 PAWS, INC. All Rights Reserved.
AND HERE'S YOUR BREAKFAST GUITAR
I'M STILL ASLEEP, AREN'T I?
YA THINK?
JIM DAVIS 6-22

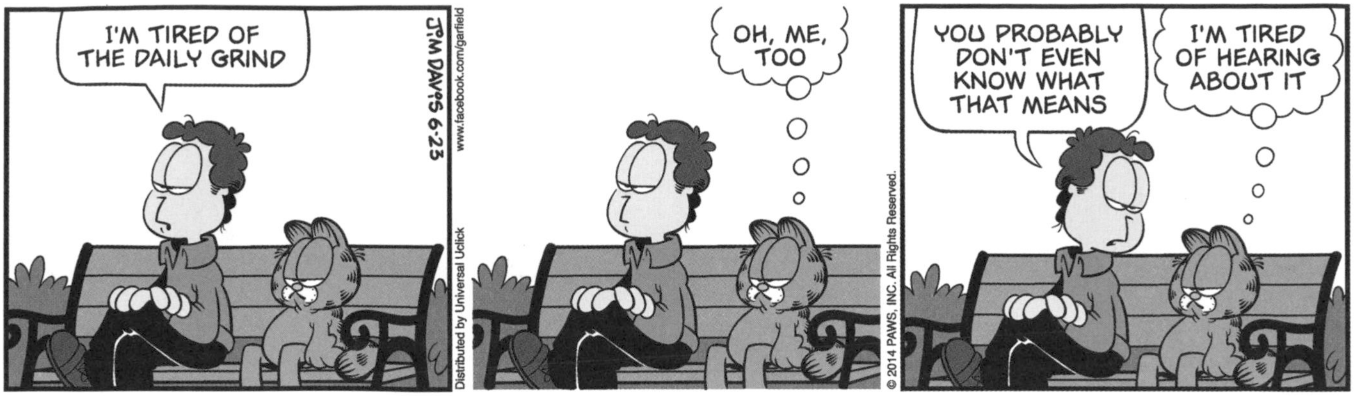
I'M TIRED OF THE DAILY GRIND
JIM DAVIS 6-23
www.facebook.com/garfield
Distributed by Universal Uclick
OH, ME, TOO
© 2014 PAWS, INC. All Rights Reserved.
YOU PROBABLY DON'T EVEN KNOW WHAT THAT MEANS
I'M TIRED OF HEARING ABOUT IT

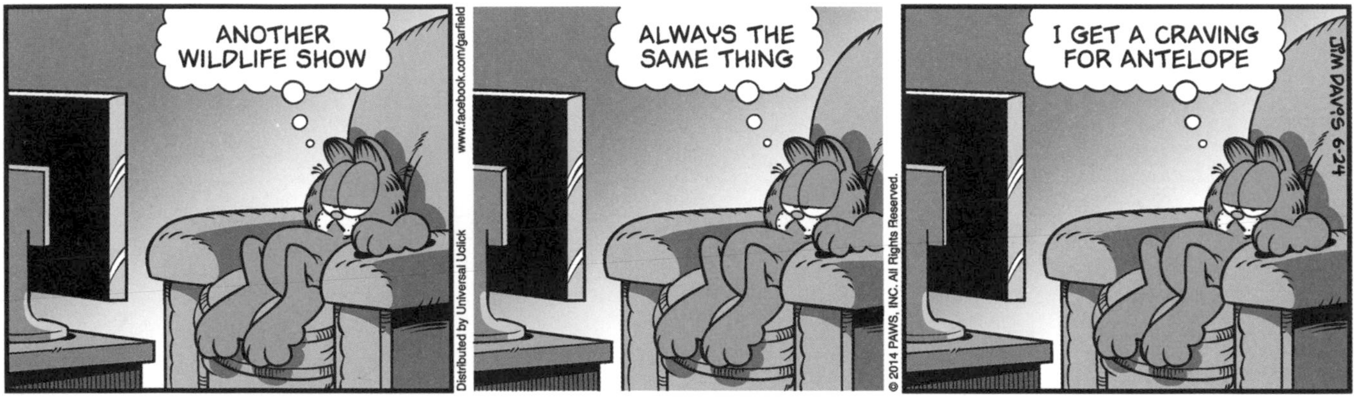
ANOTHER WILDLIFE SHOW
www.facebook.com/garfield
Distributed by Universal Uclick
ALWAYS THE SAME THING
© 2014 PAWS, INC. All Rights Reserved.
I GET A CRAVING FOR ANTELOPE
JIM DAVIS 6-24

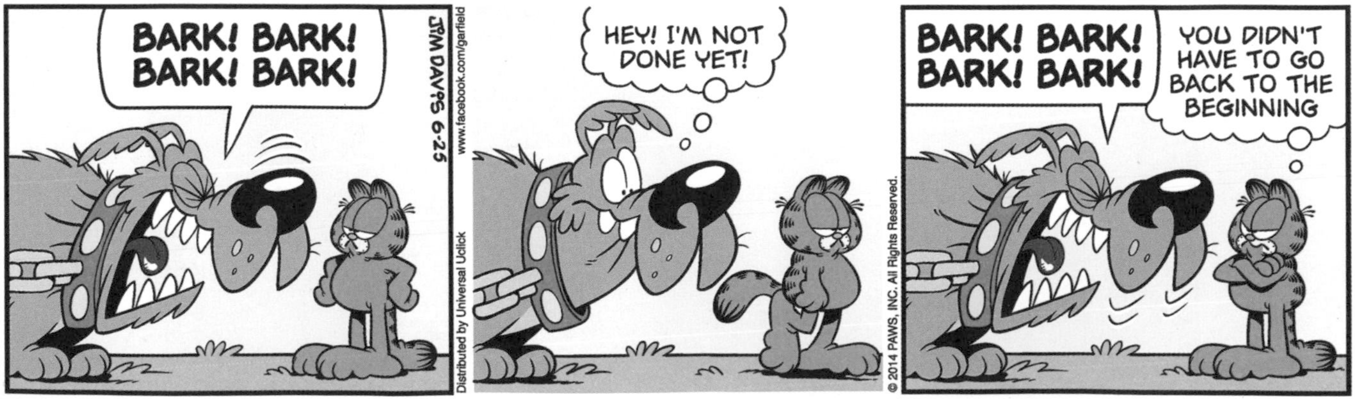
BARK! BARK! BARK! BARK!
JIM DAVIS 6-25
www.facebook.com/garfield
Distributed by Universal Uclick
HEY! I'M NOT DONE YET!
© 2014 PAWS, INC. All Rights Reserved.
BARK! BARK! BARK! BARK!
YOU DIDN'T HAVE TO GO BACK TO THE BEGINNING

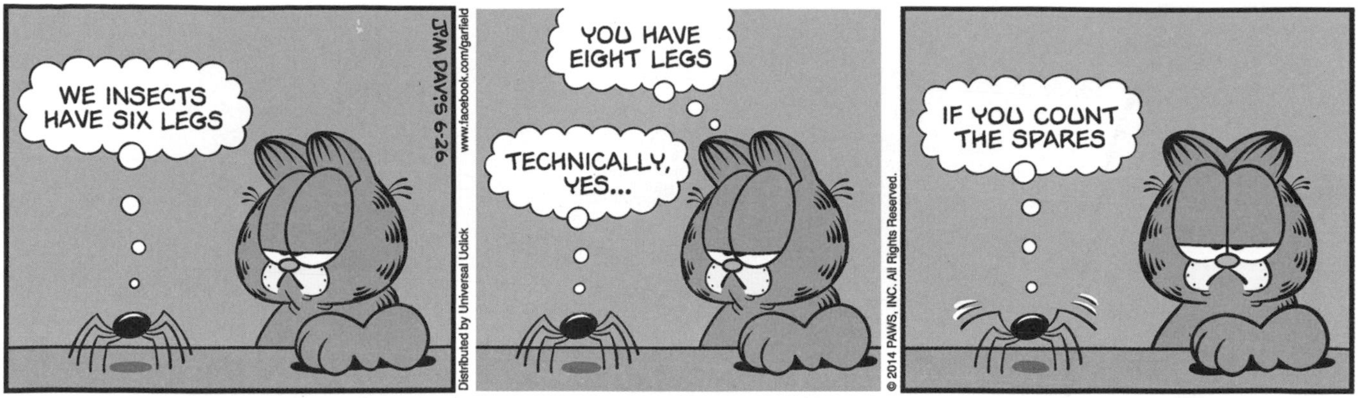
WE INSECTS HAVE SIX LEGS
JIM DAVIS 6-26
www.facebook.com/garfield
Distributed by Universal Uclick
YOU HAVE EIGHT LEGS
TECHNICALLY, YES...
© 2014 PAWS, INC. All Rights Reserved.
IF YOU COUNT THE SPARES

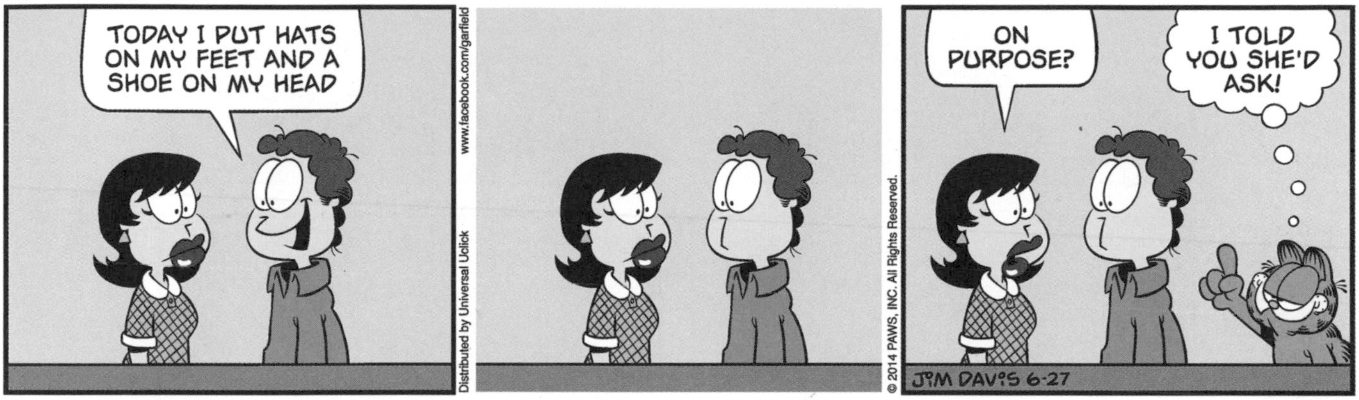
TODAY I PUT HATS ON MY FEET AND A SHOE ON MY HEAD
www.facebook.com/garfield
Distributed by Universal Uclick
© 2014 PAWS, INC. All Rights Reserved.
ON PURPOSE?
I TOLD YOU SHE'D ASK!
JIM DAVIS 6-27

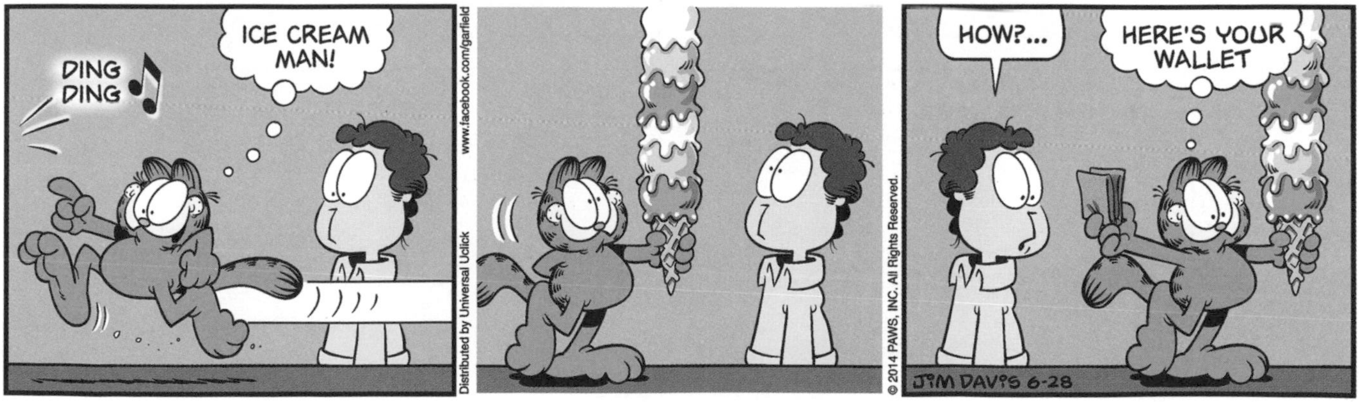
DING DING
ICE CREAM MAN!
www.facebook.com/garfield
Distributed by Universal Uclick
© 2014 PAWS, INC. All Rights Reserved.
HOW?...
HERE'S YOUR WALLET
JIM DAVIS 6-28

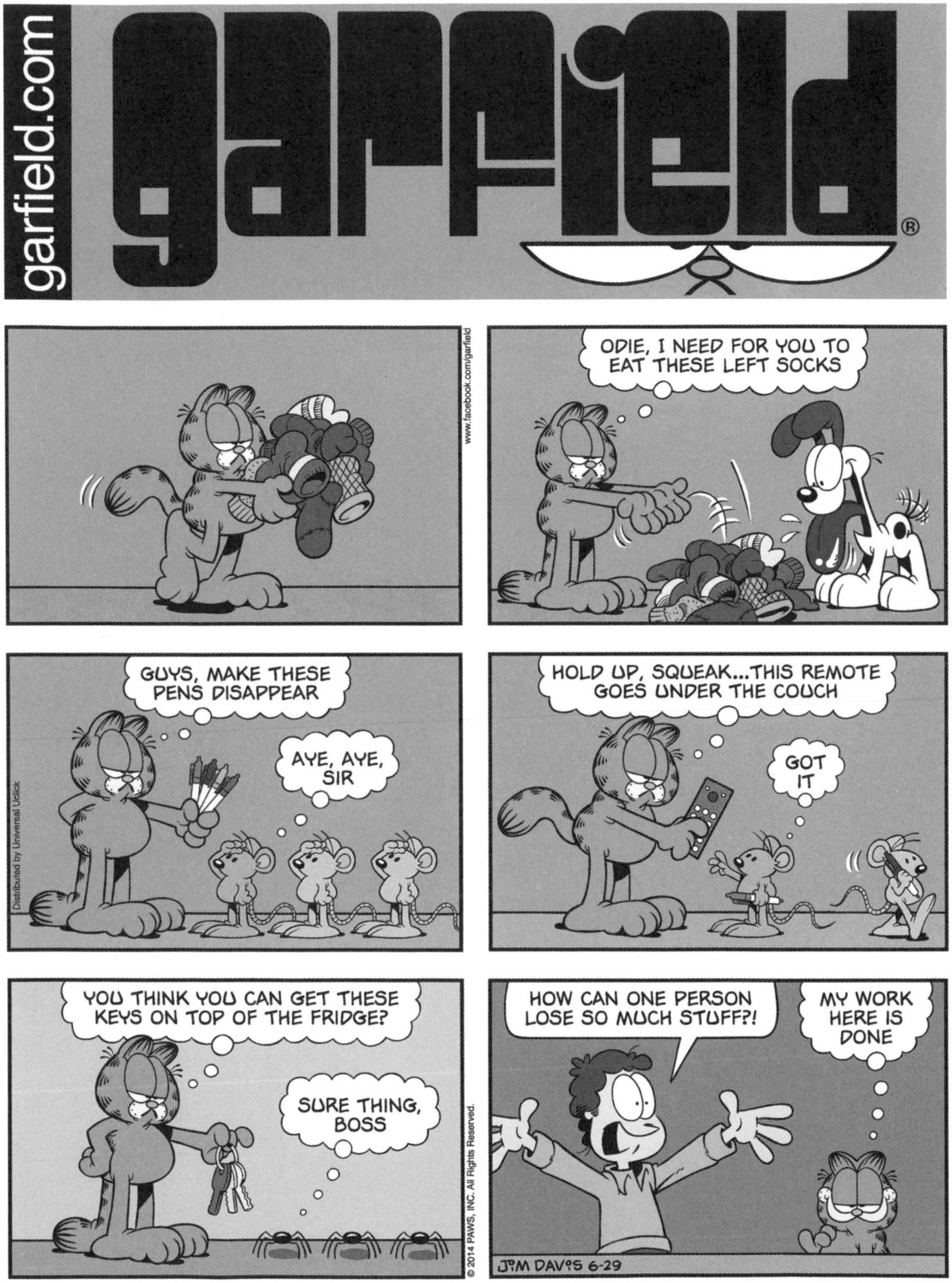
garfield.com
garfield
www.facebook.com/garfield
ODIE, I NEED FOR YOU TO EAT THESE LEFT SOCKS
GUYS, MAKE THESE PENS DISAPPEAR
AYE, AYE, SIR
Distributed by Universal Uclick
HOLD UP, SQUEAK...THIS REMOTE GOES UNDER THE COUCH
GOT IT
YOU THINK YOU CAN GET THESE KEYS ON TOP OF THE FRIDGE?
SURE THING, BOSS
© 2014 PAWS, INC. All Rights Reserved.
HOW CAN ONE PERSON LOSE SO MUCH STUFF?!
MY WORK HERE IS DONE
JIM DAVIS 6-29

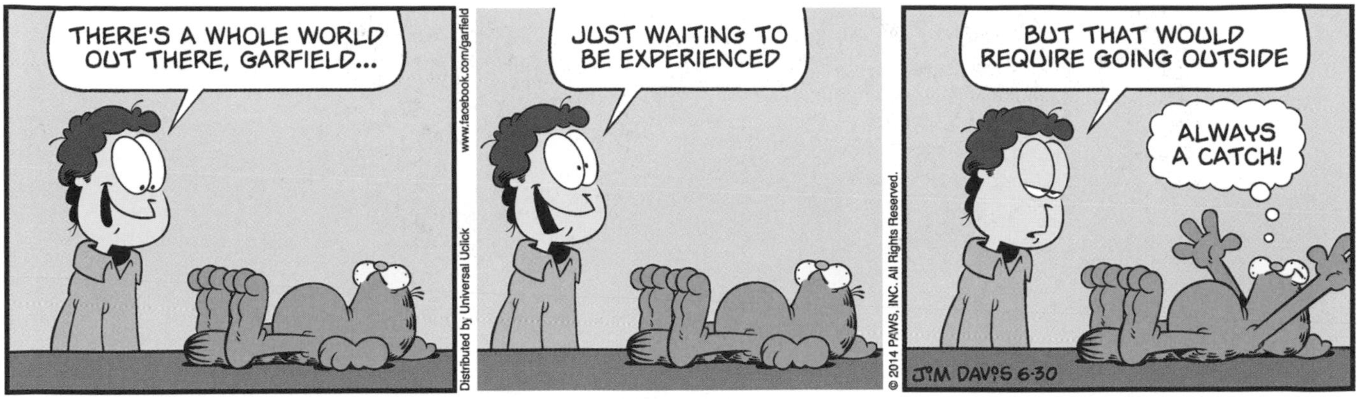
THERE'S A WHOLE WORLD OUT THERE, GARFIELD...
www.facebook.com/garfield
Distributed by Universal Uclick
JUST WAITING TO BE EXPERIENCED
© 2014 PAWS, INC. All Rights Reserved.
BUT THAT WOULD REQUIRE GOING OUTSIDE
ALWAYS A CATCH!
JIM DAVIS 6-30

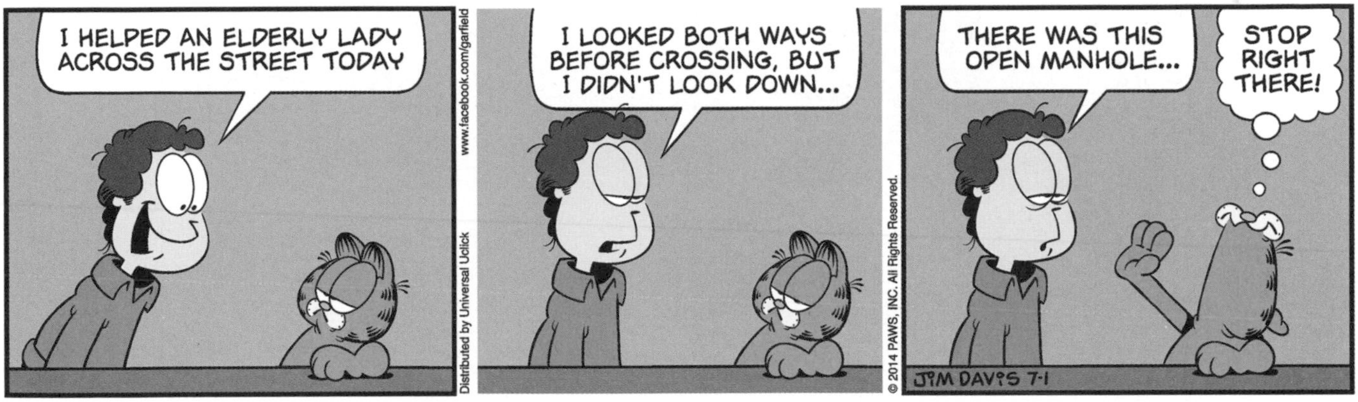
I HELPED AN ELDERLY LADY ACROSS THE STREET TODAY
www.facebook.com/garfield
Distributed by Universal Uclick
I LOOKED BOTH WAYS BEFORE CROSSING, BUT I DIDN'T LOOK DOWN...
© 2014 PAWS, INC. All Rights Reserved.
THERE WAS THIS OPEN MANHOLE...
STOP RIGHT THERE!
JIM DAVIS 7-1

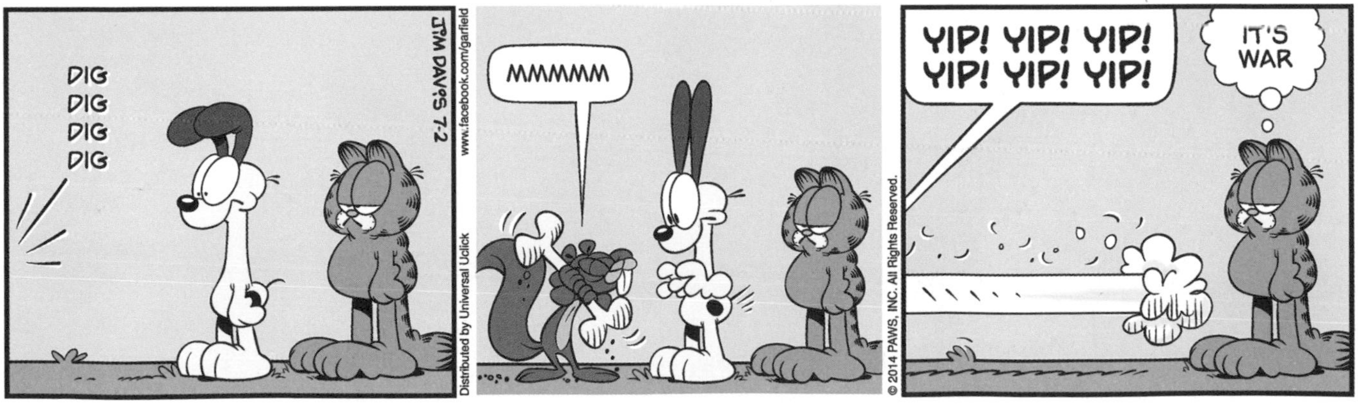
DIG
DIG
DIG
DIG
JIM DAVIS 7-2
www.facebook.com/garfield
Distributed by Universal Uclick
MMMMM
© 2014 PAWS, INC. All Rights Reserved.
YIP! YIP! YIP! YIP! YIP! YIP!
IT'S WAR

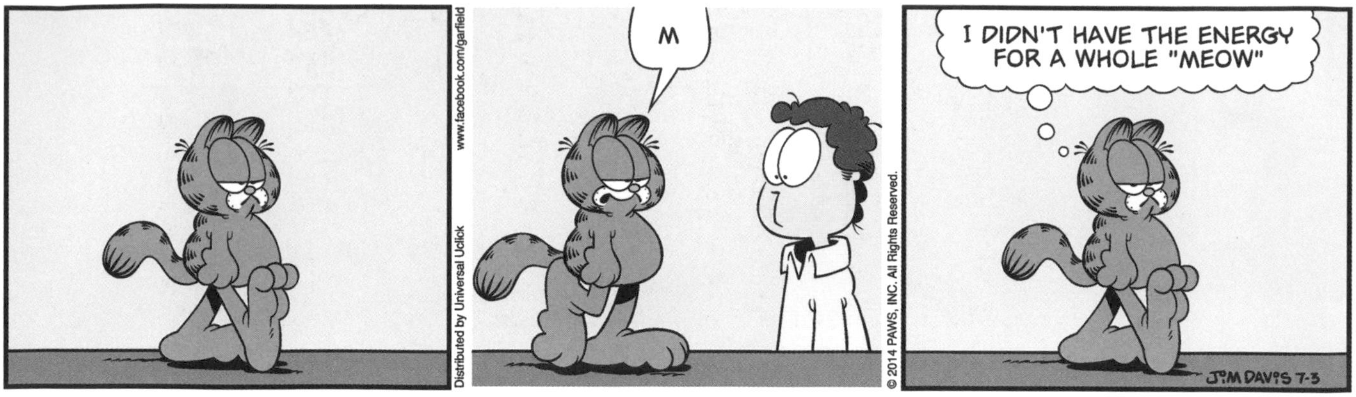
M
I DIDN'T HAVE THE ENERGY FOR A WHOLE "MEOW"
www.facebook.com/garfield
Distributed by Universal Uclick
© 2014 PAWS, INC. All Rights Reserved.
JIM DAVIS 7-3

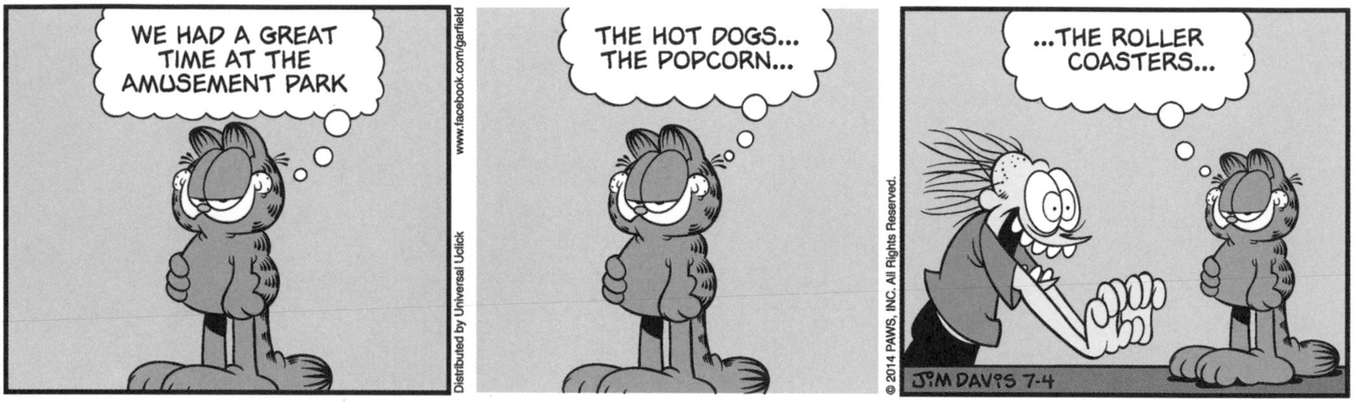
WE HAD A GREAT TIME AT THE AMUSEMENT PARK
THE HOT DOGS... THE POPCORN...
...THE ROLLER COASTERS...
www.facebook.com/garfield
Distributed by Universal Uclick
© 2014 PAWS, INC. All Rights Reserved.
JIM DAVIS 7-4

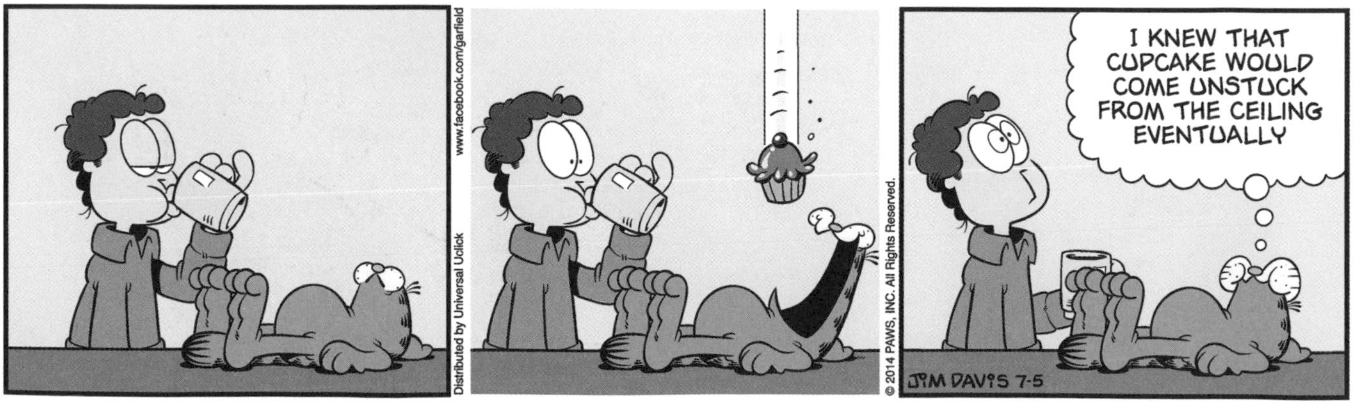
I KNEW THAT CUPCAKE WOULD COME UNSTUCK FROM THE CEILING EVENTUALLY
www.facebook.com/garfield
Distributed by Universal Uclick
© 2014 PAWS, INC. All Rights Reserved.
JIM DAVIS 7-5

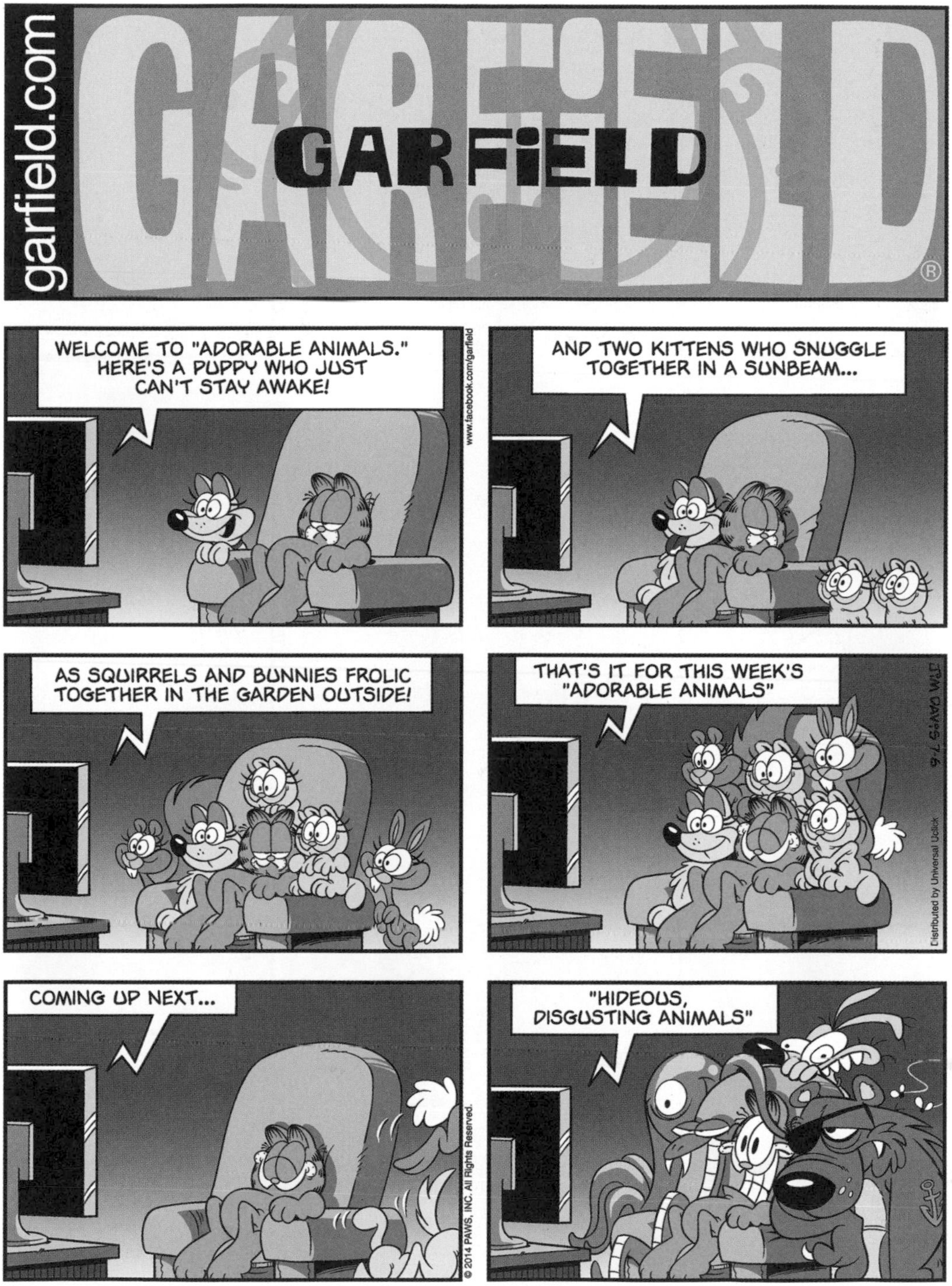
garfield.com
GARFIELD
GARFIELD
WELCOME TO "ADORABLE ANIMALS." HERE'S A PUPPY WHO JUST CAN'T STAY AWAKE!
www.facebook.com/garfield
AND TWO KITTENS WHO SNUGGLE TOGETHER IN A SUNBEAM...
AS SQUIRRELS AND BUNNIES FROLIC TOGETHER IN THE GARDEN OUTSIDE!
THAT'S IT FOR THIS WEEK'S "ADORABLE ANIMALS"
JIM DAVIS 7-6
Distributed by Universal Uclick
COMING UP NEXT...
© 2014 PAWS, INC. All Rights Reserved.
"HIDEOUS, DISGUSTING ANIMALS"

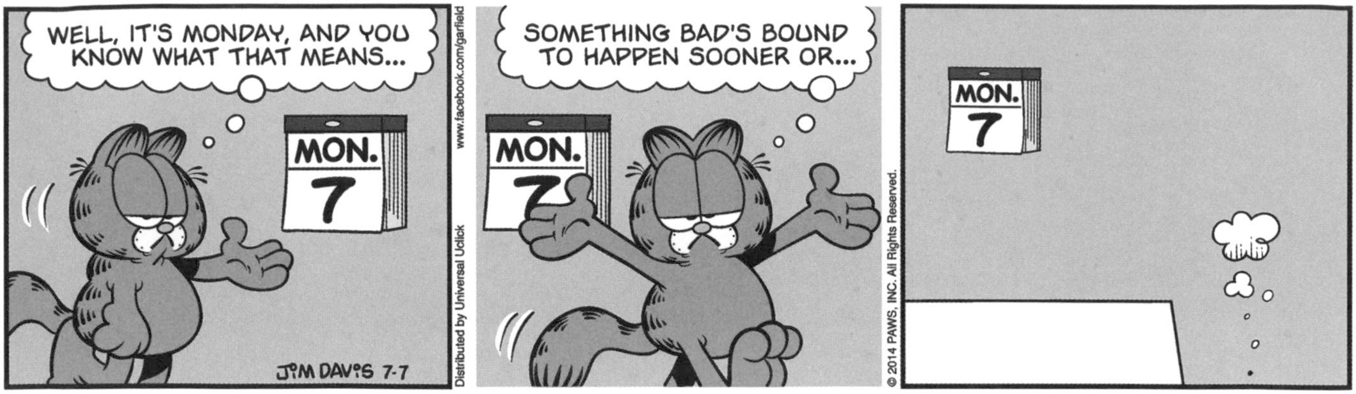
WELL, IT'S MONDAY, AND YOU KNOW WHAT THAT MEANS...
MON. 7
JIM DAVIS 7-7
www.facebook.com/garfield
Distributed by Universal Uclick
SOMETHING BAD'S BOUND TO HAPPEN SOONER OR...
MON. 7
© 2014 PAWS, INC. All Rights Reserved.
MON. 7

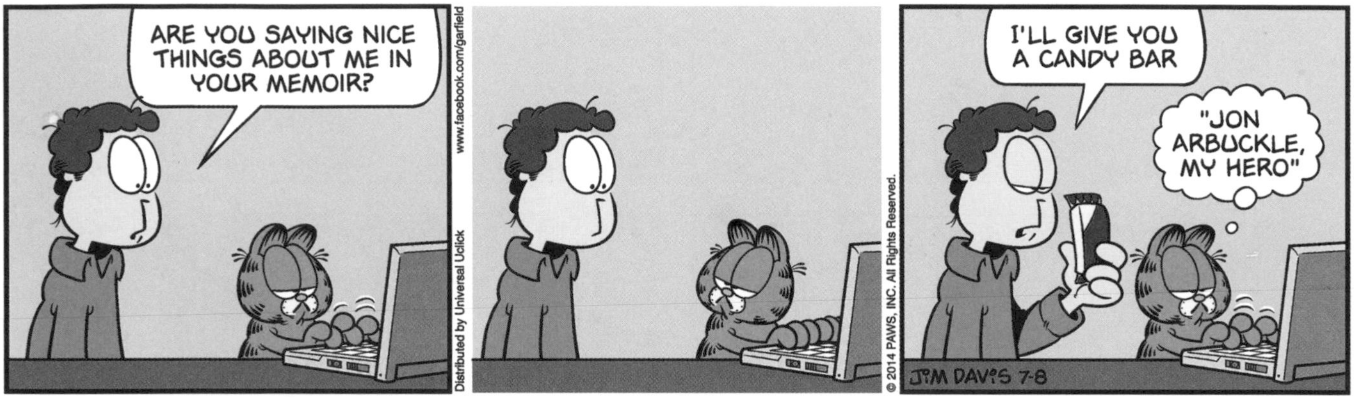
ARE YOU SAYING NICE THINGS ABOUT ME IN YOUR MEMOIR?
www.facebook.com/garfield
Distributed by Universal Uclick
© 2014 PAWS, INC. All Rights Reserved.
I'LL GIVE YOU A CANDY BAR
"JON ARBUCKLE, MY HERO"
JIM DAVIS 7-8

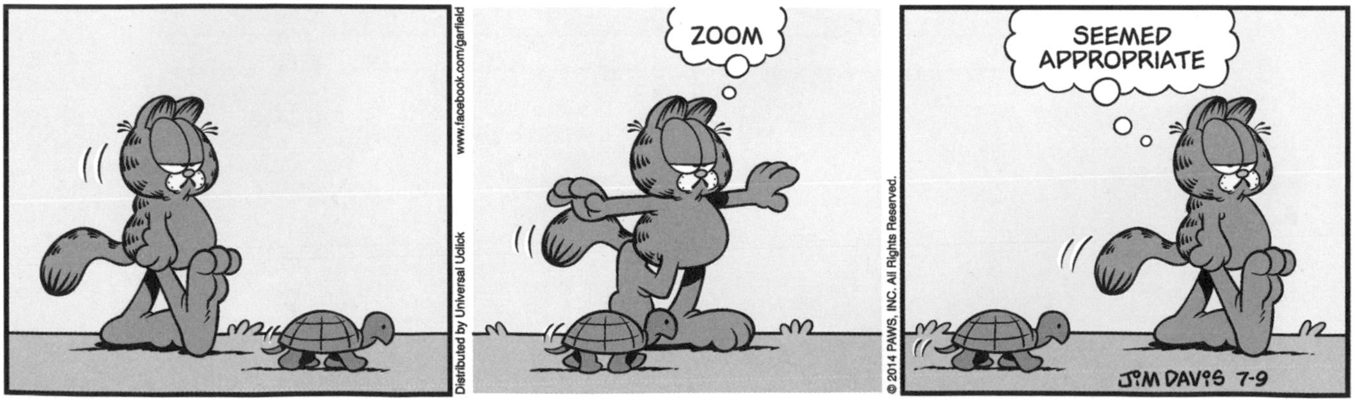
www.facebook.com/garfield
Distributed by Universal Uclick
ZOOM
© 2014 PAWS, INC. All Rights Reserved.
SEEMED APPROPRIATE
JIM DAVIS 7-9

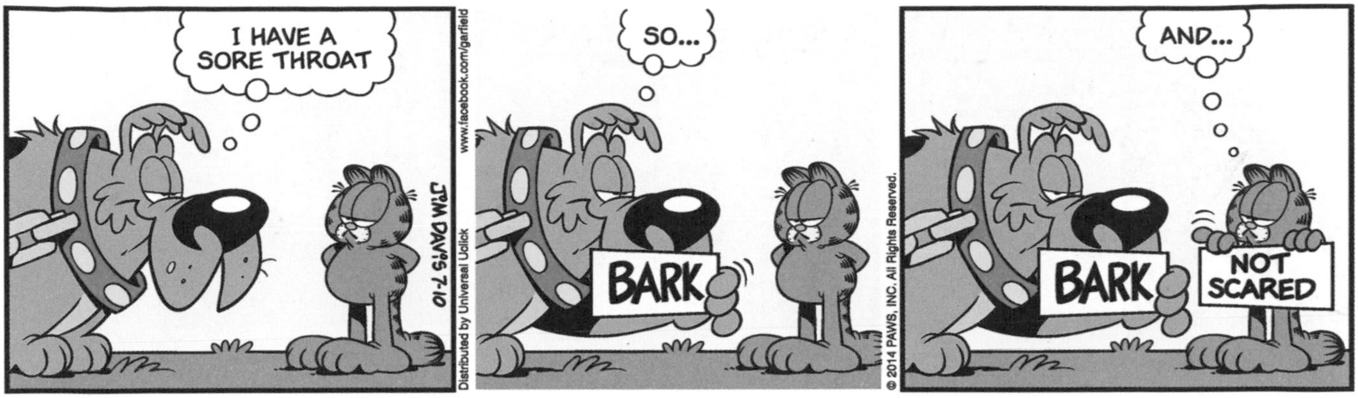
I HAVE A SORE THROAT
JIM DAVIS 7-10
Distributed by Universal Uclick www.facebook.com/garfield
SO...
BARK
© 2014 PAWS, INC. All Rights Reserved.
AND...
BARK
NOT SCARED

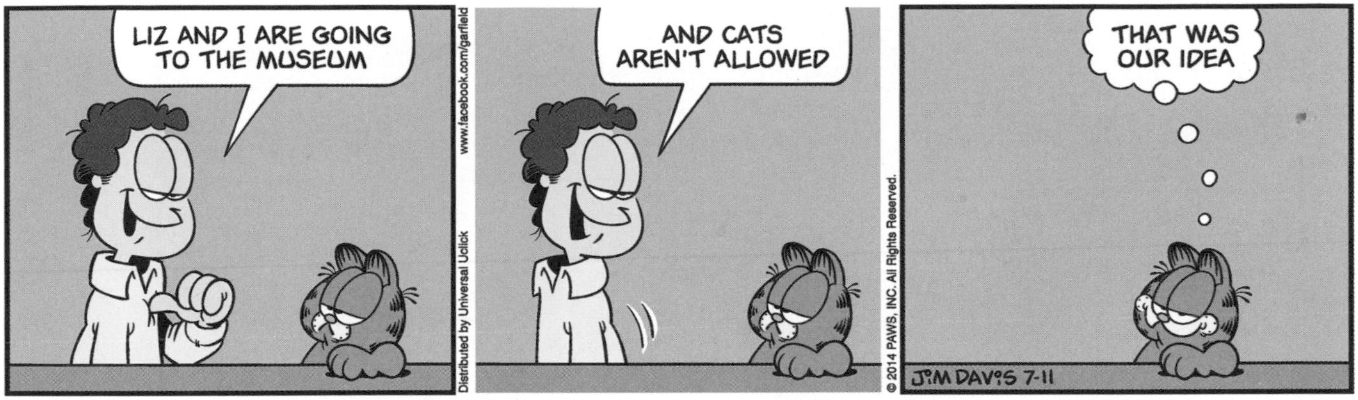
LIZ AND I ARE GOING TO THE MUSEUM
Distributed by Universal Uclick www.facebook.com/garfield
AND CATS AREN'T ALLOWED
© 2014 PAWS, INC. All Rights Reserved.
THAT WAS OUR IDEA
JIM DAVIS 7-11

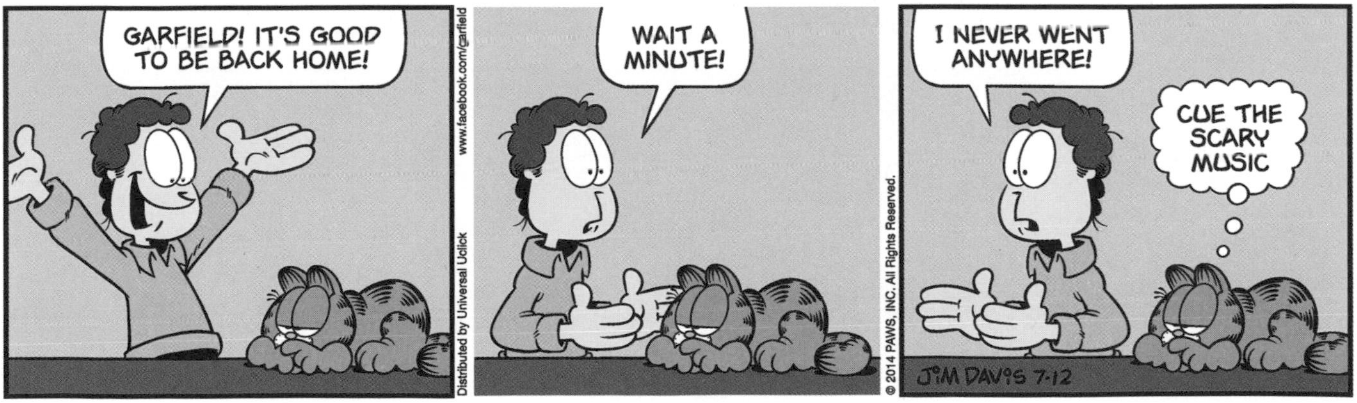
GARFIELD! IT'S GOOD TO BE BACK HOME!
Distributed by Universal Uclick www.facebook.com/garfield
WAIT A MINUTE!
© 2014 PAWS, INC. All Rights Reserved.
I NEVER WENT ANYWHERE!
CUE THE SCARY MUSIC
JIM DAVIS 7-12

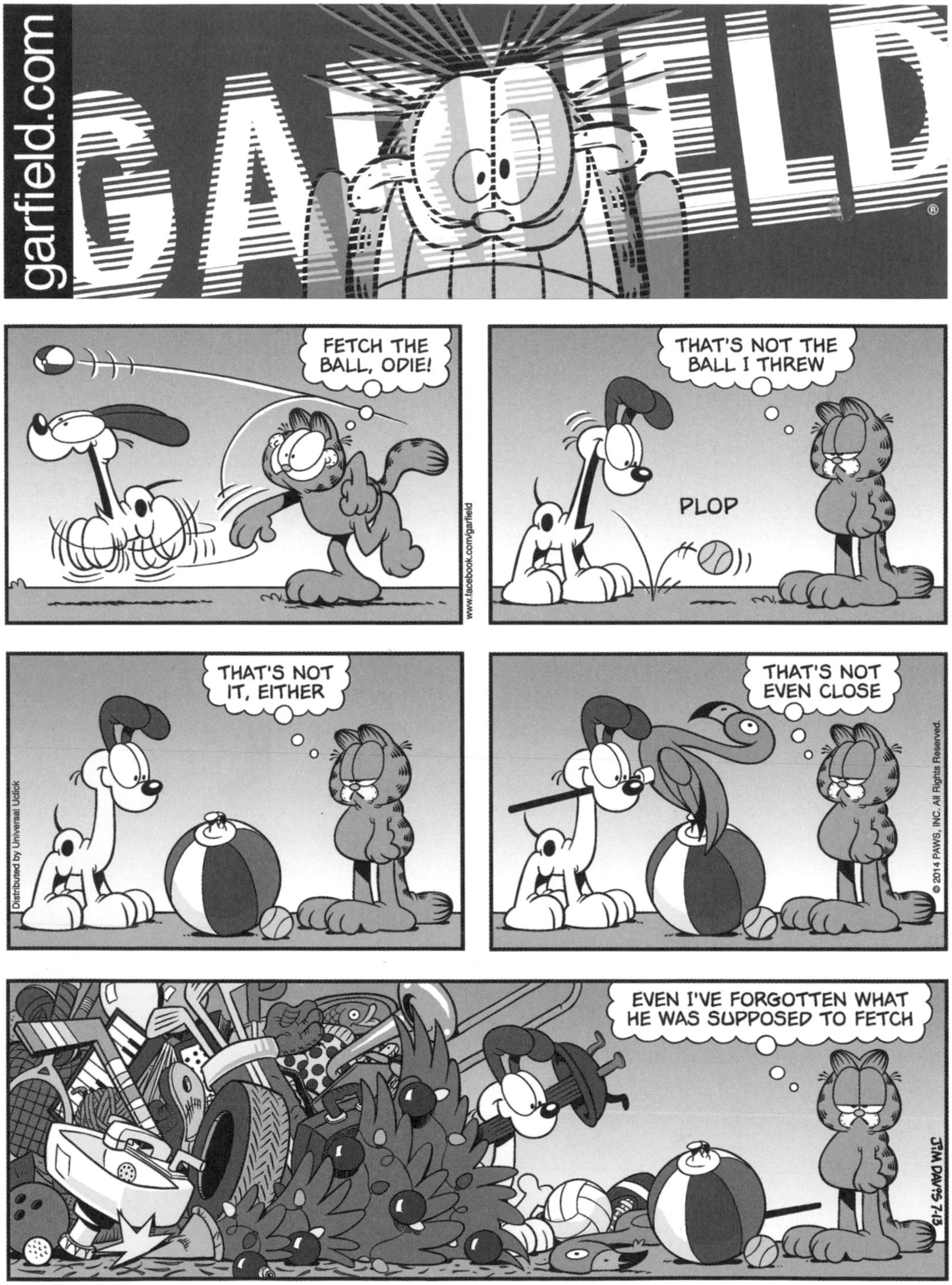
garfield.com
GARFIELD®
FETCH THE BALL, ODIE!
www.facebook.com/garfield
THAT'S NOT THE BALL I THREW
PLOP
THAT'S NOT IT, EITHER
Distributed by Universal Uclick
THAT'S NOT EVEN CLOSE
© 2014 PAWS, INC. All Rights Reserved.
EVEN I'VE FORGOTTEN WHAT HE WAS SUPPOSED TO FETCH
JIM DAVIS 7-13

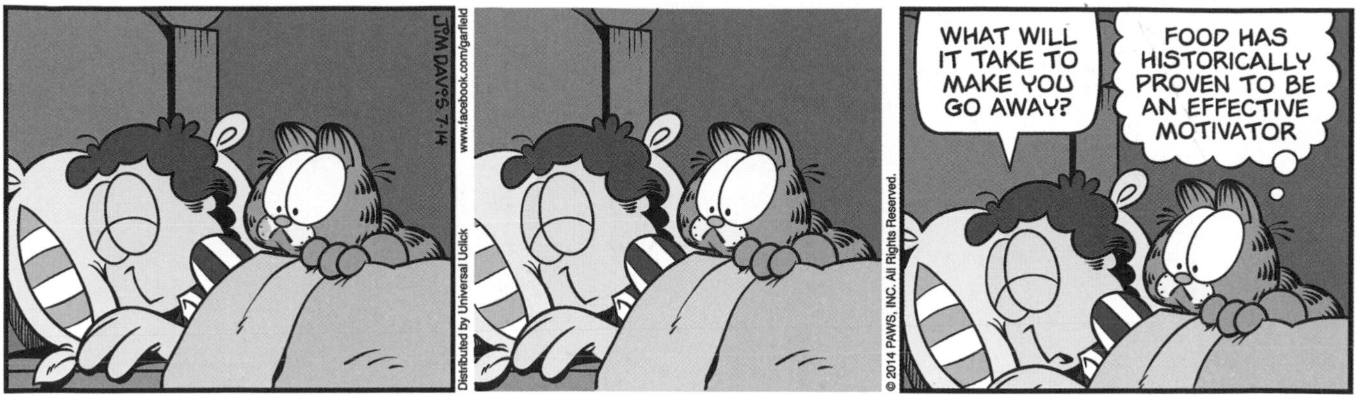
JIM DAVIS 7-14
Distributed by Universal Uclick www.facebook.com/garfield
© 2014 PAWS, INC. All Rights Reserved.
WHAT WILL IT TAKE TO MAKE YOU GO AWAY?
FOOD HAS HISTORICALLY PROVEN TO BE AN EFFECTIVE MOTIVATOR

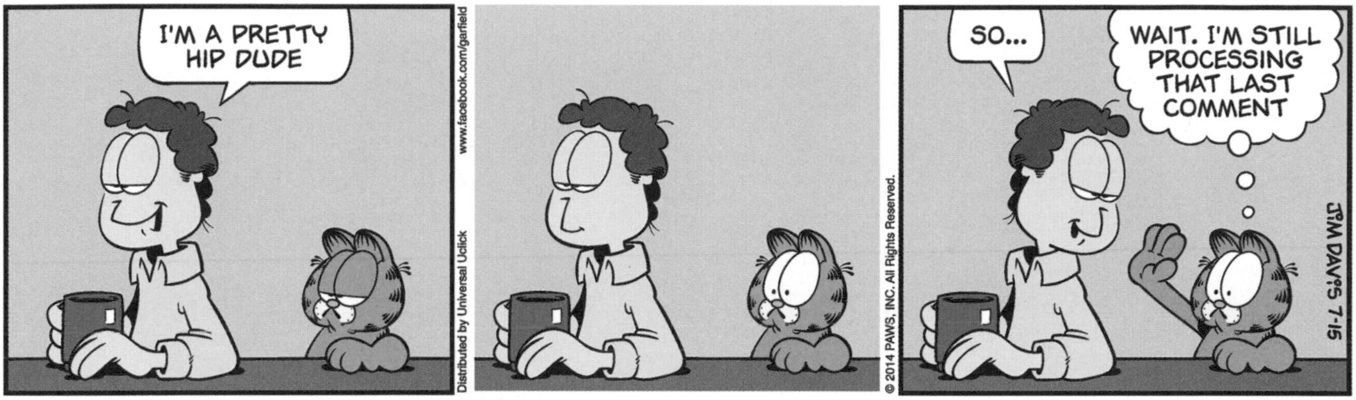
I'M A PRETTY HIP DUDE
Distributed by Universal Uclick www.facebook.com/garfield
© 2014 PAWS, INC. All Rights Reserved.
SO...
WAIT. I'M STILL PROCESSING THAT LAST COMMENT
JIM DAVIS 7-15

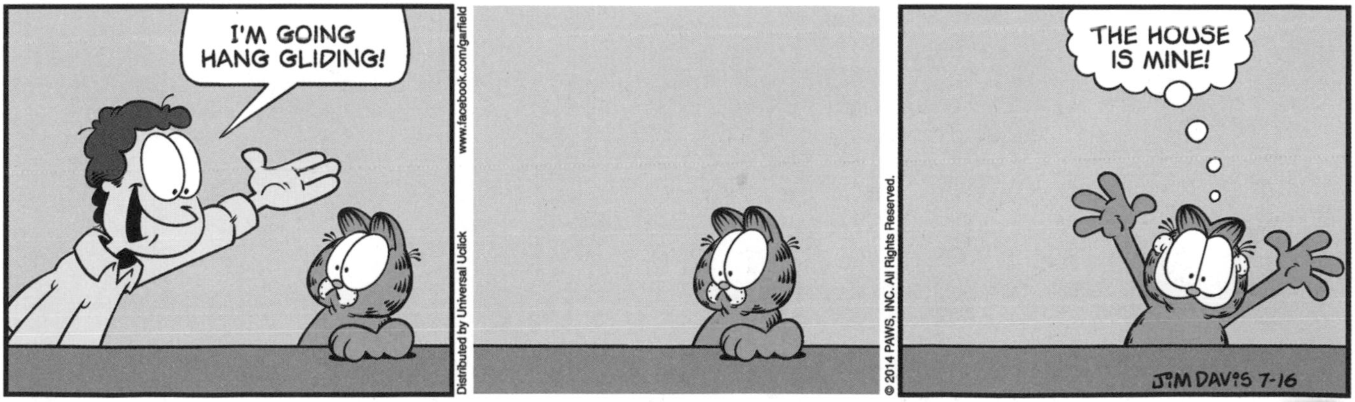
I'M GOING HANG GLIDING!
Distributed by Universal Uclick www.facebook.com/garfield
© 2014 PAWS, INC. All Rights Reserved.
THE HOUSE IS MINE!
JIM DAVIS 7-16

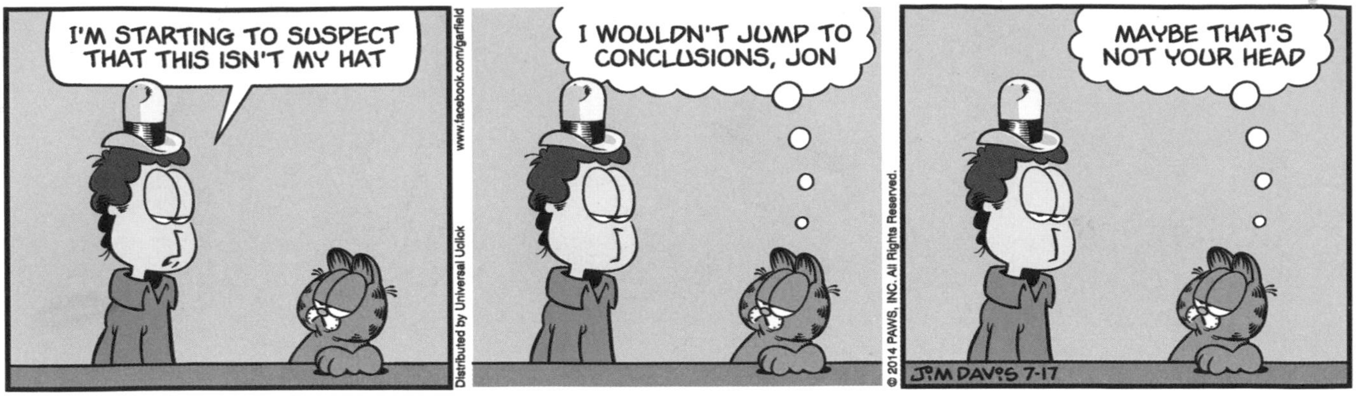
I'M STARTING TO SUSPECT THAT THIS ISN'T MY HAT
I WOULDN'T JUMP TO CONCLUSIONS, JON
MAYBE THAT'S NOT YOUR HEAD
www.facebook.com/garfield
Distributed by Universal Uclick
© 2014 PAWS, INC. All Rights Reserved.
JIM DAVIS 7-17

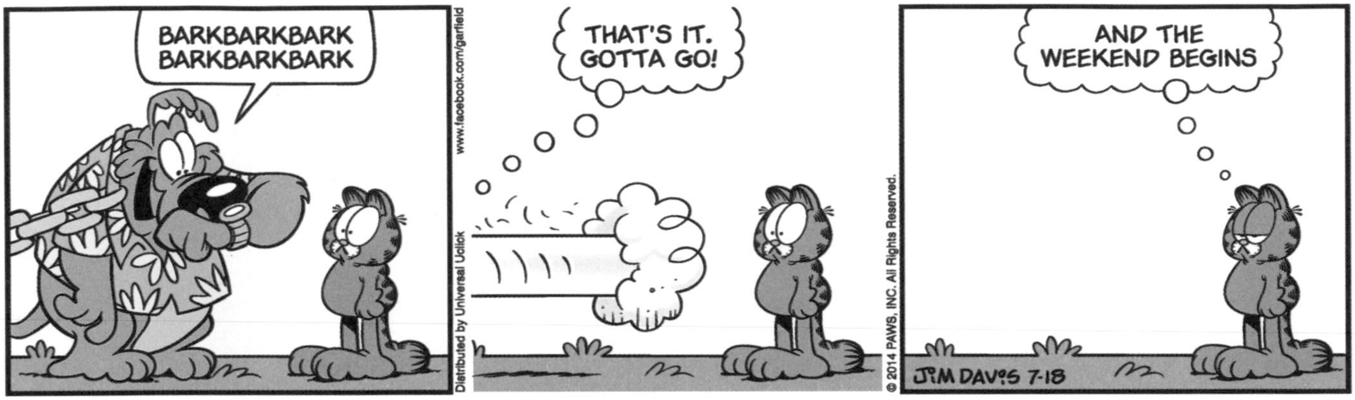
BARKBARKBARK BARKBARKBARK
THAT'S IT. GOTTA GO!
AND THE WEEKEND BEGINS
www.facebook.com/garfield
Distributed by Universal Uclick
© 2014 PAWS, INC. All Rights Reserved.
JIM DAVIS 7-18

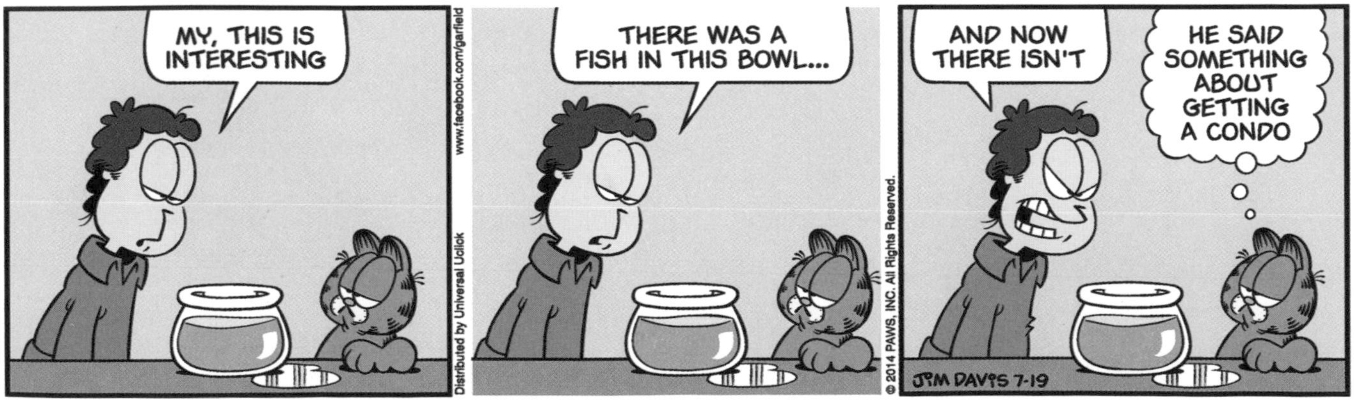
MY, THIS IS INTERESTING
THERE WAS A FISH IN THIS BOWL...
AND NOW THERE ISN'T
HE SAID SOMETHING ABOUT GETTING A CONDO
www.facebook.com/garfield
Distributed by Universal Uclick
© 2014 PAWS, INC. All Rights Reserved.
JIM DAVIS 7-19

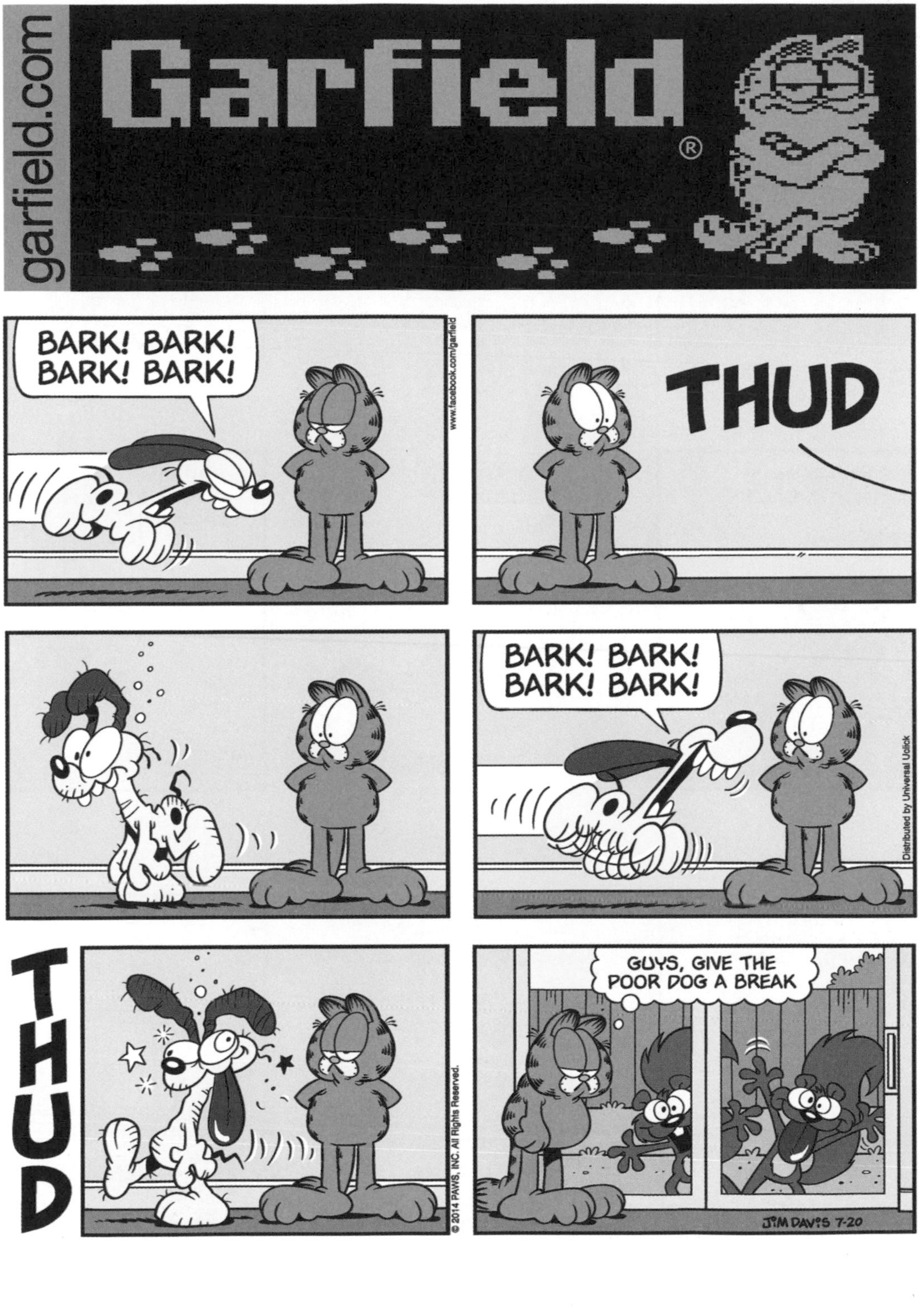
garfield.com
Garfield
BARK! BARK! BARK! BARK!
www.facebook.com/garfield
THUD
BARK! BARK! BARK! BARK!
Distributed by Universal Uclick
THUD
© 2014 PAWS, INC. All Rights Reserved.
GUYS, GIVE THE POOR DOG A BREAK
JIM DAVIS 7-20

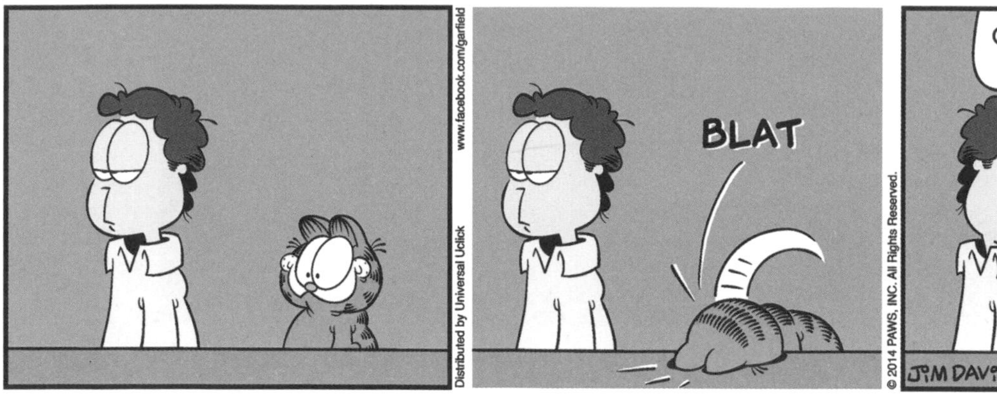
www.facebook.com/garfield
Distributed by Universal Uclick
BLAT
COFFEE WORE OFF, EH?
WHO TOLD?
© 2014 PAWS, INC. All Rights Reserved.
JIM DAVIS 7-21

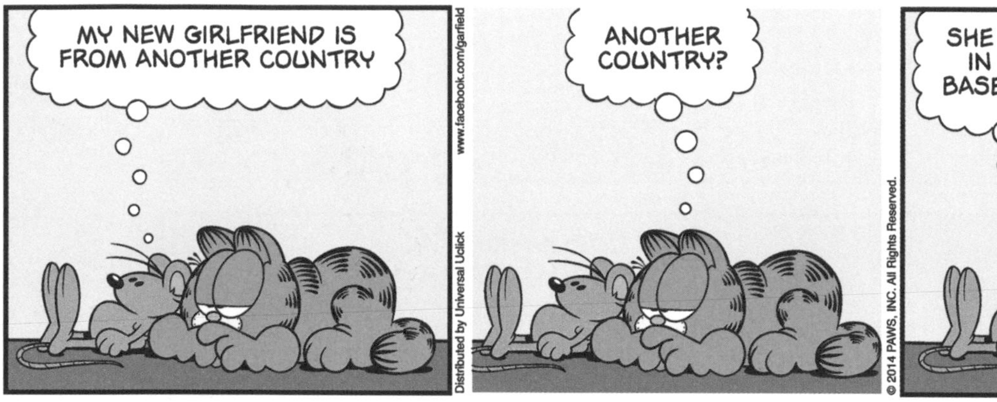
MY NEW GIRLFRIEND IS FROM ANOTHER COUNTRY
www.facebook.com/garfield
Distributed by Universal Uclick
ANOTHER COUNTRY?
© 2014 PAWS, INC. All Rights Reserved.
SHE LIVES IN THE BASEMENT
DOES SHE SPEAK ENGLISH?
JIM DAVIS 7-22

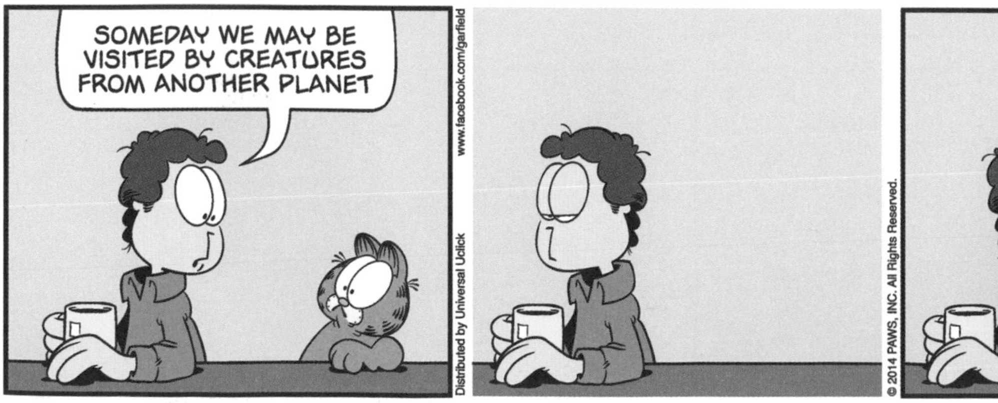
SOMEDAY WE MAY BE VISITED BY CREATURES FROM ANOTHER PLANET
www.facebook.com/garfield
Distributed by Universal Uclick
© 2014 PAWS, INC. All Rights Reserved.
I HID THE COOKIE JAR
JIM DAVIS 7-23

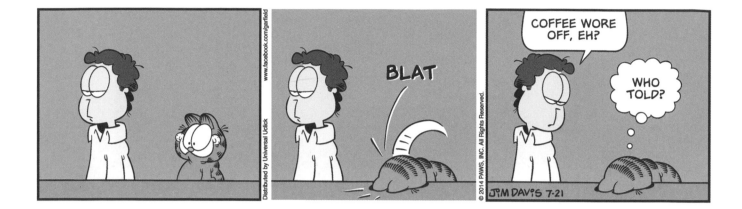

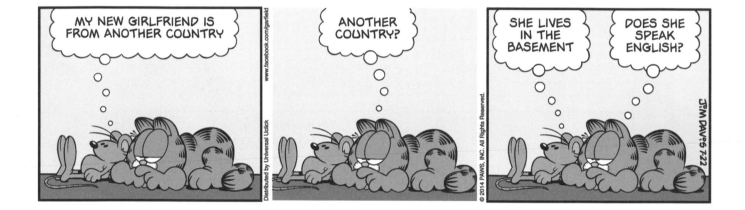

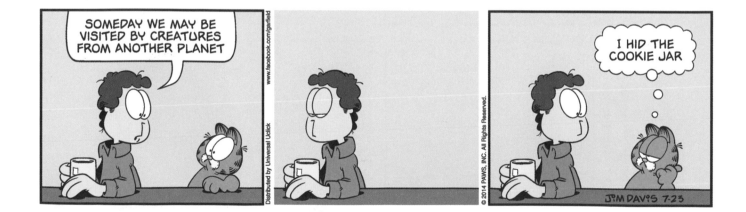

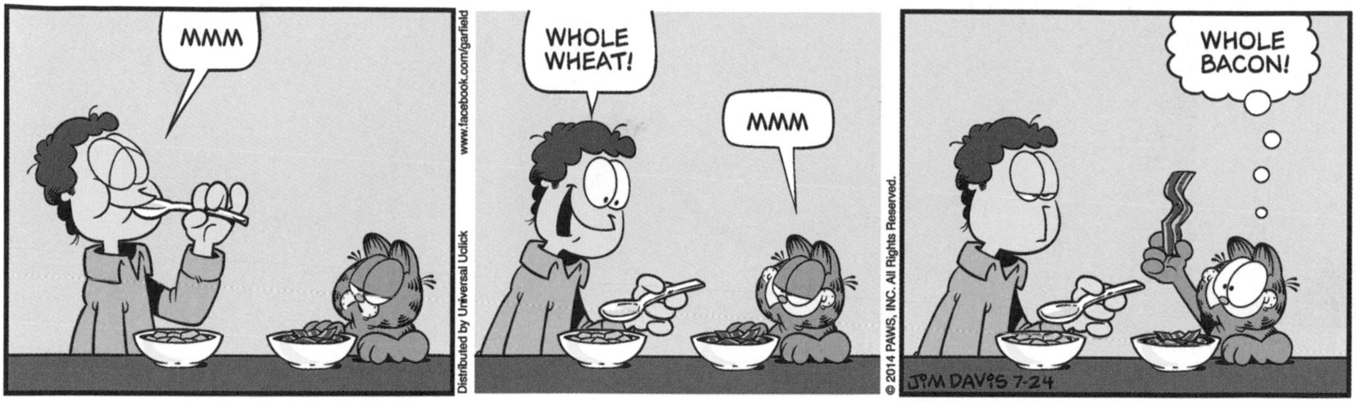
MMM
Distributed by Universal Uclick www.facebook.com/garfield
WHOLE WHEAT!
MMM
WHOLE BACON!
© 2014 PAWS, INC. All Rights Reserved.
JIM DAVIS 7-24

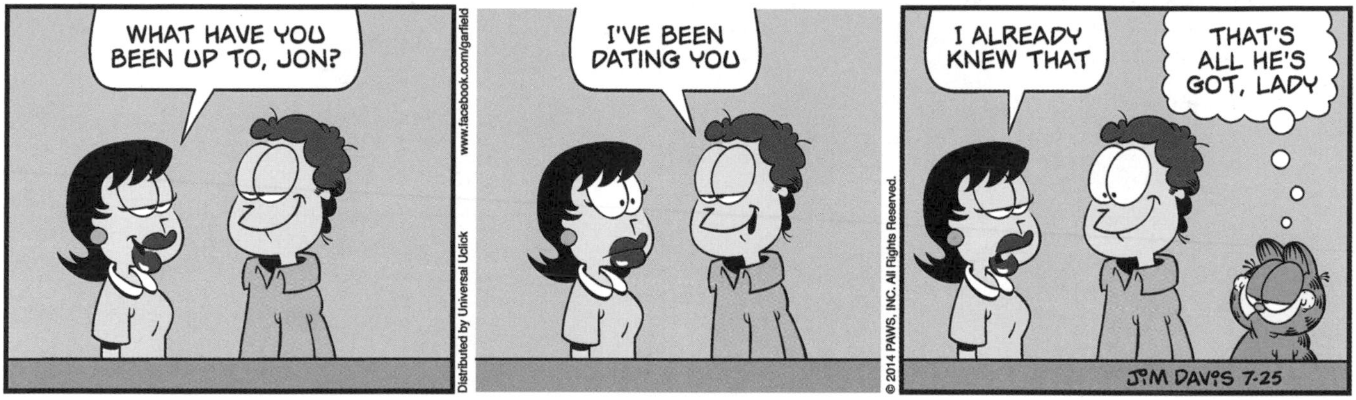
WHAT HAVE YOU BEEN UP TO, JON?
Distributed by Universal Uclick www.facebook.com/garfield
I'VE BEEN DATING YOU
I ALREADY KNEW THAT
THAT'S ALL HE'S GOT, LADY
© 2014 PAWS, INC. All Rights Reserved.
JIM DAVIS 7-25

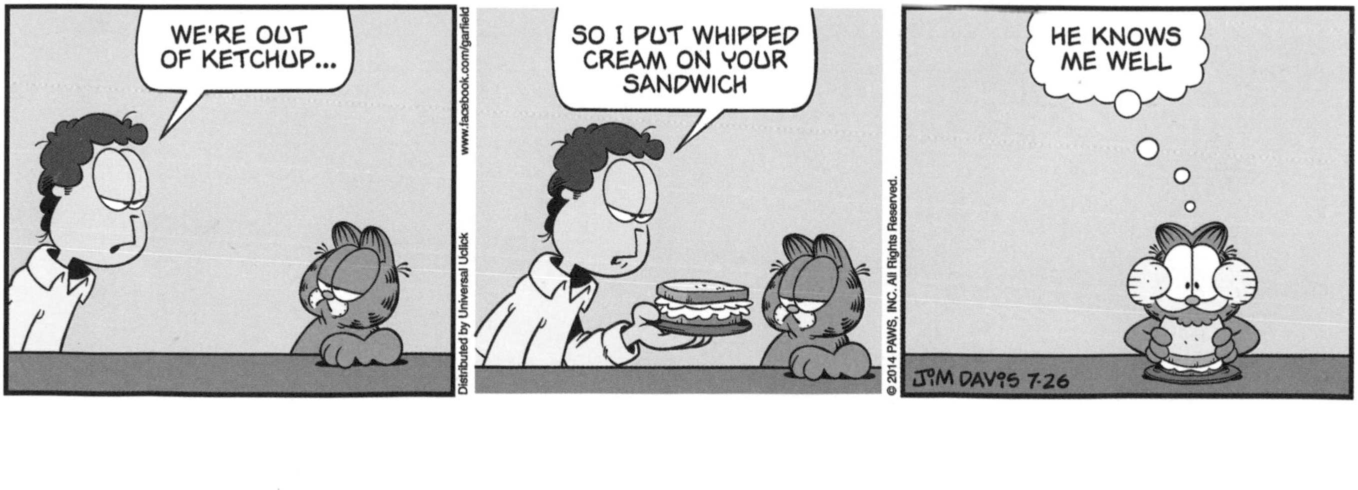
WE'RE OUT OF KETCHUP...
Distributed by Universal Uclick www.facebook.com/garfield
SO I PUT WHIPPED CREAM ON YOUR SANDWICH
HE KNOWS ME WELL
© 2014 PAWS, INC. All Rights Reserved.
JIM DAVIS 7-26

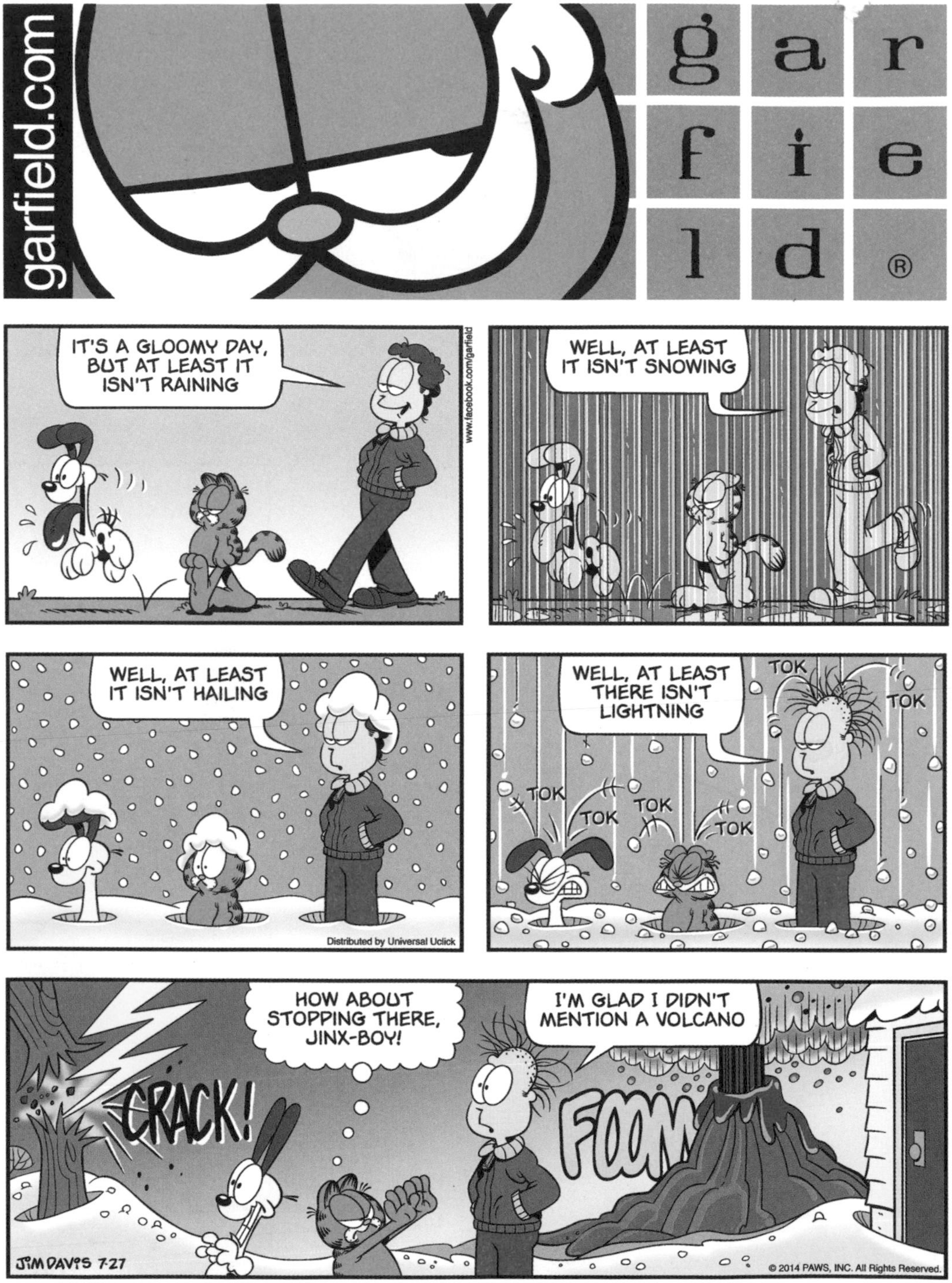
garfield.com
garfield®
IT'S A GLOOMY DAY, BUT AT LEAST IT ISN'T RAINING
www.facebook.com/garfield
WELL, AT LEAST IT ISN'T SNOWING
WELL, AT LEAST IT ISN'T HAILING
Distributed by Universal Uclick
WELL, AT LEAST THERE ISN'T LIGHTNING
TOK
TOK
TOK
TOK
TOK
TOK
HOW ABOUT STOPPING THERE, JINX-BOY!
I'M GLAD I DIDN'T MENTION A VOLCANO
CRACK!
FOOM
JIM DAVIS 7-27
© 2014 PAWS, INC. All Rights Reserved.

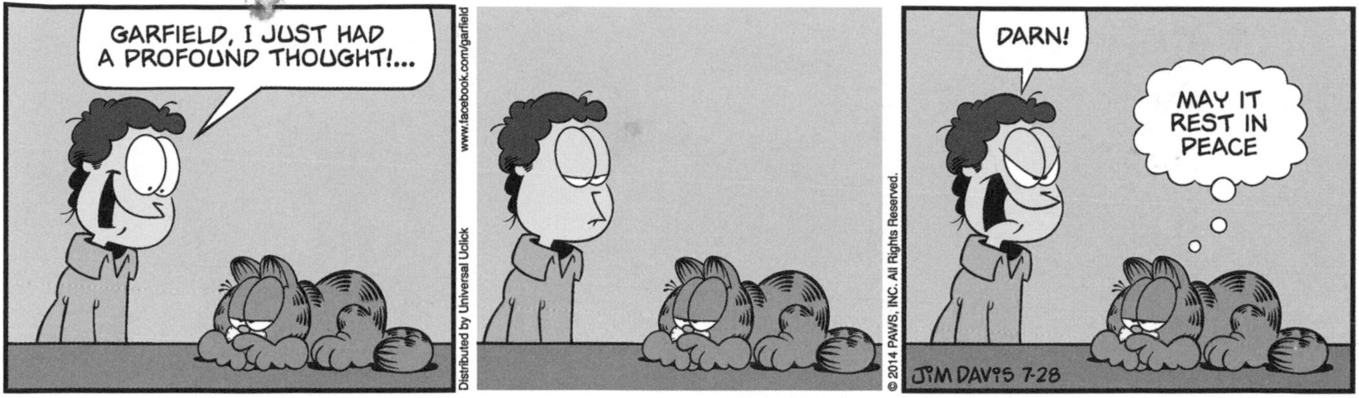
GARFIELD, I JUST HAD A PROFOUND THOUGHT!...
DARN!
MAY IT REST IN PEACE
JIM DAVIS 7-28
Distributed by Universal Uclick
www.facebook.com/garfield
© 2014 PAWS, INC. All Rights Reserved.

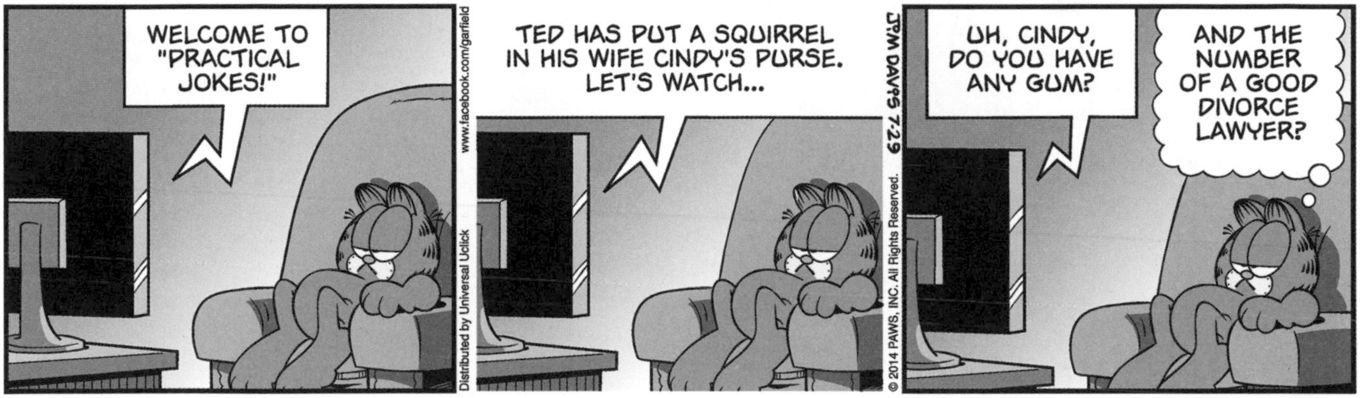
WELCOME TO "PRACTICAL JOKES!"
TED HAS PUT A SQUIRREL IN HIS WIFE CINDY'S PURSE. LET'S WATCH...
UH, CINDY, DO YOU HAVE ANY GUM?
AND THE NUMBER OF A GOOD DIVORCE LAWYER?
JIM DAVIS 7-29
Distributed by Universal Uclick
www.facebook.com/garfield
© 2014 PAWS, INC. All Rights Reserved.

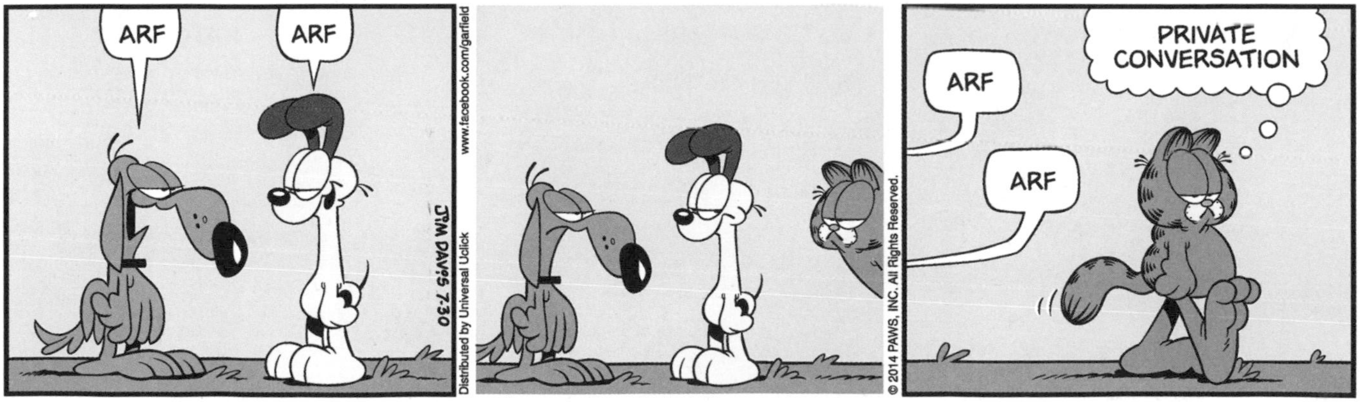
ARF
ARF
ARF
ARF
PRIVATE CONVERSATION
JIM DAVIS 7-30
Distributed by Universal Uclick
www.facebook.com/garfield
© 2014 PAWS, INC. All Rights Reserved.

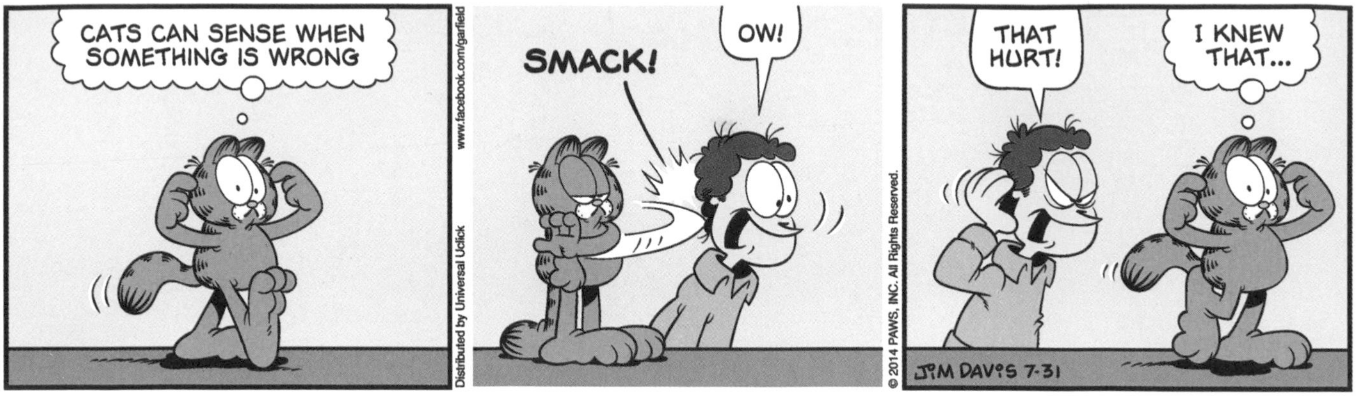
CATS CAN SENSE WHEN SOMETHING IS WRONG
SMACK!
OW!
THAT HURT!
I KNEW THAT...
www.facebook.com/garfield
Distributed by Universal Uclick
© 2014 PAWS, INC. All Rights Reserved.
JIM DAVIS 7-31

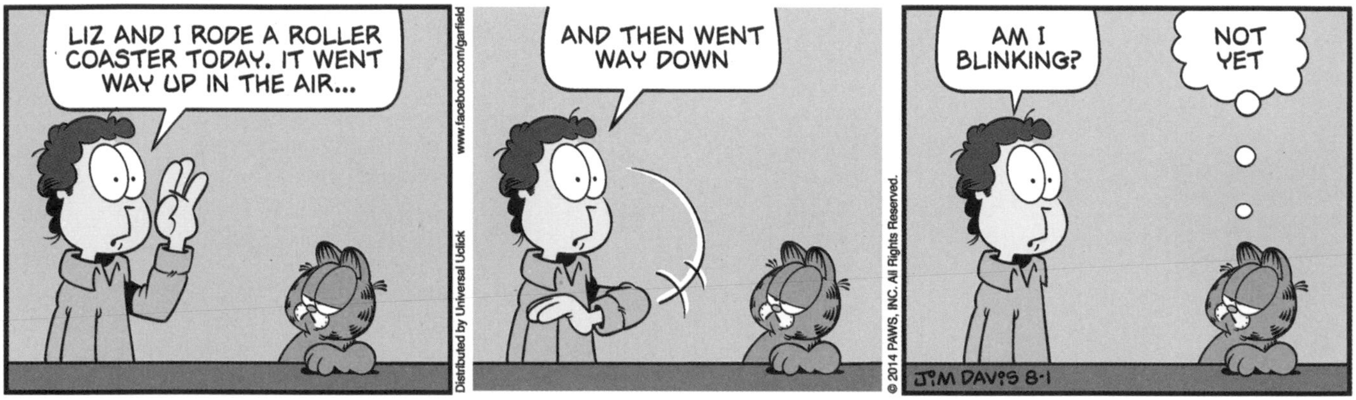
LIZ AND I RODE A ROLLER COASTER TODAY. IT WENT WAY UP IN THE AIR...
AND THEN WENT WAY DOWN
AM I BLINKING?
NOT YET
www.facebook.com/garfield
Distributed by Universal Uclick
© 2014 PAWS, INC. All Rights Reserved.
JIM DAVIS 8-1

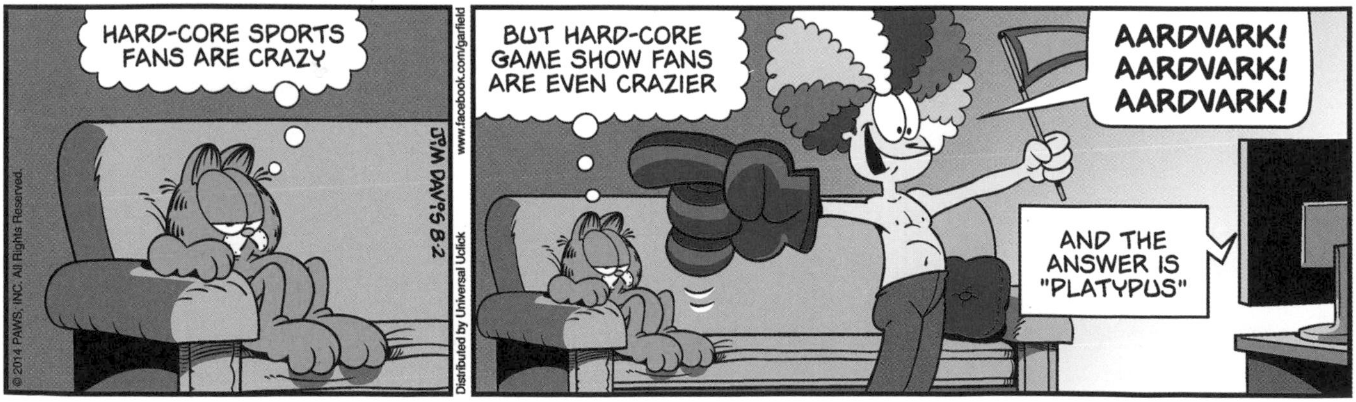
HARD-CORE SPORTS FANS ARE CRAZY
BUT HARD-CORE GAME SHOW FANS ARE EVEN CRAZIER
AARDVARK! AARDVARK! AARDVARK!
AND THE ANSWER IS "PLATYPUS"
© 2014 PAWS, INC. All Rights Reserved.
JIM DAVIS 8-2
www.facebook.com/garfield
Distributed by Universal Uclick

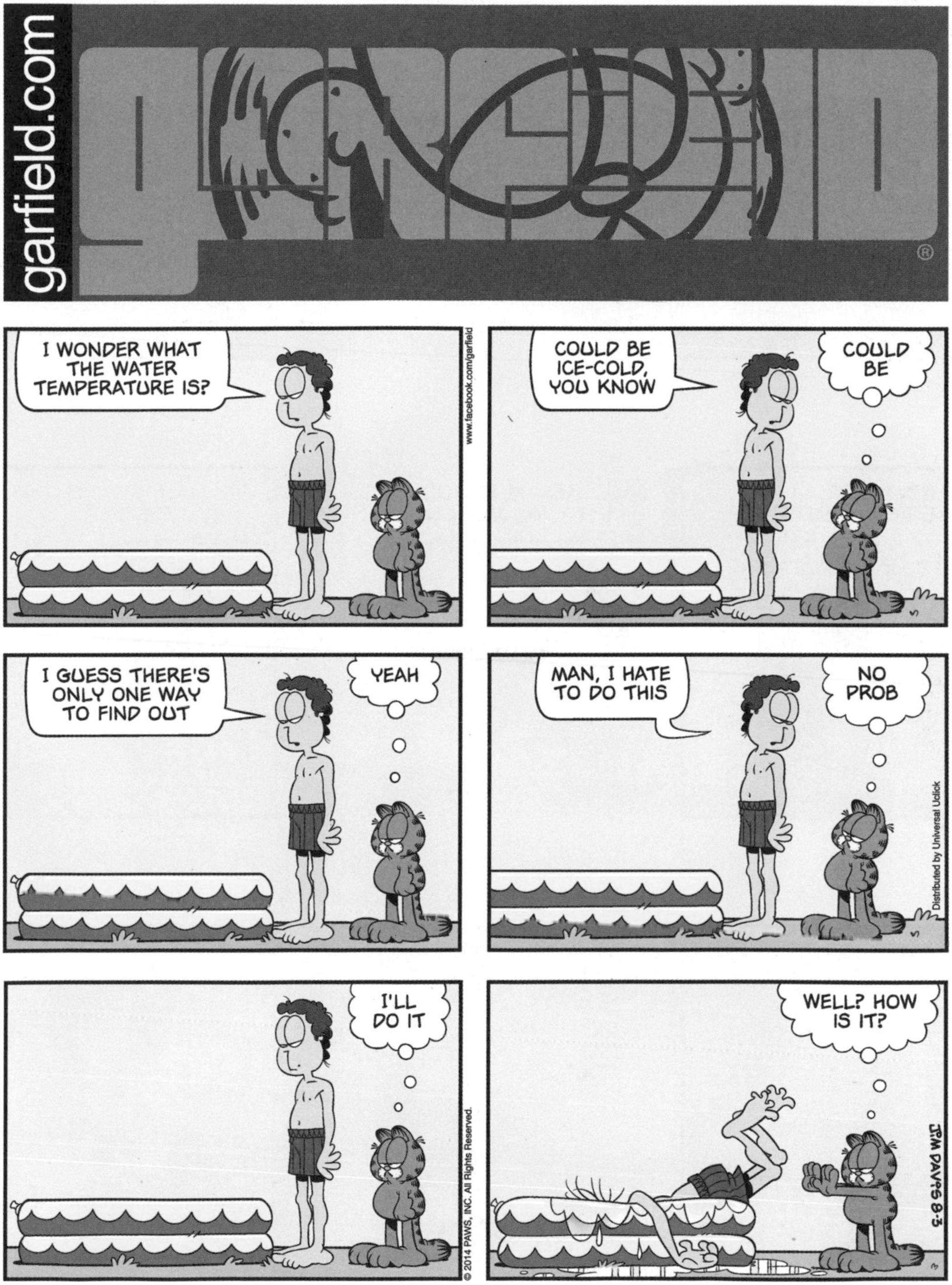
garfield.com
I WONDER WHAT THE WATER TEMPERATURE IS?
www.facebook.com/garfield
COULD BE ICE-COLD, YOU KNOW
COULD BE
I GUESS THERE'S ONLY ONE WAY TO FIND OUT
YEAH
MAN, I HATE TO DO THIS
NO PROB
Distributed by Universal Uclick
I'LL DO IT
© 2014 PAWS, INC. All Rights Reserved.
WELL? HOW IS IT?
JIM DAVIS 8-3

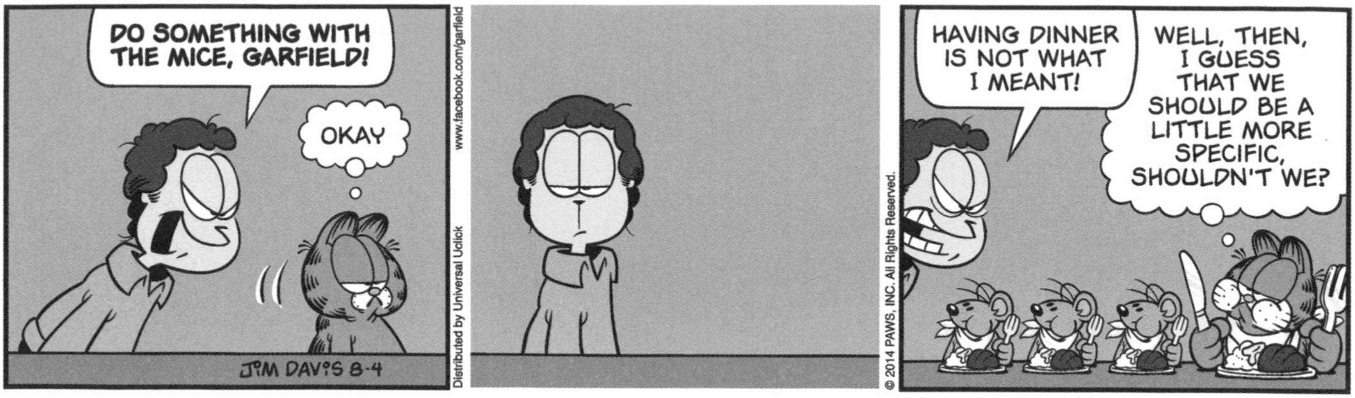
DO SOMETHING WITH THE MICE, GARFIELD!
OKAY
JIM DAVIS 8-4
Distributed by Universal Uclick www.facebook.com/garfield
HAVING DINNER IS NOT WHAT I MEANT!
WELL, THEN, I GUESS THAT WE SHOULD BE A LITTLE MORE SPECIFIC, SHOULDN'T WE?
© 2014 PAWS, INC. All Rights Reserved.

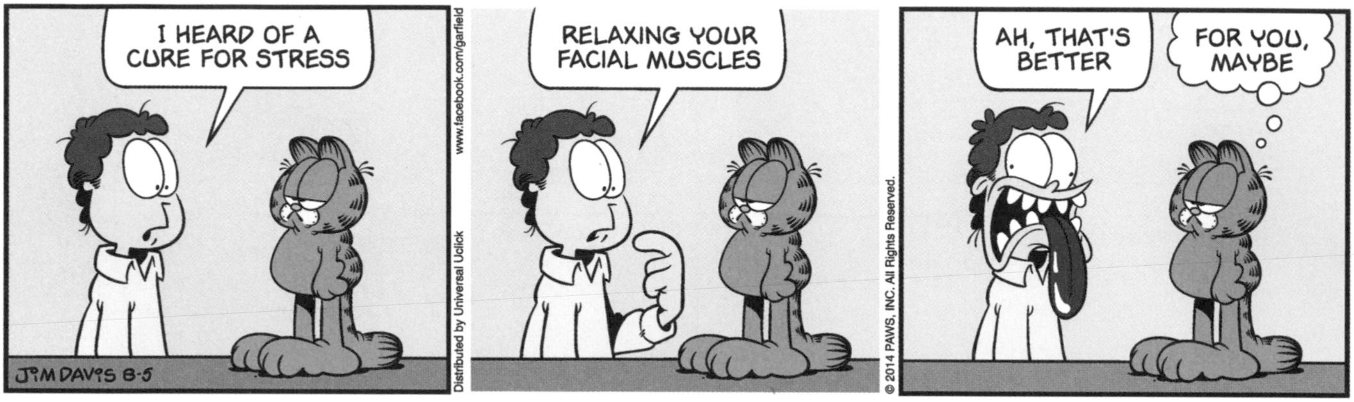
I HEARD OF A CURE FOR STRESS
JIM DAVIS 8-5
Distributed by Universal Uclick www.facebook.com/garfield
RELAXING YOUR FACIAL MUSCLES
AH, THAT'S BETTER
FOR YOU, MAYBE
© 2014 PAWS, INC. All Rights Reserved.

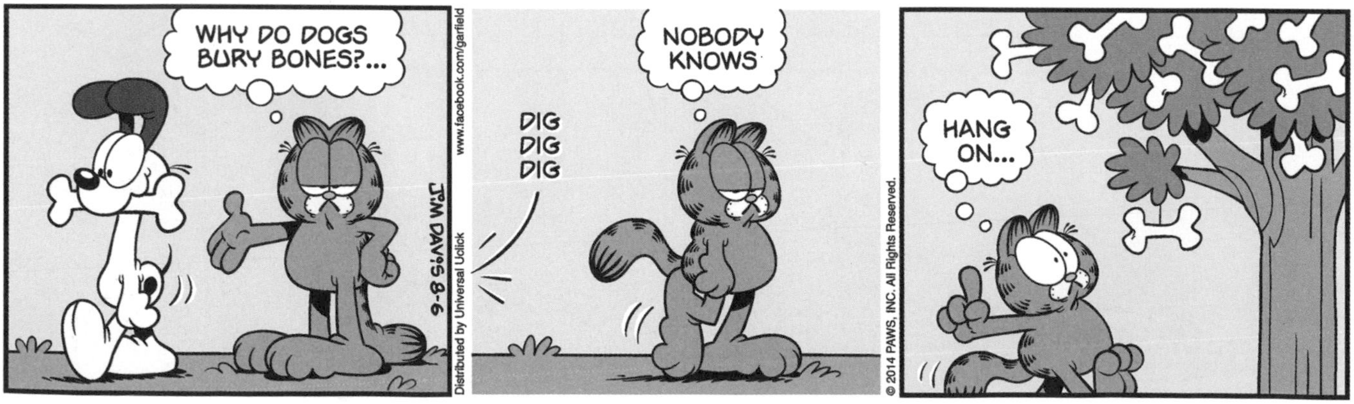
WHY DO DOGS BURY BONES?...
JIM DAVIS 8-6
Distributed by Universal Uclick www.facebook.com/garfield
DIG DIG DIG
NOBODY KNOWS
HANG ON...
© 2014 PAWS, INC. All Rights Reserved.

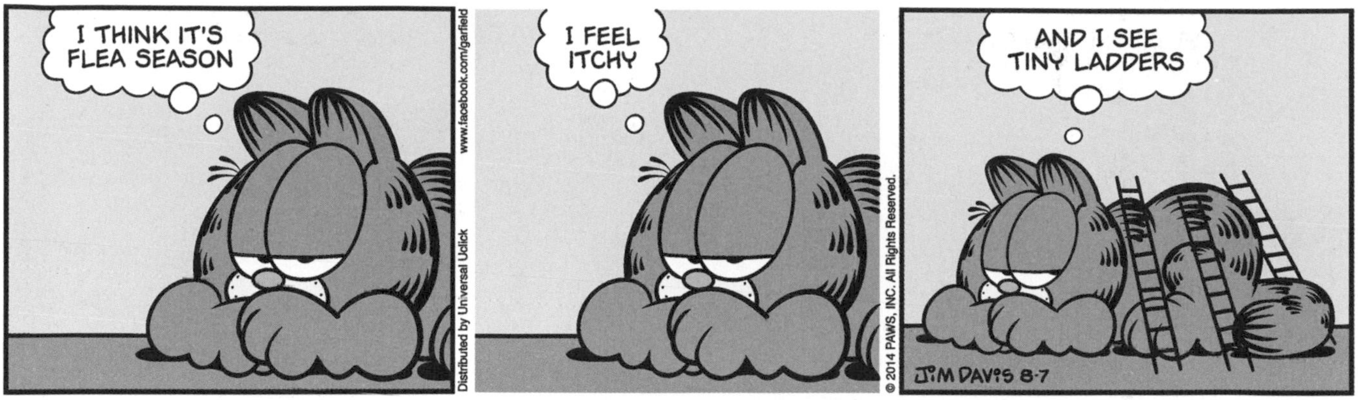
I THINK IT'S FLEA SEASON
I FEEL ITCHY
AND I SEE TINY LADDERS
Distributed by Universal Uclick
www.facebook.com/garfield
© 2014 PAWS, INC. All Rights Reserved.
JIM DAVIS 8-7

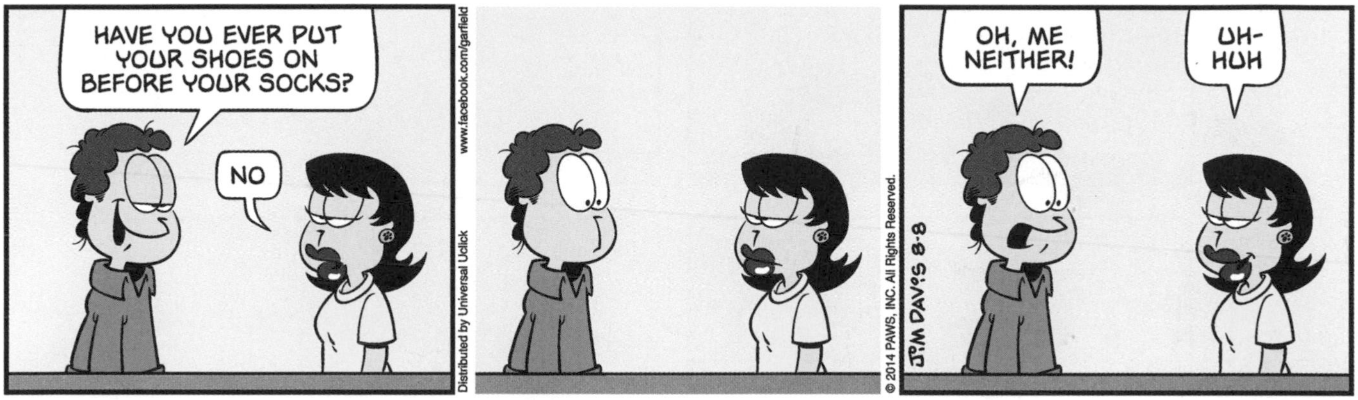
HAVE YOU EVER PUT YOUR SHOES ON BEFORE YOUR SOCKS?
NO
OH, ME NEITHER!
UH-HUH
Distributed by Universal Uclick
www.facebook.com/garfield
© 2014 PAWS, INC. All Rights Reserved.
JIM DAVIS 8-8

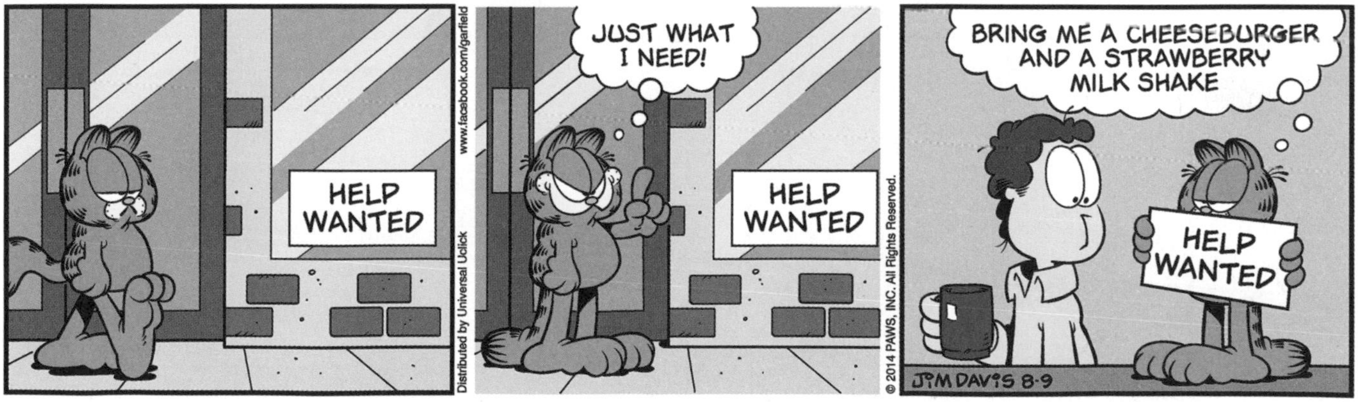
HELP WANTED
JUST WHAT I NEED!
HELP WANTED
BRING ME A CHEESEBURGER AND A STRAWBERRY MILK SHAKE
HELP WANTED
Distributed by Universal Uclick
www.facebook.com/garfield
© 2014 PAWS, INC. All Rights Reserved.
JIM DAVIS 8-9

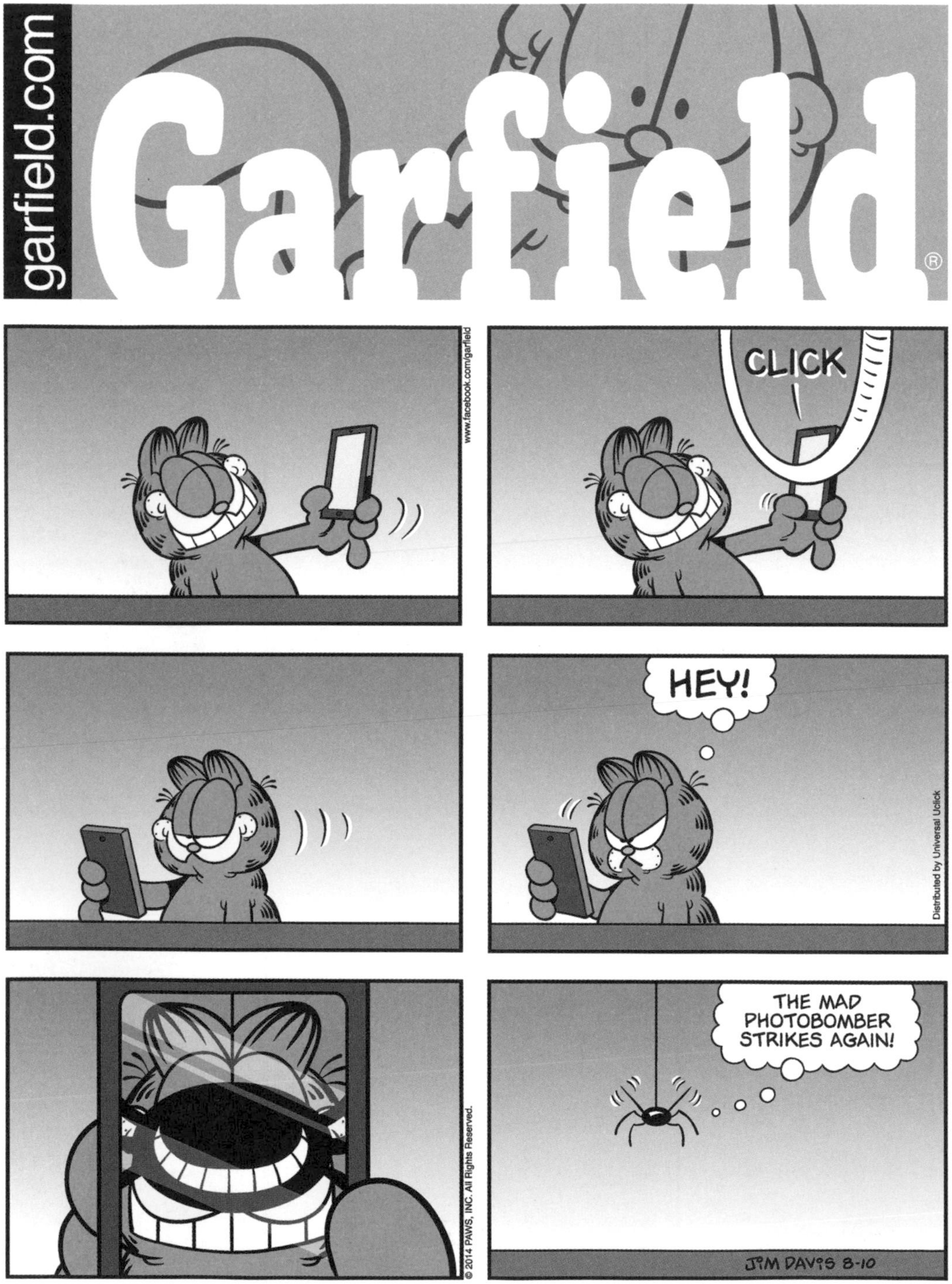
garfield.com
Garfield®
www.facebook.com/garfield
CLICK
HEY!
Distributed by Universal Uclick
© 2014 PAWS, INC. All Rights Reserved.
THE MAD PHOTOBOMBER STRIKES AGAIN!
JIM DAVIS 8-10

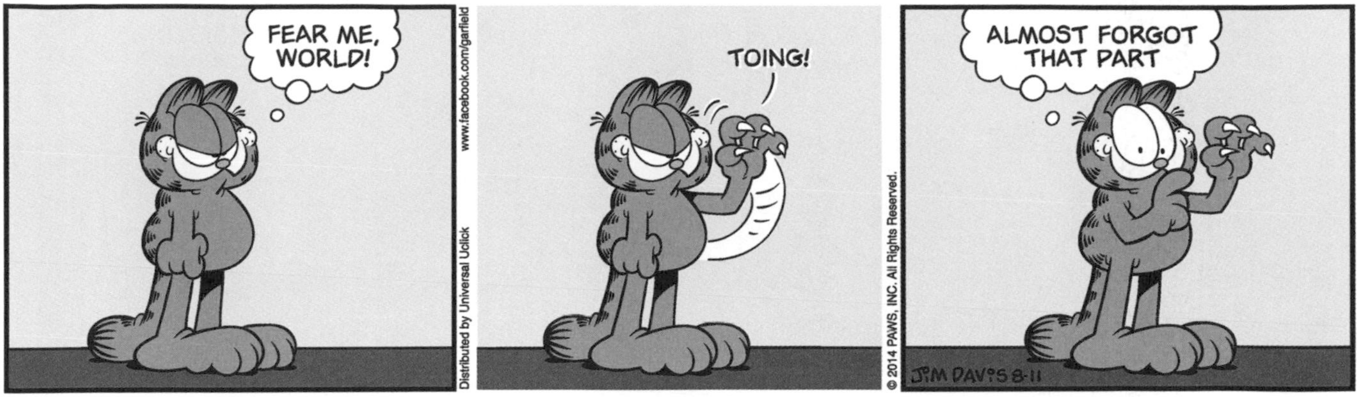
FEAR ME, WORLD!
TOING!
ALMOST FORGOT THAT PART
JIM DAVIS 8-11

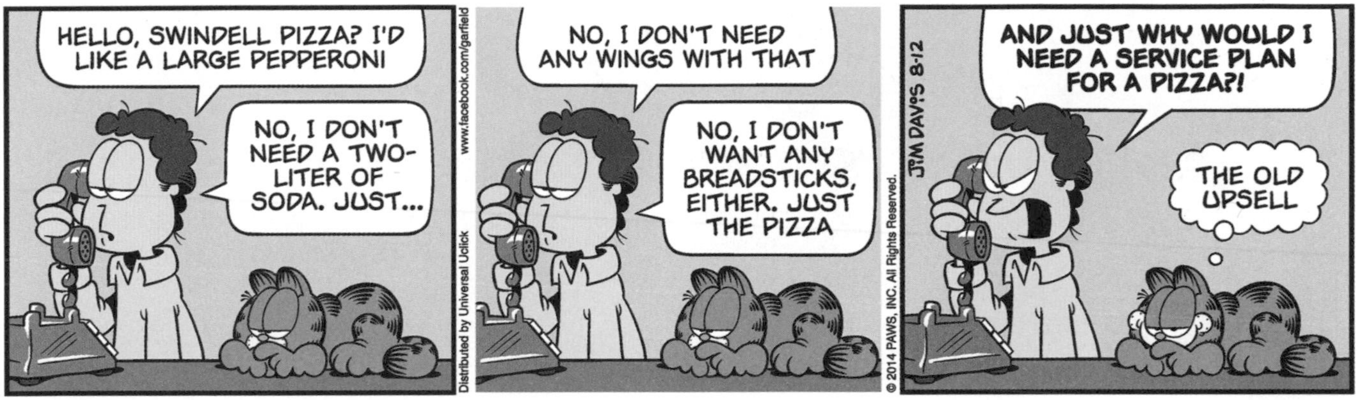
HELLO, SWINDELL PIZZA? I'D LIKE A LARGE PEPPERONI
NO, I DON'T NEED A TWO-LITER OF SODA. JUST...
NO, I DON'T NEED ANY WINGS WITH THAT
NO, I DON'T WANT ANY BREADSTICKS, EITHER. JUST THE PIZZA
AND JUST WHY WOULD I NEED A SERVICE PLAN FOR A PIZZA?!
THE OLD UPSELL
JIM DAVIS 8-12

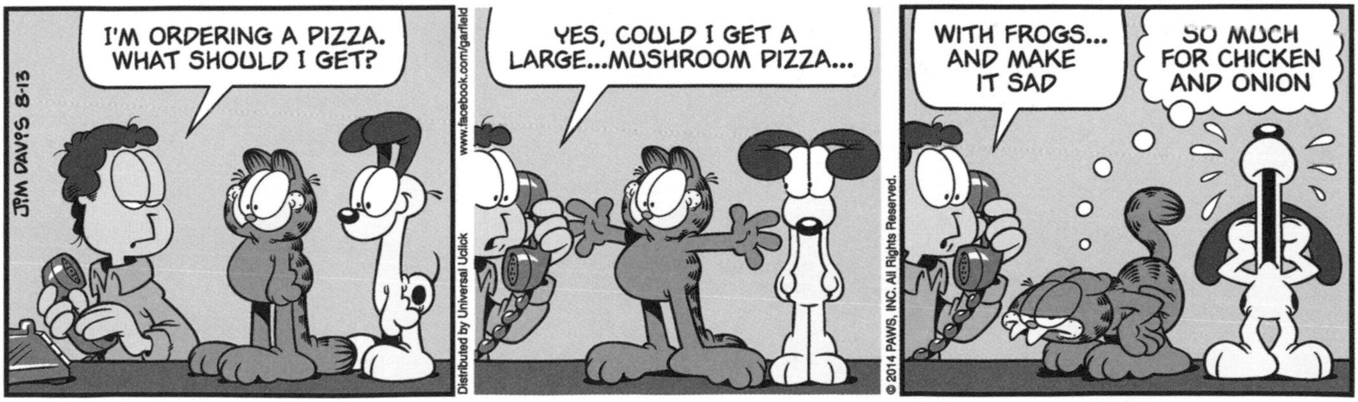
I'M ORDERING A PIZZA. WHAT SHOULD I GET?
YES, COULD I GET A LARGE...MUSHROOM PIZZA...
WITH FROGS... AND MAKE IT SAD
SO MUCH FOR CHICKEN AND ONION
JIM DAVIS 8-13

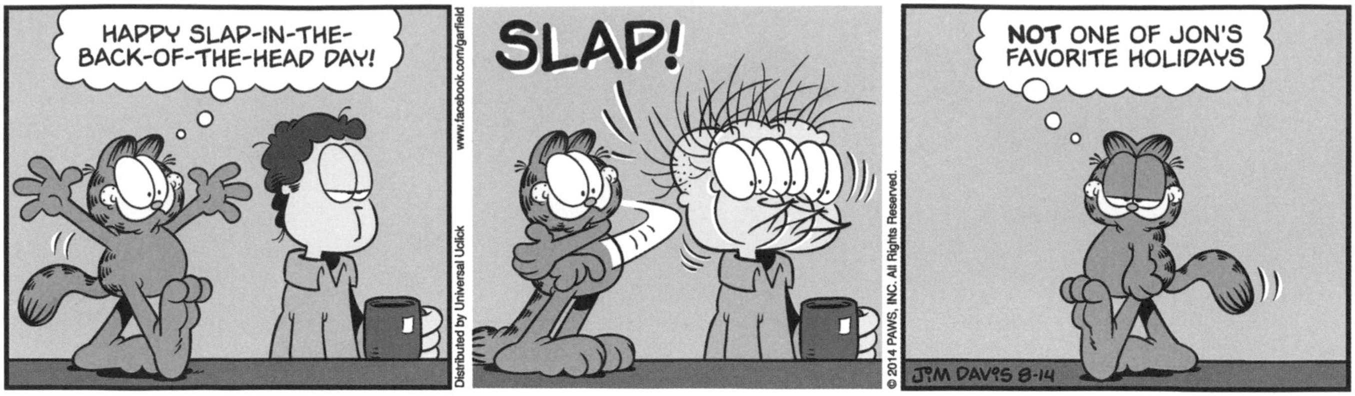
HAPPY SLAP-IN-THE-BACK-OF-THE-HEAD DAY!
www.facebook.com/garfield
Distributed by Universal Uclick
SLAP!
© 2014 PAWS, INC. All Rights Reserved.
NOT ONE OF JON'S FAVORITE HOLIDAYS
JIM DAVIS 8-14

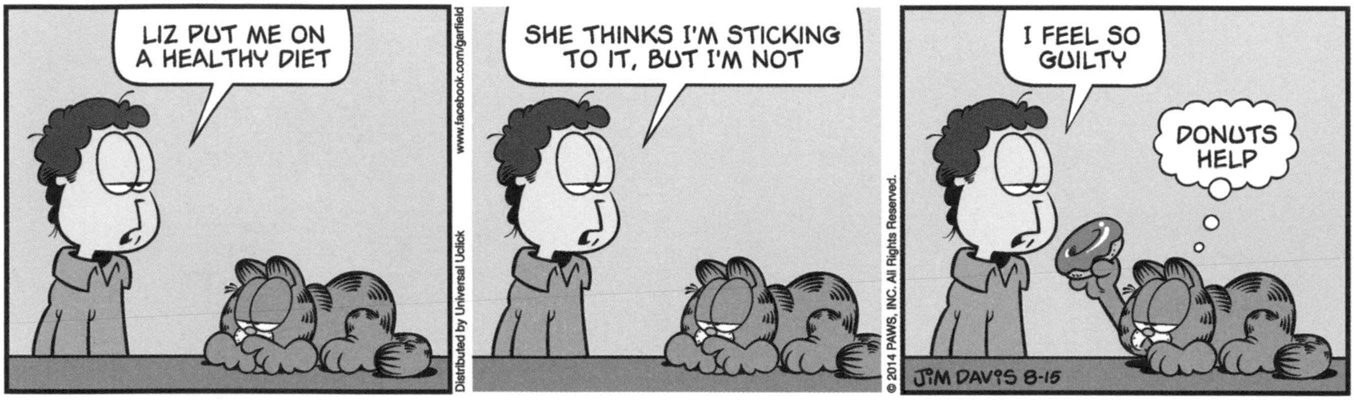
LIZ PUT ME ON A HEALTHY DIET
www.facebook.com/garfield
Distributed by Universal Uclick
SHE THINKS I'M STICKING TO IT, BUT I'M NOT
© 2014 PAWS, INC. All Rights Reserved.
I FEEL SO GUILTY
DONUTS HELP
JIM DAVIS 8-15

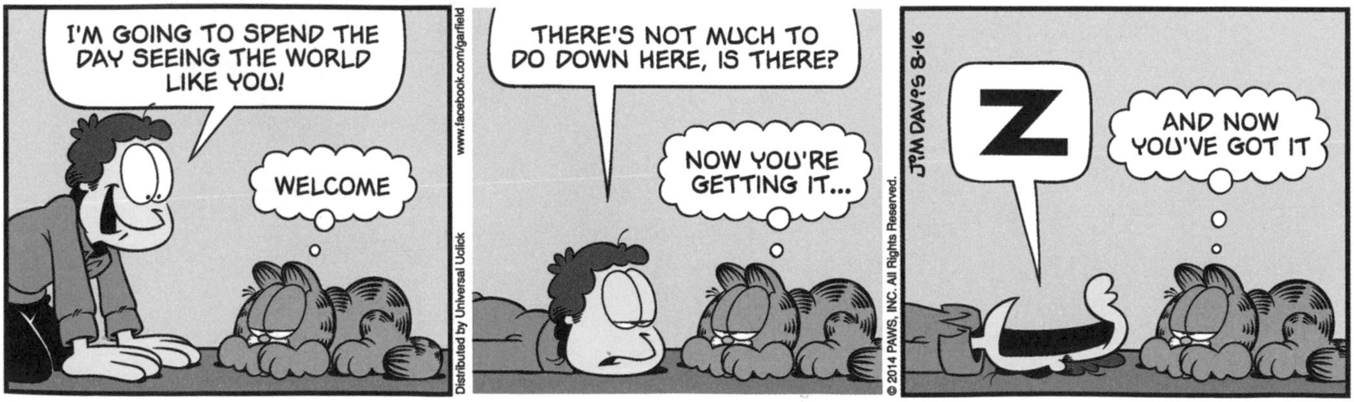
I'M GOING TO SPEND THE DAY SEEING THE WORLD LIKE YOU!
WELCOME
www.facebook.com/garfield
Distributed by Universal Uclick
THERE'S NOT MUCH TO DO DOWN HERE, IS THERE?
NOW YOU'RE GETTING IT...
© 2014 PAWS, INC. All Rights Reserved.
JIM DAVIS 8-16
Z
AND NOW YOU'VE GOT IT

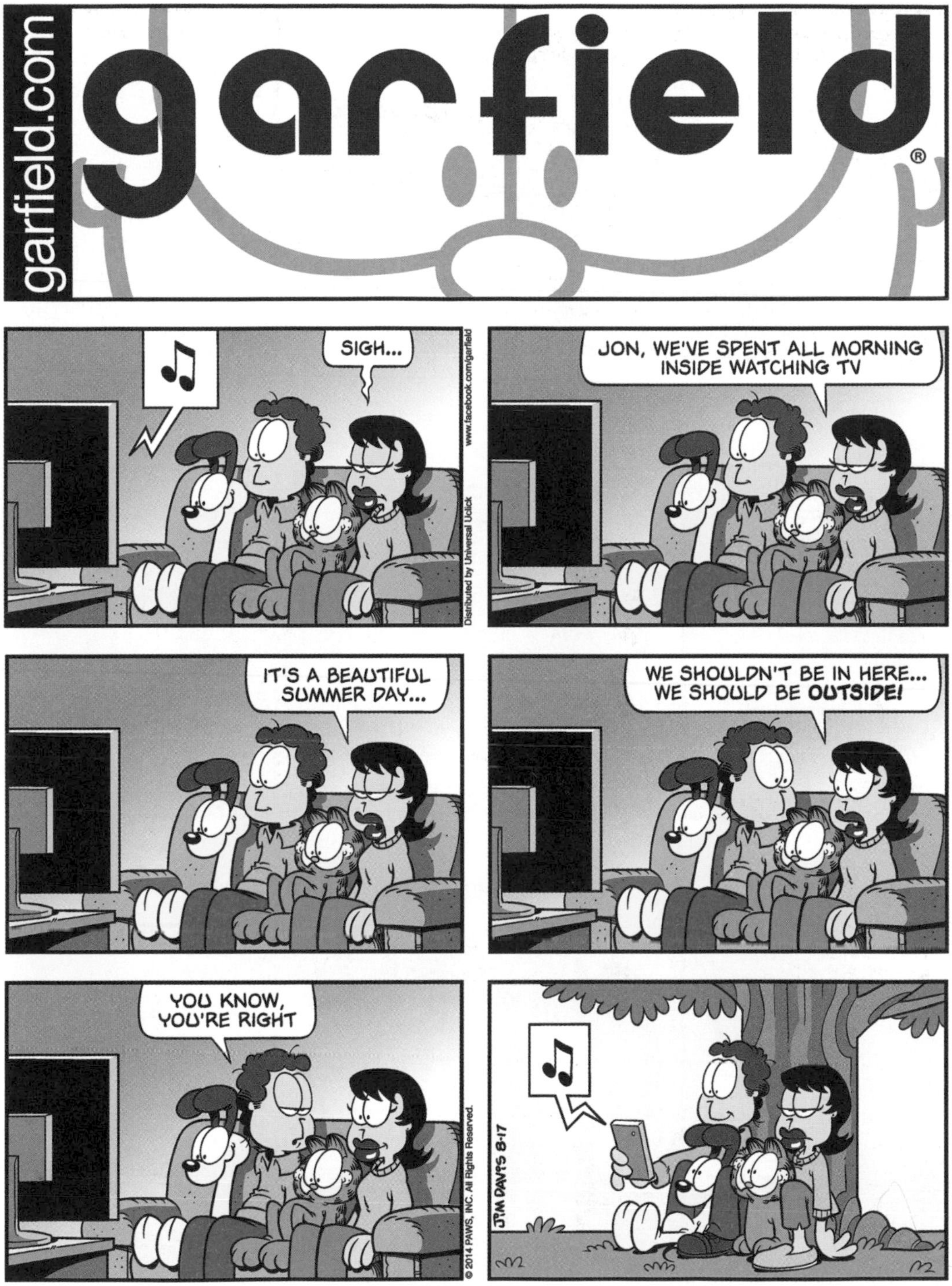
garfield.com
garfield
SIGH...
www.facebook.com/garfield
Distributed by Universal Uclick
JON, WE'VE SPENT ALL MORNING INSIDE WATCHING TV
IT'S A BEAUTIFUL SUMMER DAY...
WE SHOULDN'T BE IN HERE... WE SHOULD BE **OUTSIDE!**
YOU KNOW, YOU'RE RIGHT
© 2014 PAWS, INC. All Rights Reserved.
JIM DAVIS 8-17

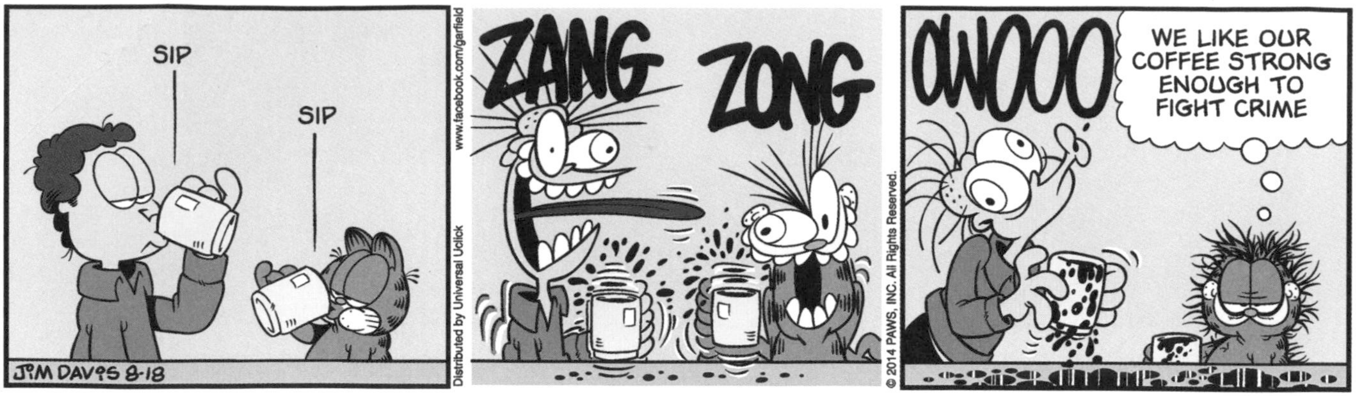
SIP
SIP
JIM DAVIS 8-18
Distributed by Universal Uclick www.facebook.com/garfield
ZANG
ZONG
OWOOO
WE LIKE OUR COFFEE STRONG ENOUGH TO FIGHT CRIME
© 2014 PAWS, INC. All Rights Reserved.

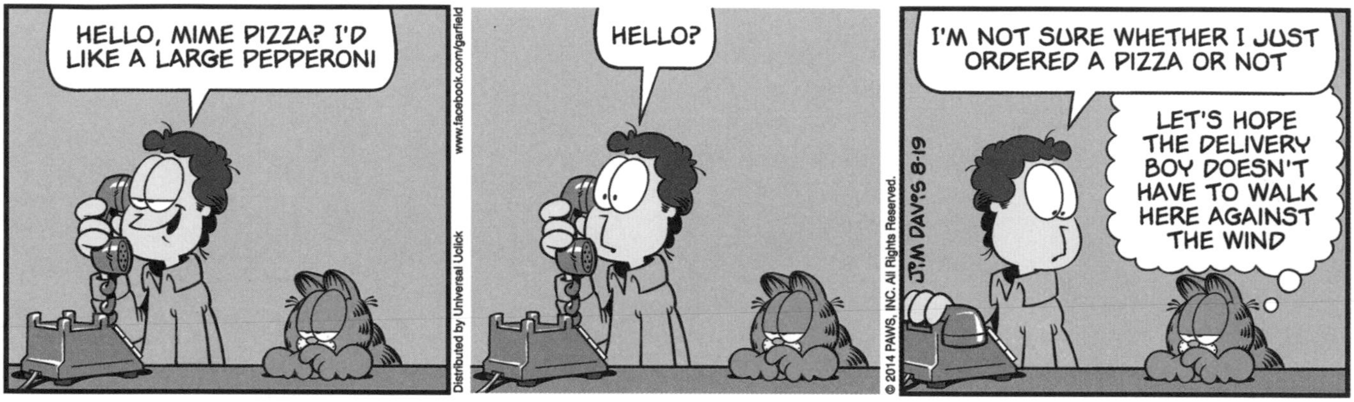
HELLO, MIME PIZZA? I'D LIKE A LARGE PEPPERONI
Distributed by Universal Uclick www.facebook.com/garfield
HELLO?
I'M NOT SURE WHETHER I JUST ORDERED A PIZZA OR NOT
LET'S HOPE THE DELIVERY BOY DOESN'T HAVE TO WALK HERE AGAINST THE WIND
© 2014 PAWS, INC. All Rights Reserved.
JIM DAVIS 8-19

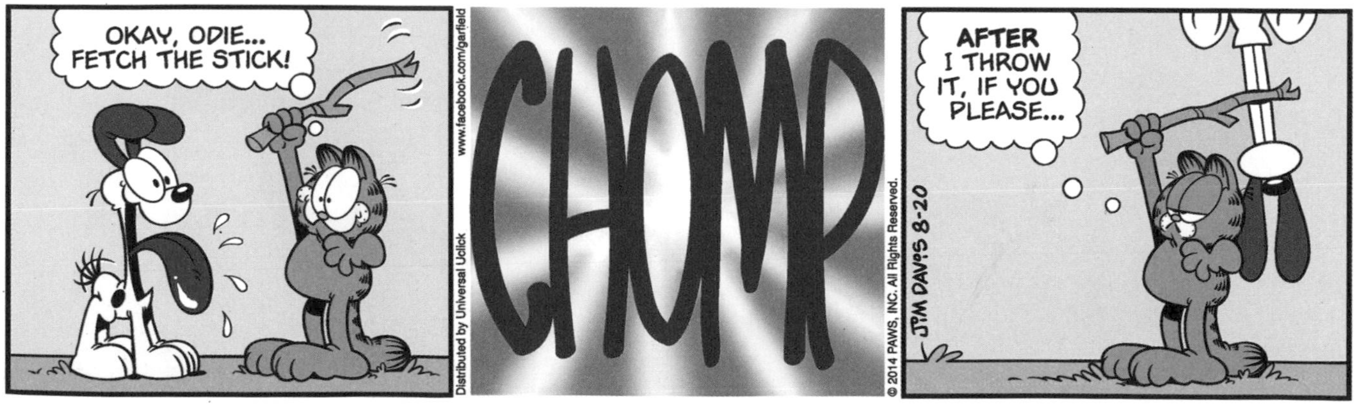
OKAY, ODIE... FETCH THE STICK!
Distributed by Universal Uclick www.facebook.com/garfield
CHOMP
AFTER I THROW IT, IF YOU PLEASE...
© 2014 PAWS, INC. All Rights Reserved.
JIM DAVIS 8-20

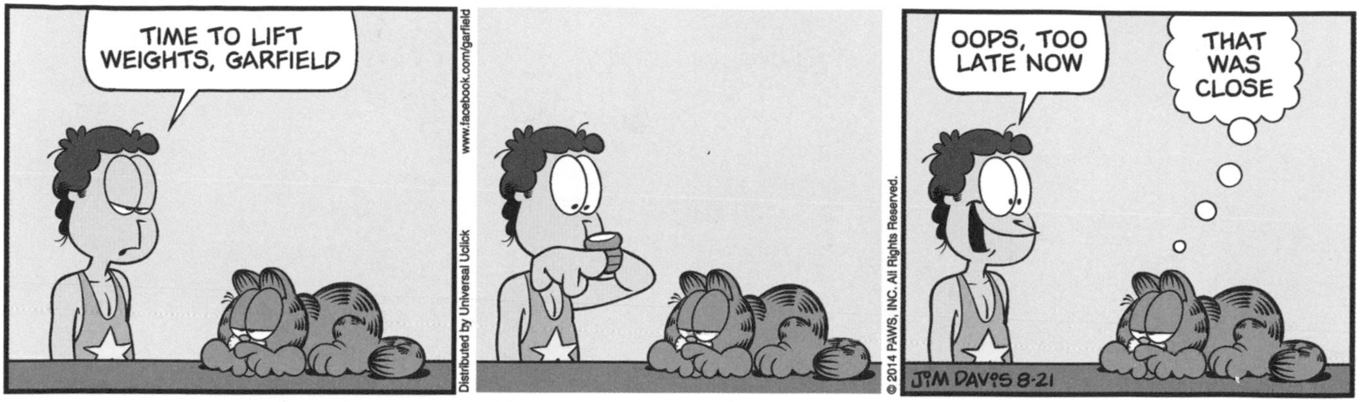
TIME TO LIFT WEIGHTS, GARFIELD
OOPS, TOO LATE NOW
THAT WAS CLOSE
Distributed by Universal Uclick www.facebook.com/garfield
© 2014 PAWS, INC. All Rights Reserved.
JIM DAVIS 8-21

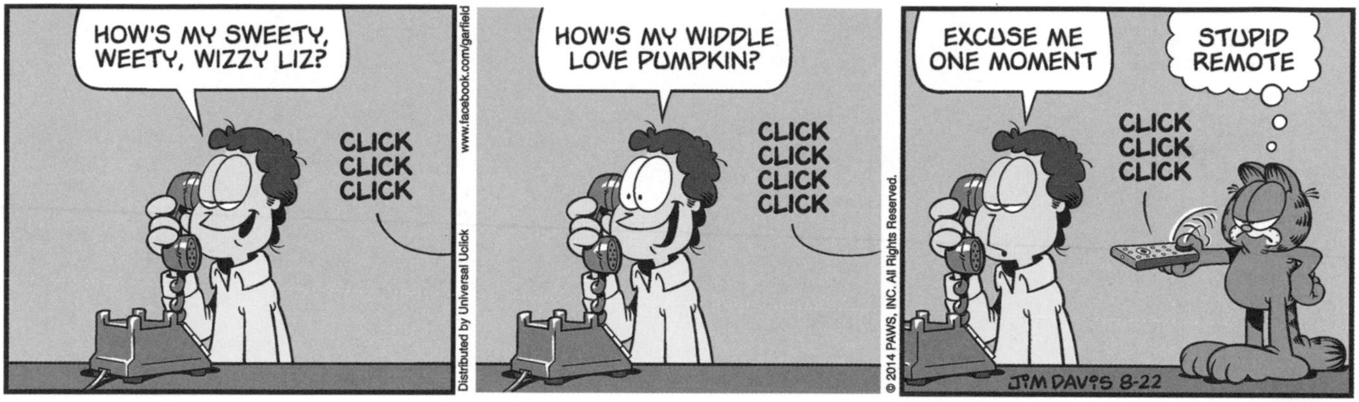
HOW'S MY SWEETY, WEETY, WIZZY LIZ?
CLICK CLICK CLICK
HOW'S MY WIDDLE LOVE PUMPKIN?
CLICK CLICK CLICK CLICK
EXCUSE ME ONE MOMENT
STUPID REMOTE
CLICK CLICK CLICK
Distributed by Universal Uclick www.facebook.com/garfield
© 2014 PAWS, INC. All Rights Reserved.
JIM DAVIS 8-22

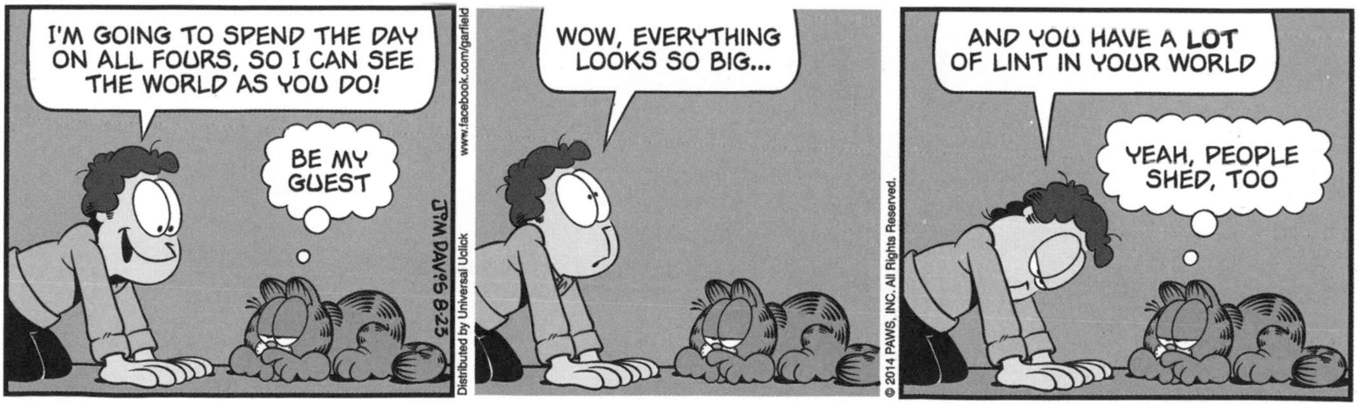
I'M GOING TO SPEND THE DAY ON ALL FOURS, SO I CAN SEE THE WORLD AS YOU DO!
BE MY GUEST
JIM DAVIS 8-23
Distributed by Universal Uclick www.facebook.com/garfield
WOW, EVERYTHING LOOKS SO BIG...
© 2014 PAWS, INC. All Rights Reserved.
AND YOU HAVE A LOT OF LINT IN YOUR WORLD
YEAH, PEOPLE SHED, TOO

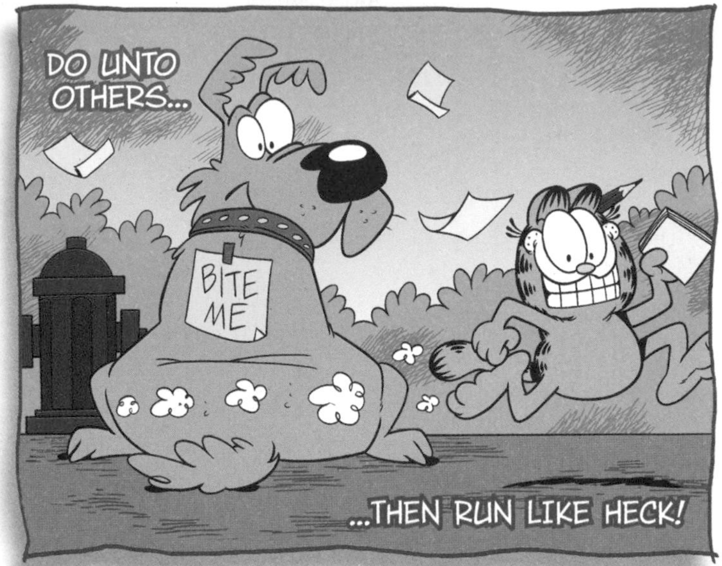
DO UNTO OTHERS...
BITE ME
...THEN RUN LIKE HECK!

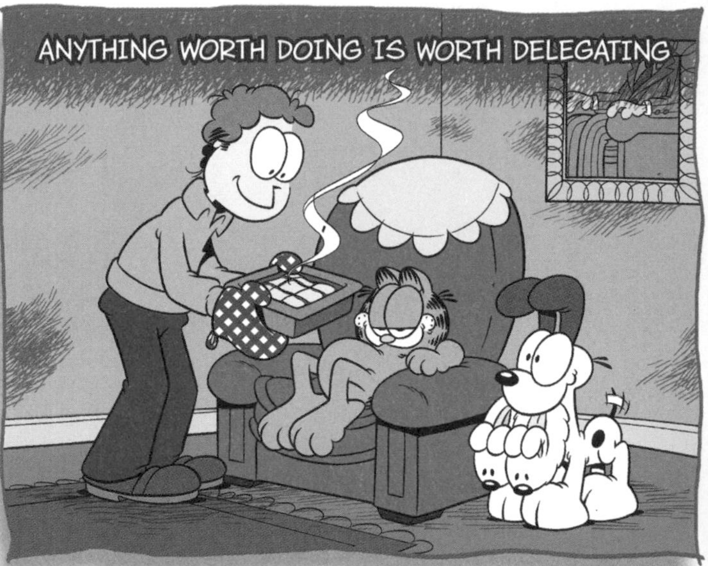
ANYTHING WORTH DOING IS WORTH DELEGATING

THOUGHTS TO CHEW ON

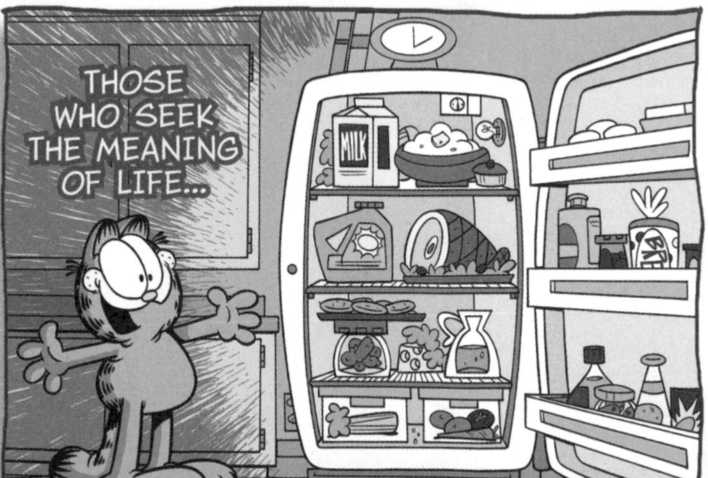
THOSE WHO SEEK THE MEANING OF LIFE...
MILK
...SHOULD CHECK THE FRIDGE!

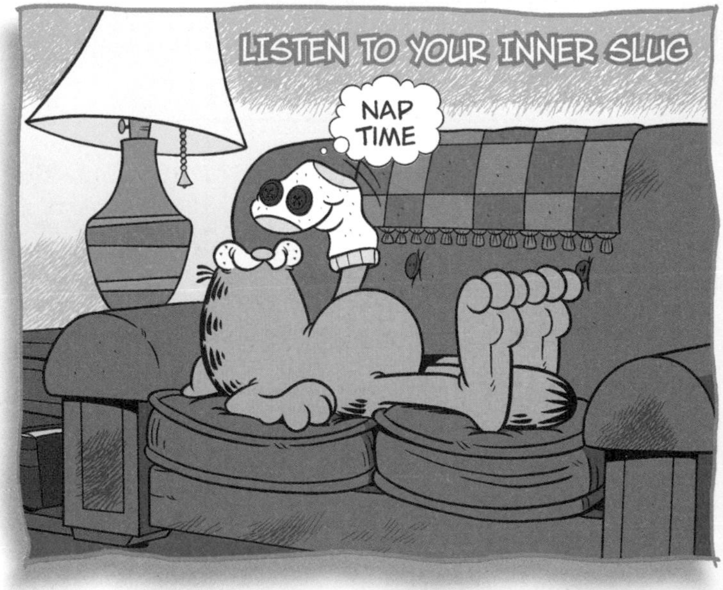
LISTEN TO YOUR INNER SLUG
NAP TIME

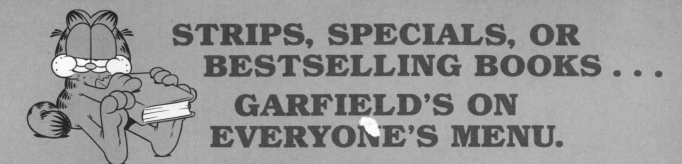

STRIPS, SPECIALS, OR BESTSELLING BOOKS . . . GARFIELD'S ON EVERYONE'S MENU.

Don't miss even one episode in the Tubby Tabby's hilarious series!

- GARFIELD AT LARGE (#1) 978-0-345-44382-3
- GARFIELD GAINS WEIGHT (#2) 978-0-345-44975-7
- GARFIELD BIGGER THAN LIFE (#3) 978-0-345-45027-2
- GARFIELD WEIGHS IN (#4) 978-0-345-45205-4
- GARFIELD TAKES THE CAKE (#5) 978-0-345-44978-8
- GARFIELD EATS HIS HEART OUT (#6) 978-0-345-46459-0
- GARFIELD SITS AROUND THE HOUSE (#7) 978-0-345-46463-7
- GARFIELD TIPS THE SCALES (#8) 978-0-345-46909-0
- GARFIELD LOSES HIS FEET (#9) 978-0-345-46467-5
- GARFIELD MAKES IT BIG (#10) 978-0-345-46468-2
- GARFIELD ROLLS ON (#11) 978-0-345-47561-9
- GARFIELD OUT TO LUNCH (#12) 978-0-345-47562-6
- GARFIELD FOOD FOR THOUGHT (#13) 978-0-345-47563-3
- GARFIELD SWALLOWS HIS PRIDE (#14) 978-0-345-91386-9
- GARFIELD WORLDWIDE (#15) 978-0-345-91754-6
- GARFIELD ROUNDS OUT (#16) 978-0-345-49169-5
- GARFIELD CHEWS THE FAT (#17) 978-0-345-49170-1
- GARFIELD GOES TO WAIST (#18) 978-0-345-49173-2
- GARFIELD HANGS OUT (#19) 978-0-345-49174-9
- GARFIELD TAKES UP SPACE (#20) 978-0-345-49178-7
- GARFIELD SAYS A MOUTHFUL (#21) 978-0-345-49179-4
- GARFIELD BY THE POUND (#22) 978-0-345-52558-1
- GARFIELD KEEPS HIS CHINS UP (#23) 978-0-345-52559-8
- GARFIELD TAKES HIS LICKS (#24) 978-0-345-52587-1
- GARFIELD HITS THE BIG TIME (#25) 978-0-345-52589-5
- GARFIELD PULLS HIS WEIGHT (#26) 978-0-345-52594-9
- GARFIELD DISHES IT OUT (#27) 978-0-345-52595-6
- GARFIELD LIFE IN THE FAT LANE (#28) 978-0-345-52600-7
- GARFIELD TONS OF FUN (#29) 978-0-345-52601-4
- GARFIELD BIGGER AND BETTER (#30) 978-0-345-52605-2
- GARFIELD HAMS IT UP (#31) 978-0-345-52606-9
- GARFIELD THINKS BIG (#32) 978-0-425-28516-9
- GARFIELD THROWS HIS WEIGHT AROUND (#33) 978-0-345-42749-6
- GARFIELD LIFE TO THE FULLEST (#34) 978-0-345-43239-1
- GARFIELD FEEDS THE KITTY (#35) 978-0-345-43673-3
- GARFIELD HOGS THE SPOTLIGHT (#36) 978-0-345-43922-2
- GARFIELD BEEFS UP (#37) 978-0-345-44109-6
- GARFIELD GETS COOKIN' (#38) 978-0-345-44582-7
- GARFIELD EATS CROW (#39) 978-0-345-45201-6
- GARFIELD SURVIVAL OF THE FATTEST (#40) 978-0-345-46458-3
- GARFIELD OLDER AND WIDER (#41) 978-0-345-46462-0
- GARFIELD PIGS OUT (#42) 978-0-345-46466-8
- GARFIELD BLOTS OUT THE SUN (#43) 978-0-345-46615-0
- GARFIELD GOES BANANAS (#44) 978-0-345-91346-3
- GARFIELD LARGE & IN CHARGE (#45) 978-0-345-49172-5
- GARFIELD SPILLS THE BEANS (#46) 978-0-345-49177-0
- GARFIELD GETS HIS JUST DESSERTS (#47) 978-0-345-91387-6
- GARFIELD WILL EAT FOR FOOD (#48) 978-0-345-49176-3
- GARFIELD WEIGHS HIS OPTIONS (#49) 978-0-345-49181-7
- GARFIELD POTBELLY OF GOLD (#50) 978-0-345-52244-3
- GARFIELD SHOVELS IT IN (#51) 978-0-345-52419-5
- GARFIELD LARD OF THE JUNGLE (#52) 978-0-345-52584-0
- GARFIELD BRINGS HOME THE BACON (#53) 978-0-345-52586-4
- GARFIELD GETS IN A PICKLE (#54) 978-0-345-52590-1
- GARFIELD SINGS FOR HIS SUPPER (#55) 978-0-345-52593-2
- GARFIELD CAUTION: WIDE LOAD (#56) 978-0-345-52596-3
- GARFIELD SOUPED UP (#57) 978-0-345-52598-7
- GARFIELD GOES TO HIS HAPPY PLACE (#58) 978-0-345-52602-1
- GARFIELD THE BIG CHEESE (#59) 978-0-345-52604-5
- GARFIELD CLEANS HIS PLATE (#60) 978-0-345-52608-3
- GARFIELD CHICKENS OUT (#61) 978-0-425-28515-2

DVD TIE-INS

- GARFIELD AS HIMSELF 978-0-345-47805-4
- GARFIELD HOLIDAY CELEBRATIONS 978-0-345-47930-[illegible]
- GARFIELD TRAVEL ADVENTURES 978-0-345-48087-[illegible]

AND DON'T MISS . . .

- GARFIELD AT 25: IN DOG YEARS I'D BE DEAD 978-0-345-45204-7
- GARFIELD'S JOKE ZONE/INSULTS 978-0-345-46263-3
- GARFIELD FAT CAT 3-PACK/ VOL. 1 978-0-345-46455-2
- GARFIELD FAT CAT 3-PACK/ VOL. 2 978-0-345-46465-1
- GARFIELD FAT CAT 3-PACK/ VOL. 3 978-0-345-48088-0
- GARFIELD FAT CAT 3-PACK/ VOL. 4 978-0-345-49171-8
- GARFIELD FAT CAT 3-PACK/ VOL. 5 978-0-345-49180-8
- GARFIELD FAT CAT 3-PACK/ VOL. 6 978-0-345-52420-1
- GARFIELD FAT CAT 3-PACK/ VOL. 7 978-0-345-52588-8
- GARFIELD FAT CAT 3-PACK/ VOL. 8 978-0-345-52599-4
- GARFIELD FAT CAT 3-PACK/ VOL. 9 978-0-345-52607-6
- GARFIELD FAT CAT 3-PACK/ VOL. 10 978-0-425-28558-9
- GARFIELD FAT CAT 3-PACK/ VOL. 13 978-0-345-46460-6
- GARFIELD FAT CAT 3-PACK/ VOL. 14 978-0-345-49175-6
- GARFIELD FAT CAT 3-PACK/ VOL. 15 978-0-345-52585-7
- GARFIELD FAT CAT 3-PACK/ VOL. 16 978-0-345-52592-5
- GARFIELD FAT CAT 3-PACK/ VOL. 17 978-0-345-52603-8
- GARFIELD FAT CAT 3-PACK/ VOL. 18 978-0-399-59440-3
- SEASON'S EATINGS: A VERY MERRY GARFIELD CHRISTMAS 978-0-345-47560-2
- GARFIELD'S GUIDE TO EVERYTHING 978-0-345-46461-3
- ODIE UNLEASHED! 978-0-345-46464-4
- GARFIELD'S BOOK OF CAT NAMES 978-0-345-48516-8
- THE GARFIELD JOURNAL 978-0-345-46469-9
- LIGHTS, CAMERA, HAIRBALLS!: GARFIELD AT THE MOVIES 978-0-345-49134-3
- 30 YEARS OF LAUGHS AND LASAGNA 978-0-345-50379-4
- GARFIELD MINUS GARFIELD 978-0-345-51387-8
- GARFIELD FROM THE TRASH BIN 978-0-345-51881-1
- GARFIELD LEFT SPEECHLESS 978-0-345-53058-5
- MY LAUGHABLE LIFE WITH GARFIELD 978-0-345-52591-8
- GARFIELD'S SUNDAY FINEST 978-0-345-52597-0

ew larger, full-color format!